A Stream of Life

A Stream of Life

BERNARD VENABLES

ILLUSTRATED
BY THE AUTHOR

ELLESMERE
THE MEDLAR PRESS
2002

Published by The Medlar Press Limited,
The Grange, Ellesmere, Shropshire.

ISBN 1 899 600 205

First published 2002

This book is from the first printing of which there are 150 limited edition leather bound copies.

Designed and typeset in 11 on 12 1/2pt Garamond by Jonathan Ward-Allen.

Produced in England by The Medlar Press Limited, Ellesmere.

Printed and bound in Great Britain by Biddles Ltd, *www.biddles.co.uk*

CONTENTS

AUTHOR'S FOREWORD

Of some of the more dramatic events of my life I have written elsewhere. But so inseparably important are they to a full definitive account of what has been my life, they cannot be omitted here. I have therefore retold these stories, sometimes editing previous accounts, sometimes re-writing them, completing a story which had its roots in the mid-19th century, and is terminating in the early years of the 21st century.

CHAPTER I

Genesis

ONLY narrowly was I not born a Victorian. The 20th century had had only seven years of being, and by only six years had the Victorian era ended. From that beginning I have lived to see the first years of the 21st century. A longer than average span of life; but how brief in the context of the immense continuity that Earth has been. So brief, so brief. Just time to catch the taste of life and worship it. Then it is taken away.

But brevity is relative - the year of one era is the moment of another. For most of the misty recessions of what has gone, the movement of time could hardly have seemed discernible. Call Earth's life a year, and it is only in the last second that the pace has quickened, then become a dizziness as has not been since earth congealed from its natal gases. In such future generations as there may be can it again be possible for such a degree of change, so vastly headlong? Perhaps then the story of my life is of some historical symbolism; perhaps in a time beyond mine it might seem so -

unless as might be, we are skidding towards history's end in terms of our species and those other species that we drag with us into extinction.

The world to which I opened infant eyes was innocent of so much of what now are the unquestioned props of the most ordinary lives in the Northern Hemisphere. Then people wrote with steel nibs and bottles of ink; most of the artefacts of daily life were still made by the craft of skilled hands. Machines, still servants, not masters, were directed by manual skills. Radio, arcane and hardly heard of, then called wireless telegraphy, had no touch on the common life. And television? What an absurdity - pigs might fly. Telephones there were; but how archaic to modern eyes, and for the use of few. There were no freezers, no refrigerators; the cooling of food, for the well equipped, was by lumps of ice in zinc-lined chests. And plastics - not anywhere in the world then apart possibly from a brittle and rather repellent substance called Bakelite. It was a world in great deprivation of glossy conveniences but contentedly unaware.

Doctors still went their rounds by carriage and pair, streets were lit by gas, and tarmac was only beginning to encase the dust of roads, and by its run-off poison fish in rivers. Oil and candles still lit the homes of more than were able to have the dreary singing of the incandescent gas mantle, and pre-packed foods were unknown. A grocer serving his customer with butter took the appropriate amount from a stock in water, moulded it with wooden butter pats which left it embossed with corn sheaves or something else as pleasant. Cars were few and for the few; man had only begun to teeter hazardously into the air. How inconceivably improbable that within my lifetime such as I could find ourselves so blindly at a loss in the electronic devilry that is the world of today. How could one life begin with the horse-drawn cab and see the ravishing of space by probes and satellites? I have the sense of having lived several lives.

Peering back over that gulf of years, small as it is historically, how placid an innocence I see, how naïve, how simply acceptant as thus it was for the ordinary citizen. Of course memory is not coherent, the earliest record comes in inconsequential vignettes within fading edges. But sometimes there emerges with sudden clarity one fragment of time. Why do I remember with tiny lucency such a moment, one anonymous moment? I think I was about two then and, it must be assumed, bombarded day by day by discoveries of life. And here is this moment, suspended for life's length, a random moment in the placid drifting in the slow current of days. I am with my mother, and in a wheel chair. It is not the steel and plastic buggy of today, but an honest old thing, a little cumbersome, largely of wood, yellow-varnished. It is strongly hinged for folding. I have found that by moving I can draw from it a whining squeak, and in the quietness that is faintly drugging in a pleasing way. In the still afternoon air my mother and I are waiting. There is a wall of red brick loftily surmounted by iron railings, because here is the school and we are waiting for my brother and sister. My mother wears a skirt which reaches her ankles over her buttoned boots; her straw hat, shiny black is secured to her piled hair by hatpins. I remember separately that the thrusting through of the hatpins makes a crackling sound. That she should so thrust them through her head holds me with fascinated horror. Now, her hand, black-kid-gloved, rests on the wheel chair handle; I recall that sharply. But no more, no moment before, none after. The haze beyond is impenetrable. That is my whole personal symbol of the Edwardian world.

Edward VII was then in his brief heyday, ending when I was three years old, so mistily far. For his funeral, and again for the coronation of George V my sister and brother had a day's holiday; that too I remember, though as something from another world - as in effect it was. What lichened cenotaphs to that departed world whose events appear at this distance; the more so because all those so remembered now are long dead. Everything recalled from that time is, inevitably, a symbol. So in its way is the incident of the milk barrow, poignant as it was at the time. Then milk was brought simply to the door, leisurely, perhaps not very hygienically. Indeed what change there has been. Slowly and on foot the milkman made his round, pushing his handcart. In it is a great churn. It is many years since last I saw one, but a highly aromatic folk artefact we would think it now - its curves of polished brass, its painted wood, its flourished enscrolling of the dairy's name, its wooden wheels. Then no mammoth Board stood between the dung-scented shippon and the doorstep. No huge tankers then, no entrapment of regulations to ensure the stale delivery of milk. The plodding milkman had in his barrow his churn brightly silver and banded with brass; that contained the milk. On a rail hung measuring vessels, half-pint and pint; they, memory suggest were pewter with handles of brass. There, in the gutter, the milkman ladled out the milk into the housewife's jug. It was slow and, characteristically, conversational. Many times I must have watched as my mother and the milkman passed the time of day over the serving of the milk and, I suppose, have sunk into a fascination - the turning of the brass tap, the gush of milk. On this morning, trapped in memory, as is a fly in amber, my mother had returned to the house. Only briefly the milkman had left his barrow unattended. There was the polished churn, there the tap. I turned the tap.

How sharply still the terror of that returns to me. The chuckling in the gutter of that flood of milk. Not until evening was the expectation of clanging prison gates assuaged enough for me to come out from under the kitchen table.

That relict world. The sense of it is flavoured far more by such remnants than by all the foreshadowing of the years that were to be. With the declining of the seasons into winter there came the muffin man. How the atmosphere of that saturated those November afternoons, with the silent rain of yellow leaves. On his head he bore his tray of muffins under their green baize cover, and as he went he rang his handbell. In summer's decline there were the lavender sellers. How may be conveyed the poignancy of that? From street to street they went, roughly but indescribably hauntingly singing their song - "Lady buy my sweet-blooming lavender, sixteen branches a penny." The hoarse melancholy searched my child's soul. Always as he sang the seller put his cupped hand behind his ear as if to catch a fading echo. Only a slight memory have I of the 'Young Lambs to Sell' man - and surely, surely he must have been the very last of his kind. I recall him in the gutter with his tray of toy lambs, singing his tinkling little song - "Young lambs to sell, young lambs to sell."

At every evening's twilight the lamplighter came. He walked through every street, upon his shoulder the hollow pole which had in its tip a pilot light. To every gas lamppost he came there with his pilot light to ignite the mantle. Can he, that far-remembered lamplighter, have been in my one life, he and the orange glare with which towns now blot out the velvet of night?

So much violence of change; disorientating, destructive of continuity, leaving little sense of kinship of past and present.

But inescapably we are the inheritors of our ancestry - how intelligible a portrait of ourselves can we contrive without some acknowledgement of the past that bred us? Without that the present is two-dimensional. An account of my life until now must have some account of the heredity which caused my being. I am the momentary phase of a long continuity.

My father then - though it is little enough I know of his antecedents. His forenames were Albert Aaron - so, in 19th century fashion, paying proper respect both to royalty and the Bible. He was born in Peckham in South London, and there he grew up in the care of his widowed mother. By what chance his knot of Venableses came to be there I have no idea - I know only that their true place of origin was Cheshire and the Welsh Marches. Rural link lay in the fact that my father's father was a gardener, a specialist in exotic fruits, as was his brother too. One grew pineapples, the other something no less tropical, but I cannot remember. In their time it must be supposed, Peckham was still a village bordering on London. But there they were - my father, his mother, five brothers and two sisters; there they were in dire poverty because no sooner had their father sired his children than he died. To his widow he left the awesome task of bringing them up in the harshly uncaring world of Victorian England. My father was the youngest. My memory of my father's mother is slight; but it is vivid. She, then in her eighties, was little, birdlike, like a starling, eyes bead bright and

Albert Aaron Venables

black, with not a hair of her black head touched with white, the hair dragged back from a central parting. Her father had been a Frenchman whose name was Lefevre, and that her appearance plainly showed. My child's eye picture of her shows her as hard-bitten. How otherwise could she have been? I think I was slightly afraid of her. My father's brothers were earthy men, only he lived with sensitivities beyond the immediately material. I must guess that his gropings were incoherent, entirely without guidance; but instinctively he had an awareness of music partnered by a tenor voice which, it was said, was beautiful onwards from the breaking of his voice. In some more than usually harrowing trough of poverty, to help his mother he went into the public gutter to sing for money. There he was accosted by a man who introduced himself as a teacher at one of the great schools of music. He begged of my grandmother that she should let him take her son that he might be musically trained. She, hardened in the school of survival, was obdurate, dourly hostile to such insubstantialities. What was she to do without such contribution as he could make to her tenuous budget? The vision passed.

As I recall my father he was of middle height, thin, eager of manner. He saw the world through hazel eyes, full and lustrous behind pince-nez spectacles. They left purplish concavities either side of his nose when they were removed for his fidgety cleaning, and left him owl-like myopic. He was an untidy man. His cheap worn-shiny suits, with trousers barely reaching the tops of his boots were so much bagged at the knees that he appeared always to be standing with bent legs. His zest for living induced in him a wish to be very erect; he strove to that as almost to be leaning backwards. The wish alas was vain, not compatible with his inescapable shape. He was delicate; he was pigeon-breasted; his shoulder blades were painfully prominent. Instinct urged him to vitality; I believe he would have had himself adventurous, rangy. Inexorably he was pinned down, trapped in an ailing body, and an imprisoning context. Had there been opportunity almost certainly he would have been a writer.

As it was he wrote letters. Formidably he wrote letters. He wrote them with love on foolscap sheets in a neat copperplate hand. When, occasionally, having the luxury of a correspondent he was lavish with such sheets. He was not a practical man; indeed no handyman was he. Consummately he was inept. Few jobs about the house were beyond his mishandling. His tools were few. He had a saw, 'the saw'; its teeth were dull and brown; before use he rubbed it with dripping.

He had a watch, by nature not reliable. For its vagaries he had two remedies; he would rap it sharply on a hard surface, or he would pour paraffin into its inner mystery. Such treatment long pursued, had given it a face of dusky yellow. It was a pocket watch; without the security of a chain he carried it in his waistcoat pocket. Returning one day from work he was worried about his watch. When in his tripping fashion he had been descending a stone staircase, his watch leaped from its pocket. Down the stairs it preceded him jumping from stone step to stone step.

It fell to him that economy compelled his repairing of our boots. His work was not pretty; it did just serve its purpose. He came to the work with hate, with loathing so profound that long wear was all of his concern. The soles he gave us were thick, tipped with iron. Sunday morning was the time for it.

At the back of the house was a lean-to, roofed with that thick repellent glass that is ribbed for semi-opacity, fronted in the upper half with trellis. This was 'the glasshouse'. Descent into it was by a very deep cemented step. On that day my father would sit, bitterly crouched, the cobbler's last gripped between his knees. In a bowl of water at his side a sheet of leather would be softening. With brads held in his lips he would secure the leather to the boot on the iron foot of the last. With the cobbler's knife, which he had given a rough sharpening on the step, now he set to paring away the surplus leather. Already he had hit his thumb with the hammer and was smouldering, swearing quietly, fervently through his teeth. Drawing with the knife he cut the leather to the sole's shape. So on better days; but mishap was never distant. There were days when the knife slipped. All would explode, knife, last, and my father. "Blast, blast, damn and bloody blast," he roared. But his words were indistinct; he was sucking his thumb, spitting blood. A little later, snarling, roughly bandaged, faithful but with hate, he returned to the work.

Had he been a spectator, though quick with aid, secretly and guiltily he would have found it funny. His was a world very full of things that were funny. His sense of humour was uncomplicated, bubbling, often bawdy. He fell easily and unpredictably into clowning. Once on a sunny Sunday morning he burst from the parental bedroom scuttling on thin legs, dressed only in the long-sleeved vest and long pants that then were the mode. On a box he set one foot, threw back his head, threw up his stiff arm with clenched fist. "Ajax defying the lightning," he explained.

He was gregarious, characteristically warm towards his fellow men, but often not tolerant of them. He was gentle, abhorrent of cruelty; he treasured his ideals. Also he was richly prone to prejudice. His threshold to irritability was low. Offence to his principles - or his prejudices - could throw him into scalding irritation. But essentially his character was one of sweetness, pinched and thwarted though it was by the meanness of his life. And, it must be said, life with my mother could tax the most even temper. His background, his lack of education - he left school at the age of twelve - inhibited the growth of (as I now perceive) a strong intuitive intelligence. He needed his giggling sense of humour. He was a clerk in the chemical firm of Burroughs Welcome; there his routine was dull and grossly underpaid. People today cannot guess the scarifying poverty then of a man in full employment.

My father's marriage to my mother was improbable. My mother was a maverick. As the wife of a poverty-ridden uneducated clerk in a working-class environment she was grotesquely improbable. She was no less at variance with her own heredity - though indeed that heredity had a steady tendency to eccentricity. Her name before marriage was Adelaide Constance Maud Harcourt-Perrotte. The path from her hereditary origins to the married state was tortuous.

Perhaps its unravelling should start with the two barrels of that surname. Of the Perrottes I know less than of the Harcourts. Family lore received in my childhood was vague, but such substance as it had began with Sir John Perrotte - a shadowy figure, but my mother swore to his undoubted truth. He, the story is, was a bastard son of Henry VIII - one of a large brotherhood. Also the story says, this Sir John found himself in trouble with Elizabeth, for which his sentence was despatch to Ireland there to attempt the bludgeoning into submission of the Catholic Irish. This he was said to have done with verve.

Beyond that Tudor fragment there is no more of the Perrottes until the time of my great great grandfather. Now we find the Perrottes in Buckinghamshire in the vicinity of Stony Stratford. But of all their life there nothing emerges but the story of the great pike. Great great grandfather was an angler. Among the anglers of that locality there had long been much vying for the capture of a notoriously great pike. The story was told to my mother, then a small child, by her grandfather, my great grandfather, Henry Harcourt-Perrotte. He told of that day when he, a small boy went with his father on a fishing foray destined to be epic. Of detail I know nothing but that my great great grandfather did so gloriously hook and land the pike, and it was indeed enormous. There it lay, on the bank, legend no longer. Small boy great grandfather stooped in awe to stare at it. The pike, thought to be beyond further activity, leapt suddenly to fix its multiple teeth in the calf of great grandfather's little boy leg. At this point in the story great grandfather pulled up his trouser leg. "There Adie my child," he said, "you see I still bear the mark of the great pike." There the scar was, livid still.

This great grandfather can be pinned down, so to speak, by the fact that he was first cousin of that Sir William Harcourt who was Chancellor in Gladstone's Liberal governments of the late 19th century. His father was Archbishop of York, whose sister was my great great grandmother.

Though of the Harcourts I know more than of the Perrottes, it is only confusedly so; my mother's accounts of family history were rambling rather than precise. Of Sir William I know that his full name was William George Granville Venables-Vernon Harcourt, and that he was issue of an ancient descent. In the year AD 876 the family was founded in Normandy by Bernard the Dane, he being of those men of Danish origin who had become Norman by invasive conquest. His son Angeraud d'Harcourt, came to England in the train of William the Conqueror, thus to found the English family Harcourt. For my line the nineteenth century brought connection by marriage to the great industrial families. My great grandfather, Henry Harcourt-Perotte, married a daughter of the ascendant family of Cubitt, then becoming an industrial giant. In a way I have never learned, my mother was also related to the family of Hoare - she spoke often of her favourite cousin, Naomi Hoare. It was a happiness to my mother that my daughter's second name is Naomi - it might have been her first name but for the certainty of our pain at hearing her called NaOmi rather than NAomi. Naomi is too beautiful a name so to be made ugly.

Family tradition says that marriage to my great grandfather was thought then to be socially excellent for a rising family. So in principle no doubt it was. But, there was the man.

Fortune had been fair to him, so it was said, endowing him well. It gave him talent; he was an architect, but a civil engineer too, and could almost as well have been an artist. It was expected of him that as an architect he would ascend. But he was lazy, feckless, by nature a parasite. He was too well established in a way of privilege, unquestioningly he assumed a right for tastes of luxury and looseness for which he lacked the money. The record is shadowy, but I was told the Perrotte family fortune had been at least in part in ownership of stage coaches and coaching inns, too vulnerable to the coming of railways. My great grandfather was too arrogantly idle to restore fortune thus damaged. As my mother recalled him he was small, very elegantly precise, walking with a slight forward inclination from the waist. In manner often he was contemptuous, regarding from under lowered lids those whom he considered his inferiors - so he considered many more than not. His victims he withered or stung to fury.

His descent was basis for his arrogance; it was otherwise unsupported. Very cosily surely he could have lived in the warm nest of his wife's family's wealth, so it appears at this distance. But it seems as a wastrel he was ingenious. He had come to being a down-and-out sleeping by night on a bench on the Thames Embankment. There, collapsed and hungry, he was found, taken to hospital. In delirium he revealed enough to identify himself. He was restored to his family; with how much gratitude he was received is not recorded. But how perversely almost as by talent he came again to an Embankment bench, again to be restored. Now the family, accepting the inevitable, maintained him thereafter as he considered was his right. He was long enough in the conventional frame to produce a family. Of those one was my grandfather, Henry Harcourt-Perrotte. Another was his brother James, my mother's

Henry Harcourt-Perrotte

Uncle Jim

Uncle Jim, and there were the sisters, Alice, Constance, Kitty. From the beginning Uncle Jim was turbulent. At fourteen he ran away to sea, and, being recovered, did the same at sixteen. Then, and for good, his life was a wild vagrancy about the world, a doing of many things in many places, few of them safe and decorous. By the smallest chance he evaded becoming food for cannibals; and this being the time of the Wild West, inevitably to that he came and as surely was a gunman. When last he was heard of he was editing a newspaper at Maple Creek, Montana Territory, USA. A surviving daguerreotype shows him swaggeringly posed, hand on the handle of a logger's axe. In the fashion of Buffalo Bill he wears the cowboy hat, flowing hair and beard.

His lawlessness was as fundamental to him as his skeleton. His random returns to England were often eventful, never without his six-chambered revolver and a readiness to accept any provocation. There was a day when he walked with his sisters through a street market. Passing a greengrocery stall with no warning he flung himself upon the stall holder. Women screamed, police whistles blew, as they rolled fighting in a sea of tomatoes, plums and greenstuff. Uncle Jim explained later; he had not cared for the way the man had looked at his sisters. Who better than he to assess such a look? It was his way on these returns always to sing a song, always with unction:

> *"Sailing home, sailing home*
> *Across the wild and rolling main*
> *Sailing home at last to England*
> *Sailing home dear land to thee."*

He was never long again forsaking the dear land.

My grandfather was born in the Green Dragon Hotel in Hereford. Probably his father was involved with the rather dubious Victorian work on that glorious cathedral so close to the hotel. If that is true, it induced no sanctity in my grandfather. He was a painter, red-bearded, aggressively blue-eyed, seldom a very peaceful man, always belligerently ready to respond to a glance, a word, a touch. He was small, excessively strong and as men were then, tough. Every morning, summer or winter he put himself under the yard pump, working it with one hand while he scrubbed with the other.

Even the rather hostile family allowed that the girl he married was beautiful. Her father was Irish, from Connemara; her mother was a Spanish opera singer of tumultuous temperament. She was foreign; she was on the stage; she was far from being self-contained - not indeed a formula to have the approval of an English 19th century aristocratic family. Of that she was contemptuous. Aristocratic mushrooms she declared them to be. Did not her own descent come directly from the Spanish kings of Granada before the Moorish conquest?

"Black ones?" asked Aunt Con.

Her Irish husband was strong in his taste for other women; to which her response was simple. She called upon him at his office; she summoned his staff, so witnessed she slugged him with an office stool. Out of such turbulence came my grandmother - gentle, beautiful, sweetly yielding. She was too tragically yielding. To my grandfather she bore one child, my mother. Only six months after that birth there came Uncle Jim storming home on a visit. He discovered the beauty and delight of his brother's wife; he seduced her, bore her away, then soon abandoned her. My mother recalled that she, then a small child, was accosted in the street by a woman whom she remembered as tall, slim and beautiful. She pressed my mother with questions as to her life and that of her father, tears welling from her eyes. Never from then was there further trace of her. There was much matter for questioning. For a child, a girl, to be left in the sole charge of an unpredictable father, insecurity and unhappiness were probable. So it would have been if he had been averagely responsible. He was not.

Perhaps events would have fallen out less appallingly had he not suffered the incalculable pain of the loss of his wife, and by such means. Through many nights my mother heard her father pacing, muttering, sometimes crying his wife's name. But he needed no such causes. He was unstable, erratic; a prank in his youth had made him no less so. Being dared he climbed to the roof of a house, there to run along its ridge. He fell; that fall, on his head normally would have been fatal. Still concussed but living he absconded from hospital to all seemingly mentally unharmed, just his eccentric self.

Calamity waited. One of its results is that I, his grandson and a painter too, have never seen the least stroke of his work. What its quality was I must, tantalisingly, guess. Family tradition is firm that it was brilliant. Why then has his name left no echo? How can all his life and work leave no relict sign, no least memento? Were his rambling eccentricity and his early death so erasing?

My mother's recalling of his work was incoherent, though it did convey a sense of sombre wildness, of large Titianesque canvasses of satyrs. But it might be that that darkness which haunted her came from the shadowy frenzy of his working. He worked only by the torrential urges which swept him, working day and night without pause, without consciousness of all else. When exhaustion claimed him hardly could he bear the sight of a brush. His refuelling was largely by wine and company of friends, mostly painters. One of them, my mother said, was from France; it was at that time she and her father were living at Upper Norwood, and then it was Camille Pissaro too was living and working there. How tempting it is to suppose that he was the painter from France.

Out of the fog of uncertainty there is some evidence of commissions of consequence. Of those was one to paint a large mural in the Carlton House Terrace home of Sir Ernest Cassells, friend to Edward VII. It is said to have been on the staircase wall, and I, on occasions have brought suspicion upon myself by peering through open doorways there. But vainly. I have found nothing.

His intervals of lucidity brought awareness of the wider world of people. So particularly, came awareness of his daughter whom he had forgotten entirely. His paternal sense awakened; he was all urbane care - how was she eating, how was she faring. Had she suitable clothes? He bore her off to Fortnum & Mason; there on a typical occasion he ordered for her a dozen pairs of lavender kid gloves; for which of course he never paid.

"Adie my dear," he would say, "you are a lady. We must be sure that you are dressed as you should be."

That she had survived with no serious damage was due to her inherent toughness and immense capacity for survival - a legacy passed on to me. In his episodic concern he had care too for her speech and hearing; he reproved lapses.

"Now Adie my dear - what did I hear you say? 'That is awfully nice,' You said. How may it be that something is both awful and nice?"

His own modes of behaviour were little concerned with accepted standards. Under stress he swore fluently, though not coarsely. For him was his own oddity, though its spirit was the same. "Nebuchadnezzar, Jehoshophat, Ahab and Beelzebub!" he would roar. He dropped easily into unctions of self-pity, seeing himself as a hapless pawn of ill fortune. "I never loved a dear gazelle but it was sure to die," he would lament.

His prejudices were violent; for soldiers and for undertakers he nursed deep hatred. "Hired assassin!" he would hiss at the passing of an innocent soldier. "Vile body snatcher!" he shouted at undertakers. With what sighs, what shaking of her head my mother recalled outings with her father. Some were peaceful but never with certainty, often were outrageous. Thus, lamentably, was the incident of the bus - it of course being the horse-drawn bus of that time. At the coming of the conductor her father bought their tickets. Later, the conductor came again asking for their fares.

"I have already paid our fares," said her father. Other passengers declared they have seen the buying. "Prove it," said the conductor. "Show me the tickets." "You have my word; others have confirmed that I have paid our fares. I will not show you the tickets." It was stalemate. At their point of alighting, as they stepped down, the conductor put an arresting hand on my grandfather's shoulder. In the instant they were locked, rolling, fighting in the gutter.

"Adie," my grandfather would sometimes say, "most people are extremely silly. The silliness of most people is endless and extraordinary; you may lead most people into almost any absurdity. Now Adie my dear, observe - I will demonstrate. You shall see how silly most people can be."

Taking her urgently by the arm he led her to the pavement's edge. There, staring intently, he pointed, appearing to talk in excitement. Others stopped, staring too. The few grew to many, intently rooted. Then his crowd assembled, my grandfather withdrew quietly, chuckling.

"There Adie, there you see - observe their asinine excitement. Let us leave them to their idiocy."

As the years passed so the more his oddities possessed him, his painting turned more to its shadowed half-world. Growing into her teens, so the more my mother's life was warped by neglect, his episodic love, his wild moods. In her distress she turned to the warmly offered kindness of a neighbouring working-class family. They befriended her. Being one day with them, she received a message - would she please go at once to her father's house; he was ill. She found the house silent, dark. Then she heard her father's voice, very quietly, brokenly. "Adie," he whispered, "Adie," then as she passed through a doorway, from behind the door he sprang screaming. He gripped her throat, strangling her. She was young, supply strong; she struggled fiercely. Her friends, sensing danger, had followed her. Her father was overpowered.

Decline now was rapid. He was certified, removed to an asylum. There soon he died. He was forty-five years old.

On that day, immediately upon his removal, some people of the locality, knowing my mother to be without defence, came plundering. They left nothing. My mother was sixteen years of age; she was entirely destitute. Her befriending neighbours took her in, making her as of the family.

How curious it was my mother used to say; within six months disaster overtook every one of those who had plundered. Death by cancer and fates as draconian had come to all.

CHAPTER II

Under the Marsh Sky

SUCH heredity as was my mother's might be expected to bequeath idiosyncrasy. She was widely divergent. That so she was became evident to me only retrospectively. Adolescent children may suffer hot shame for the least parental difference from the common way; but with younger children it is otherwise. Their parents are the standard by which others, rightly, conform or, wrongly, do not. When school age came to us my mother had imbued us with her infallibility. Any differing from her was a fall from verity. That conditioning must have been exceedingly strong; my mother differed so obviously from those about us. To them she must have been idiosyncrasy made flesh. But so clearly she saw herself as the very model of reasonable normality - if perhaps wiser, more deeply perceptive, more compassionate than can be the common gift.

No tidy definition could be put upon her; how is one to be defined who slips so unpredictably among so many irreconcilables? Pre-eminently she was an egoist, sometimes falling into wondering admiring of the figure of herself which she saw. Genuinely she had a compassionate concern for others; a burning intolerance of injustice. As compulsively she must amend all circumstances to her need to live with drama. She was passionately combative, quick to fiery challenge, as quick to quixotic kindness. But always, through all there must be drama and she its vibrant or emotional centre. She could slip from lofty optimism to tragedy at the instant's demand of her script. Her cheerfulness was buoyant as birds in spring, her miseries, transitorily, black as pits. Her waking hours rang with her loud clear laughter, but when calamity fell she would throw the back of her hand across her back-flung brow, then cast it despairingly to her leg. In the face of injustice she was furious and sometimes physically aggressive.

To what extent the whole shape of her character had emerged at the time of her father's death I cannot say, though I think it must largely have done so. When about twelve she saw several boys dangling a live mouse by its tail above a cat. The cat sprang, wrenching the mouse from its tail. In a bound she was across the road to fling herself upon the boys, felling one, scattering the others. A passing elderly gentleman gave her sixpence.

Her independent spirit must already have been evident, expressed in her high-flung head and erect bearing. In what, at that time, must have been the scandalous circumstances of her father's end, she received a letter from the husband of Aunt Con. He whose surname was Gilbert-Cooper, was late of the Colonial Service; he had been a magistrate in China and, I believe, India. 'I must ask you,' he wrote, 'not to let my name come into this affair.'

'You need have no worry,' my mother wrote back, 'my own name is good enough.'

That so far as I know was the whole of her relatives' expressed interest in her predicament; it established a gulf still unbridged. It set a course which led to my father. Now in the care of that neighbouring and befriending family she was in a working-class context; she must have a trade. She was put to dressmaking. That must have had little to do with the assembly-line rag trade of today which feeds the high street shops. The dresses then, in the 1890s were elaborate; they were built; much of the work on them was pitilessly patient handwork. My mother recalled the endless hours of hand stitching seams, ruffs, panels, the flouncing, the padding, the ache of eyes exhausted by long hours in poor light. Subsequently the trailed trains of those dresses swept the dust of summer streets and the mud of winter.

Of first meeting of my mother and father, at what age they were married, I know nothing. Probably it was earlier rather than later; she must have wished for the establishment that marriage and the marriage home would give her. But in some respects, whatever was her age, she was not ready for marriage in the most fruitful sense. People of recent generations cannot grasp the atmosphere of the late 19th century's acceptances regarding sex. It was fuzzed, its biological nature slipped out of sight in a cotton wool of euphemism suspended over embarrassing fact. Love must be 'pure'. Decent women did not experience sexual desire - unless of course they were of upper and more aware classes. Respectable young women of working or lower middle classes were under the moment-to-moment scrutiny of an austere God who would allow no besmirching of His creation. That it was indeed just such a blasphemy which ensured God's purpose of continuity was decently obscured. There were women who admitted and obeyed their instincts. They were said to have 'gone gay'. My mother had no illusions as to God's right to rule her private life, but her biological promptings were as throttled as were those of most of her contemporaries. To a point men could be accepted with respect - though only a superior minority.

For the appalling majority the frontier of acceptability was their sexual impulses, so lamentably close to the surface, so little repressed. How clearly that demonstrated women's superiority to men - a fact unquestionable. Only look at the shape of men, she would say - those absurd narrow hips, not the splendid broad hips of women. But the sight of a broad-hipped man caused scalding scorn. "Ugh," she would say, "like a woman." No less was she offended by a man with powerfully developed pectoral muscles. "Like the breasts of a woman." Her way of enunciating 'breasts' gave the word an extra fleshly sound. Men were 'beasts'. A woman to whom a man made an amorous suggestion had been 'insulted'. How deplorably often women were so 'insulted'.

During their courtship my father had given her as a Christmas present an umbrella. She one day was carrying it when in the street she was 'insulted'. So great was the purity of her anger that in beating her accoster over the head with the umbrella she shattered it. It was long after, after marriage, that my puzzled father came to learn how his present had been destroyed. How could a decent young woman speak of such things to the young man who was to be her husband and the father of her children?

The first of those was my sister Violet Adelaide; next came my brother Albert Henry, two years younger. Then, three years more and it was my turn. They called me Bernard Percival; it was a compromise. Greatly as in early life I deplored that second name, it was an escape from worse. My paternal grandmother pressed strongly for Percy. Though in childhood it was with such difficulty I endured the shame of Percival, in maturity I have come to hearing the three names as making a pleasant sound.

Of my own first five years of life I have given such a sketch as memory allows. When I was six my father came home one day with a dog. The dog was nine months old, sprawlingly large, black and tan, half Airedale, half bloodhound, vastly amiable. He had neither the pendant jowls of the bloodhound nor the blood-hung eyes, nor the magisterial mien; but his voice was a hound's, an imposing bay. His name was Gyp. After first nervousness of his boisterous size, he started in me a love never to have been exceeded. There was soon another event; it had a connection with the advent of Gyp.

"Would you," said my mother to me one morning, "like to be a country boy? Would you like to leave the streets and houses? Would you like to live with the fields and woods?"

So, just so quietly when I was six the change came that was to reveal to me the meaning of life. From the half-life of south London we went into the sky-filled distances of south-east Kent; it in that far time was still deep country. Still then no touch of London's proximity had impinged. The grubby insulations that had muffled the textures and smells of life were dissolved away. We went to the village of Ham Street, just lodged on that brink where the roll of wood and meadow gave way to the watery levels of Romney Marsh. Our house, alone, out a little from the village, lay within the web of dykes and sedgey quakes.

Cypress House was its name though not a cypress was there. It was a little starkly set in the marsh, rather crouched as if feeling the immensity of sky. Very large it seemed to me, and now, between eighty and ninety years later, still I recall the enchantment of going from one to another of its rooms, each named - the blue room, the green room, each one large and light and square. They looked out on the shimmering light that lay on the marsh. I think now that my parents awarded to the rooms their delighting names for our greater pleasure. The kitchen was stone-flagged, in its corner a great pump. In the beams of the ceiling were hooks black with ancient being; they, my mother said, with the certainty of what she wished them to be, were for the hanging of flitches of bacon. A squeaking oaken door gave on to a paved yard and outbuildings; in the yard, splendidly, another great pump. Outside, in front, beyond a wicket fence the little road made its knife-cut into the marsh's distance, running all the way with a brimming dyke. Removed some way further on the road another house shared the solitude.

For inspection and arranging of the tenancy, before our coming, our parents had been down. They returned enraptured by the house and as much by its elderly owner. So gently patriarchal a man, so dignified by his silver hair and courtly manner.

For its water the house was dependent on its pumps. So rurally charming my parents thought that. How aromatic a thing compared with the urban dullness of taps. Aromatic it proved to be. The pumps yielded water that was yellow; it was opaque, its smell repellent. Other revelations were as disturbing. The sum of all was that the house was not habitable. There was a state of war between my parents and the saintly owner. But habitation however onerous must continue until an alternative were found. For my parents how stressful that must have been; how more so for the cold douche of disillusion. But what interest could I spare for all that? How could

I have heed in the midst of so much revelation? The marsh was spread to the eye's limit; its sky quartered by flights of wildfowl, even sometimes they said storks came. Along the dykes, leaning pollard willows had clustered crowns in which I could cradle to watch the vastly moving sky. The boundless air was sweet, humming and singing in the drowse of wind. In London life had gone from day to day; here suddenly, was ecstasy. Now I knew, if not just in those words, I had been born a countryman, by fate casually mislaid in a London suburb.

Behind the house lay the last small meadow before the marsh. In it lay a pond, small, shallow, insignificant as I now see. Over it spread the lean shade of a stunted oak, last of its kind before the dank-footed willows of the marsh. A poor little pond it was, but in me it stirred agitations - what hardly imaginable creatures moved secret ways beneath that green concealing surface? What lurking things? Could even there be fish?

I went with my pennies to the village shop. The shop was double-fronted in an old-fashioned way, its windows small-paned with slender glazing bars. From its door it went into far recessions of twilight storages. Its smell was of that kind unique to rural emporia, unforgettably mingled of camphor, leather, drapery, paraffin, pickles, and the miscellany of stocks left by the years, stacked, parcelled, beyond all possibility of inventory - leather boot laces, stout boots, rabbit wires, cartridges, bill hooks and sweet jars, bucolic ladies' underwear, fire lighters, candles, patent medicines and groceries. My pennies bought me a garden cane, a fishhook and a length of twine. Those and worms prepared me for revelation. By the pond in drugged bewitchment I stayed for many hours of many days, not tangibly rewarded but never diminished in faith. Minor fauna seethed within that green stagnancy - in its little compass a jungle, an ecology which gripped me with a deep fascination, making of me who knew nothing of such things, a naturalist. Much small life I did draw out, snails, crawling things that squirmed in my palm, slightly alarming beetles. Even I had half glances of newts for which I hungered obsessionally. But of fish never was there a sign. Probably not even a stickleback could flourish in that rich turbidity. But for faith there was food enough beyond the pond.

The whole marsh glimmered with its skeins of water, and no doubt in all there were fish, but never were they at any risk from me in my bewitchment. The Royal Military Canal threaded the marsh, so ringingly named, but really the most bosky forgotten-seeming waterway of immeasurable peace.

Spring came that year to Ham Street as presumably so it came every year; but never before in my brief life had it come as now it came. Perhaps there were days less than lovely; memory does not acknowledge them. It records only that each day the sun rose smiling to mornings hung with scents and sounds that trilled in the blood, that all day marsh and woods and fields pealed with birds' ecstatic voices. Never before had grass been so lucently green, leaves so tenderly hung on burgeoning boughs. A golden shine of kingcups spread upon the marsh; speedwell, celandine, violets swept the verges and over the fields. Thrushes and blackbirds sang without ceasing deeply into twilight each night; every aisle and clump and thicket rustled with life. I had never seen primroses before; they were tussocked, cushioned through the glades, over every bank. "Blossoms like pennies," my mother said in wonder. She was speaking of those robust old pennies that then we had, an inch or more across, not the pygmies that now we call pennies.

In the woods the anemones crowded under the trees, frail and fey, and after them the bluebells, knee-high and blue to the eye's limit, the air swimming with the fragrance that was theirs. More than an average lifetime later that scent in a moment slips me back to those distant woods of Ham Street. Unforgettably, almost anguishingly, of that spring's miracle were the nests of birds and the astonishing perfect fragility of the eggs that lay in them. I wish that first incredulous pang of discovery were recoverable now. I remember it; I cannot recover it. First of my discovery was that of a hedge sparrow, a dunnock. In the innocent ingenuity of the nest there lay the eggs, tiny, of the flawless distant blue of an early summer sky, the texture of a petal. In the herbage of a bank one day I found the nest of a robin, careless and downy with moss and feather, without the treasuring minuscule craftsmanship of some. The eggs were hazily freckled, warmly pinkish, brownish. As I stared enraptured, there came before my nightmared eyes a rat savaging the nest for the eggs.

Acute though was the worry of Cypress House my mother was not less joyously transported than I - though deprived by maturity of the most finely thrilled edge. Fresh brown eggs from her own hens probably symbolised her dream of country living; I wonder if she was aware as I was of the airy tranquillity of the sound of them? Free-range they would be called now; they had the range of the marsh. In that sky-soaked space they disposed their eggs - as did our neighbour's hens. Eggs were for the most diligent searchers.

Relief came at last from the incubus of Cypress House. We went to a house of quite another kind, off the marsh, at the upper end of the village; much at odds with the dream which had drawn my parents out of London. It was one of a short row, semi-detached, called Orlestone Villas, not in the least rural-seeming, but of a kind urban-looking which at the turn of the century had dropped incongruously through the villages. Sad fall for my parents though this was, for us compensation was ample.

The road dropping into the village passed the slope of the rather pinched little front gardens of the row. Opposite and beyond a small paddock was the railway station. It in country fashion was tiny, but on the main line to Dover. Gloriously a consequence, the most splendid locomotives of that time were to be seen - there, little beyond our windows. There they would be, with god-like panting, soft and vast, as they stood waiting in their power. Who would understand now what were the marks of their aristocracy that belonged to those stirring days of steam? They were green, darkly gleaming, brass-banded, squat-funnelled and, finally thrilling insignia, they had outside cylinders. Clouds of steam, firm as cotton wool, shrouded them as at the beginning of motion, with enormous sighings the silky steel of the pistons slid back and forth. To be near them then as with slow majesty the wheels began to turn was awed delight. Recent generations programmed to diesel and electricity cannot know what was the glory of those vanished locomotives. Compared with the utilitarian things of today they were almost sentient. For me it was a quiet but curiously intense pleasure to wander very privately on warm days in the sidings, dawdling bewitched among the rails and sleepers, smelling sun-warmed oil and creosote. As in the performances of a rite I would sit on the rails, then slowly, with reverence touch, actually touch the wheels of the wagons.

At the back of Orlestone Villas their long gardens ran down to a field that, in season, was a hop garden. Beyond that lay, first cherry orchards, then the woods. The house had no such undreamed of aids as electricity or gas. Regularly paraffin lamp wicks must be trimmed, paraffin topped up and, once a week, brushwood faggots were delivered for the feeding of the brick oven. Urban those houses appeared from without; inside they were intactly rural. Our neighbour on the right in that prim row was, incongruously, a farmer, a kindly man. His name, so aptly, was Garner. He was of a kind with few counterparts now, so small a farmer that he had no farmhouse, but must ply to and from his land from Orlestone Villas. It was just out of the village, just beyond the station, beyond the ugly little chapel. Twice a day from his yard he came, two buckets of milk suspended by the chains of a wooden shoulder halter, as for centuries men had carried milk, and now have so utterly ceased to do.

In the low huddle of the yard there was a shippon, a mouldering barn, a cart lodge, all anciently scented of milk, cows and, pervasively, dung. Domed in the yard's centre a lofty midden was sinisterly riddled with the holes and galleries of rats. That, from time to time, was purged, and I once was the dumbfounded witness of that. Mr Garner, kindly man, took me to stand by him to watch. I guessed that others there were small farmers too, coming on a basis of mutual help. To one side of the midden all stood with their guns in an arc. From a basket was taken a small animal, sinuously white, slinkily long, short of leg, exuding pretty menace, the first ferret I had seen. Put to the midden it slid in. Almost at once a loathely vomit of rats tumbled out. Over my head Mr Garner's gun burst with shattering sound beyond my imagining; a rat jumped, rolled, and lay twitching. Then all the guns were firing, a rending thunder spreading rats inertly everywhere.

As unimaginable as the gun's outrageous clap was its capacity for distant effect. I walked one day with Mr Garner over a slight rise of meadow to sight of the margin of a spinney. There, feeding out on the grass were rabbits at seeming invulnerable distance. Over my head the gun exploded; I, seeing nothing coming from its barrel but a slight puff of smoke, saw an incomprehensibly distant rabbit fling up, drop, lie still, entirely dead.

Spring melted into summer; still, memory tells of no weather not benign. The outside world continued to augment its delight - strengthening my sense that all that is worshipful is in the air, the fields, hedges, and the pagan temple of the woods. Briefly I did put conformity to the test. Other children of the village went Sabbath-clad and clean to Sunday School, the boys imprisoned in Eton collars rising in glazed slope from the shoulders to scrape the ears, in dark blue serge, black-polished boots. Thus to the ugly little chapel, not willingly but impelled by parents wanting the privacy of the Sabbath afternoon. No coercion was put upon me, my parents being at least as sceptical, as much inclined to the sweet pagan pleasure of nature. I perhaps was pushed by a faint sense of not belonging. I too would go to Sunday School. For three Sundays I did go. In the chapel the air was dusty, its smell stale. It lay dead in the depressed interior. I remember little else of those sanctified afternoons beyond my wistful consciousness in that sterility, of the flowering world outside. Opposite the chapel a yard interposed between Orlestone Villas and the woods, the fields. In the yard were great tar barrels because this was at the time when the old dust of the roads was by tar surfacing being sealed away. The barrels lay on their sides, so invaluable for the games of village boys. On the fourth Sunday to the yard I went. I lay, in a barrel, there unseen, commanding a view of the chapel. I saw that reluctant trail enter, the joyless door close upon it, enhancing my sense of freedom in the lilting air. I left my barrel. I went into the woods. To Sunday School I went no more.

It came in June to hay time, which had the nature of a festival, the first of those of summer. It was for everyone, men and women, children and the quite actively old. Through the day's long hours of sun there was a unity touched with festival. There was my mother, in a sunbonnet, tireless with a hay rake. The hay was tossed, turned, offered to the sun. Then, cocked, it waited for the wagons which came as beautiful as wooden ships, each curve and piece evolved from ancient usage. Sweating men with pitchforks swung trusses to men on the wagons until they were piled as high as reach would go. The slow return to the rick yard behind the rolling flanks of the great horses, on top us children half drugged by sweet scent of hay, drowsy with summer's pleasure. It was good hay, sweetened by sun and dew and humus. No taint was there then of chemicals to make it bitter.

Then to the orchards came ripening. Into the dappled alleys of the cherry orchards, every bough lusciously pendulous, came the pickers. Through the days the big circular baskets were filled, born away, replaced and filled again. The days were fruit-besotted. We were there, we and the Garners' small son, at first plundering unseen. Edging in, timidly plucking, we allowing ourselves to be seen. A young picker, elaborate with contrived clumsiness, overturned a basket.

"Oh bugger," he said, "tipped un over oi 'ave. Spilt all the bloody churries. Can't pick 'em all up again. Better be yourn. You 'ave 'em."

Then, hotly, exuberant, it was hop time. The trains came packed from London bringing the pickers - men, women, children, suckling babes. From the station the noisy throng flowed into the cloisters of the hop garden beyond our garden gate. The shade that had known nothing louder than hum of bees became uproarious. Women squealed, men chaffed, children shouted, babies cooed and cried in parked prams. Under the twine canopy canvas troughs were set up for the picking. Men with poles hooked down swags of hops; picking began. On the enclosed air lay the heavy pungency of bruised vines. Day by day in the hot lusty gout of humanity so it went.

Then it was done, the last hop picked. The shade that had

thrummed with lusty life became naked, with no stir left within the skeleton of wires and poles. Ham Street was emptied of its pickers. But not all of summer's events were over. To the summer-dry margins of the marsh came a convergent multitude of sheep and drovers. The uproar now was not of London voices but of hollering of drovers and a sorrowing thunder of sheep. This was the great annual sheep fair.

Desperate fellows my mother thought the drovers to be, and rather alarmingly rough they did look to me; and as the fair matured some did become rather extensively drunk. No doubt out of fair time they went their ways placidly enough. My mother was at first sight of a world of which she was hardly less ignorant than I; and was primed with her urban and dramatised misconceptions.

After the sheep fair, a culmination, there was The Fair, inheritance from all the generations of husbandry; all harvests gathered, a time for thankfulness and fun. Quite early in the day a blissful sense lay on the air, an unaccustomed look touched everyday things, as if with a different light. Everyone for that day must wear fancy dress, and in the warm September dark of evening there was to be a torchlight procession. My mother, erect with a high-held head, looked slimly proud in her dark green and braided velvet as a woman of the 17th century. I was a bluebell fairy; it brought me to the benign attention of Joseph Conrad and his wife. They lived a little out of the village at its upper end. Coming down to see the roundabouts they found me timidly at the edge without confidence or pennies. Each by one hand, they conducted me, providing pennies.

To the village Conrad was a figure of mystery, eccentricity. A writer he was then - what sort of a queer living was that then? Doing all his work at night too, when other people slept. Nobody must make a sound in that house by day, they said. Didn't seem right. On occasions, as the guest of the driver of the water cart, I had been to the house. The water cart had a boiler-shaped tank mounted on the frame and wheels of a cart; it went its trudging way behind a horse for the delivery of household water. Then in that whole place there was no such thing as piped water. The driver, a kind and dawdling man, took me on the slow ambles of his round. Where anywhere now could be found the fathomless tranquillity of that?

To a fund-raising sale in the village Conrad had given an autographed copy of one of his books. Though marked down it did not find a buyer. He was of the early motorists, his car a thing of fume and clatter; he drove hard to wring from it perhaps thirty miles an hour. Its passage out of the village raised clanging dust clouds from the road still then not tarmacked into submission. To this Gyp, a dog of his day, was not conditioned. With thundering voice he pursued it, almost belly-flat to the road.

By that and other happenings there fell upon Gyp a notoriety. "Savage bloody dog 'e is - didn't ought a be free about bloody place. T'aint safe for folks." But that falsity on his good name was not without value. We were incomers, strangers. Ham Street saw few of such a kind. Adults, not hostile, not overtly unfriendly, were cool. My parents tried with warmth to play their social part, singing in the choir, all that they could. Perhaps in home privacies adults talked - undoubtedly they did - equally certainly children were attentive. So much was to be sensed at the school.

The school was at the upper end of the village, where the roll of wood and meadow began. It was little, low, ugly, held from the woods by a small asphalted playground. It seemed to me always to be twilight inside. The teaching staff was two, Mr and Mrs Farrer. Their mental field extended little beyond the school's windows, and it was plain they saw us with little favour. Bert, nine, and Vi, eleven, were in the loftier level in the room ruled by Mr Farrer; I in the other room had the rule of Mrs Farrer. I recall her as dimly dressed, pinched.

In both rooms, senior and junior, we wrote on slates with slate pencils which squeaked, setting my teeth on edge. In the juniors, among my contemporaries, five and six, I suffered no hostility; acceptance among us, so young, was unqualified. But in the seniors some were evolving, growing towards hobbledehoy aspirations for which in school they lacked scope. Outside its taint could have expression. It fell not upon Bert, not on me, but on Vi. Ham Street in the way of Kentish villages then, could be subject to clots of first symptom sub-pubescent youth seeking assertion. Such a one Ham Street had. It was in want of a target; there was Vi. It was less providential that Vi, walking abroad, went often in the company of Gyp. Gyp was a dog who knew what he should do.

So one day, when Vi was waylaid, surrounded, hands laid upon her, Gyp was impressive. He prostrated the handler, stood on his chest the better to thrust his thunderous snarl, his slavering teeth closely into the helpless countenance. The offenders dispersed. A few such incidents were salutary. Gyp and Vi were secure in his reputation.

It would be false to let such minor factors suggest a dense atmosphere of rejection. Most people were kindly and of good intention. But then, in the very early years of the 20th century in such a village as Ham Street, in such a place as rural Kent then was, there was an ingrown isolation as people of today cannot guess. It might well be that never before had they had to adjust to the coming of a family not of the local kind. Most people did their friendly best; but to their instincts our effect was of another species.

I, most of the time, was without consciousness of these immaterial factors. Life's dear revelations of every day did not stop. When summer went there were sweet chestnuts ripened in the woods - so lovely was that discovery - the shining nuts in their prickled satin-lined cases, bewitching to touch. That they were so delighting to eat was the more so for being illicit. It was in Mr Maleham's woods the chestnuts grew; they were on his farm. When we, a little raiding party, saw his distant angry approach for the thwarting of us, we lay in a ditch while his legs thudded by on the other side of the hedge. When he was safely away and to home, happy to have defeated us, we gathered our nuts.

Mine I took to the village baker and greengrocer shop. I invited them to buy my nuts; they gave me a penny for them. It was the first money I ever earned, my first venture into crime.

CHAPTER III

The End of a World

THE PARADISIC pleasures of Ham Street sadly were fugitive; it had been an idyll, no more. Idylls, in their nature, do not translate easily into common solidity. The end was inevitable; the Ham Street experiment had run its course. It had disillusioned my parents; it had set for me a future pattern of life.

Though then I had no terms for so defining, it had revealed to me that life could be acceptable only in a context of nature. Though I could not so express it, I now knew that I was, and could only be, a countryman. I knew I had fallen into a worship of nature. Of that I knew too that its most poignant expression was having succumbed to fascination by water, by merest ponds, the canal, the seethe of life that so mysteriously was in them. Though unacknowledged, a brooding sense of that had haunted me from earliest consciousness. Not until the coming to Ham Street had I seen living water; then almost as by the seeing of a vision, came passionate awakening.

Bernard, middle row, centre.

It was not in the least as an experiment that my parents had come to Ham Street. They came drawn by a sanguine vision; theirs was an inspired departure from which there was to be no return. The shabby past was ended; no more was there to be suburban frustration, the grey treadmill. All that was done, left. They were to make of life what would justify the having of life.

With what idealism they must have discussed it - I can imagine the visionary bulge of my father's hazel eyes behind his pince-nez; with what joyous ignorance they must have talked of what lay beyond. But how little their lives till then had been a preparation for the realities of ruralness. My father's wistful vision had been of the dewy ways of country life. My mother, no less poignantly beckoned, was swayed by visions much enlarged by her ardent mind. The delights they found were real; but in their Arcady were other factors. Not all was of delight.

Bucolic simplicity they were to have found. My mother would keep chickens that laid brown eggs; my father, so good a gardener, would grow delicious vegetables in their own soil by their own garden path. I think that in their vision a time was to come when my father should shed his London shackles. They planned for no less than heaven.

Of heaven they found small gleams; but darknesses soon lowered. The enforced separation of the weekdays could have been only partly lightened by the glow of weekends; and then, weekends began at midday on Saturday. Pressure of money weighted the wings they had hoped to spread in the sun of rural delight. Nor did they find the kindly welcome into rustic society that they had expected.

In such distant days the pattern of exodus from town to country had not begun. The closed-shop of rural life had not then been breached. My parents, coming with their hearts on their sleeves, were not rebuffed. But they were not absorbed. Sad return to London became inevitable.

During the latter months at Ham Street there were portents. The year was 1913. Probably foreshadowings had touched my parents. To us children, probably to most rural adults, it was an exciting extenuation of the summer's sequence. When all seemed done there came this recurrent passage of soldiers - troops so impressively massed that again the road into and through the village was choked, not now chaotically, but with military order. Under our very hedge, wedging past hours at a time, khaki soldiers, horse-drawn wagons, great guns on their rumbling wheels. They came not as a cavalcade, with no blood-stirring trumpeting, no drumming, but purposeful. The soldiers were jolly. Some sat straddled over gun barrels wide as the back of a big horse. I found that immensely impressive.

Perhaps nothing beyond could compete for my memory, but there ends for me all that was Ham Street. That there was an interval is certain; it was a dark evening of November when we came to South Norwood. Of the weeks or months between I know nothing. But here I was, tired, emptily forlorn, sitting on an upturned dresser drawer, in a little empty kitchen. My mother was silent. Slowly she gazed round the pinched meanness.

"Dad - Dad," she said at last. "You've brought us to a slum."

The light was dim, a candle; probably my father was without a shilling for the gas meter. The close walls pressed more closely because they were papered with deep red simulated brocade. My father looked disheartened, a little sheepish. His large eyes looking larger behind his glasses. But how could I, then but six remember? I do, with dreadful clarity.

No more than that; nothing of arrival, of furniture coming, not of going to bed. Exhausted sleep must have been immediate. But not to last. I was awakened by a sound so queerly sinister as to throw me into dread. It ululated; was like no sound I had heard before. I began to think it had a sound of children, but what children of earth could have a sound of such nightmare? On successive nights it came again. But, my mother told me, it was nothing but the cries of lust-ridden tom cats. Thereafter I came to know them well, for they were legion, beasts of such ugliness that their sound could not have been otherwise. They were lean, rank, huge of head and crop-eared, battle-tattered. Their drear caterwauling of the first night was fitting for what morning's light revealed.

Could the fields and woods of Ham Street be in one world with this? Could we have left them for this huddle beyond the window? Under the window was the glass-roofed lean-to, beyond it a cramped few feet of sullied soil, on either side enclosed by an open-palinged fence, at the end by a solid fence. So was our garden separated on either side from its replica and from another glass-topped lean-to. With such identical twinning either side was made the street's short length. That I saw on that first morning at No. 20 Aylett Road, a terraced house in an obscurely mean cul-de-sac. For an illusion of privacy in front of each pinched house was a narrow concreted space bounded by a low wall topped with iron railings. Its other function was to contain the dustbin on refuse collecting days. Aylett Road at its blind end was crossed by an alley, beyond it a fence and a squalor of gardens and housebacks very like our own. That was the rear of what I was to know as the hostile territory of Whatcomb Road. Our neighbours beyond the back garden fence were of Notson Road, neutral territory of respectability greater far than Whatcomb Road.

At the street's open end it formed a T-junction with a crossing road; there a right turn took you in a few yards on to another street that paralleled and duplicated Notson Road and Aylett Road. This was Albert Road, its squeezed little houses running into a vista throwing off other streets; the first of those was the infamous Whatcomb Road. But Albert Road's frontage gazed not at another mirror row but over a hawthorn hedge to wide green spaces, at first sight a prospect. It was illusory. Officially and euphemistically the filter beds. By any name its smell was no better. In all but hard freezing the sewage farm stank; on summer's most balmy evenings smell made of the air almost a solidity.

Aylett Road and its neighbours lay in the low belly of South Norwood. Northwards the ground rose; with its rising the air cleared until attaining the relatively salubrious High Street. Beyond, rising still, it came to Upper Norwood where still was a residual aura of 19th century gentility. The mellow reaches of its chestnut-shaded streets, the vistaed drop; of its steep ways from the central ridge, the stately stucco of its houses, was dominated by the Crystal Palace. It, though then bereft of all but ghostly emptiness, was magnificent.

Back in the slough of South Norwood there was little saving distinction, nor ever was, it may be guessed. Apart from its heights. Its greater part, that low trough, was built on original marsh. My mother recalled that she, when a child at Upper Norwood, knew it not as South Norwood but as The Marsh. Probably the cause of its building had been to provide labour for prosperous gentlemen of the City who resided genteelly on South Norwood's high ground. In our earlier years most larger houses - and some smaller ones - were still decorous with white-capped maids. Still a coachbuilder was in supportable business.

In the belly of Norwood squalor was confined. South Norwood valued its working class respectability. Its citizens sharply divided downwards to dwellers of restricted slums where throughout winter ragged children went barefoot. There secluded were relict reminders of a country past. A cottage row almost rurally intact had been trapped by a meanness of building which had swarmed over it.

From the more exalted heights Portland Road pitched down steeply to where by probing through a hinterland of small streets Aylett Road could be found under its pall of odour. By back roads from there, with slight acknowledgement of a country past, there could be found an open green space. Curiously its name was the Carcasses. At its far corner there fell away a road, unmetalled, often muddy, still half rural, regarded most dubiously. Its name was Love Lane.

That name once probably had been appropriate. It could be seen how bosky, gently shaded had been its nature. Now its dwellers were ragged, warily regarded; their only sin was poverty. Round the corner from Love Lane was the cemetery, starkly posted by Lombardy poplars. Beyond lay the noisome wastes of the sewage farm.

A track crossed it which could take you to Elmers End. There still in spring the air could be sweet; on fine days of May still a way could be taken through grasses and wild flowers to catch minnows and fill jam jars with frog spawn from a streamlet by the railway. Still then Elmers End had wistful remnants of a rural past. Beyond its straggle of houses a way could be taken across potato fields to the village of West Wickham, so pretty then and countrified as to charm the heart. At the T-junction of its two streets a huge elm all but filled the road's width, imposing on traffic a caution which was of those slow times. All of that gone now, tree and tolerance

South Norwood, eight miles only from London Bridge, belonged then to London's outer southern suburb; within easy reach of a good pair of legs lay country. By the walking of five miles the feet could tread meadow grass, ears hear the sigh of wind through woodland. So, tenuously, there was a thread to the revelations of Ham Street.

That was of later discovery; memory of the first months mercifully is faint. Perhaps they brought some solace of acceptance, possibly even to my parents. Probably my mother's sanguine resilience brought her soon to the surface after that bleak initial immersion. But in Aylett Road even that left need of support more solid. All the circumstances pressed upon her, but one was central. It was Carter. Carter was the agent; he collected the rent. He was small; red and swelled at the neck. He was bulbous; his voice, constant for all occasions, was a bubbling boom. On Monday of every week he left his house at the corner of Notson Road to make his rent-collecting round. Between him and my mother in very little time war was joined. It was to be intermittent but inevitably recurrent. Combat though often lusty, was without bitterness. Carter, great as was his thunder, was a not unkindly man. He had a well-loved mongrel dog; friendship was soon established between him and Gyp. But Carter was accustomed to the having of his own way with tenants; his was the thunder of authority. He came in innocence to first encounter with my mother.

"I'm not one of your browbeaten tenants," she told him at an early affray. "You'll get as much as you give."

She astonished the hitherto unchallenged Carter. To us most horrifyingly the house had bed bugs. I remember my own revulsive sickening at the sweetly horrible smell of them when crushed. So infested was every house in Aylett Road.

"You have the impertinence to come asking for rent for these infested hovels?" my mother demanded when he came bawling on his rent round.

"Have to put up with that, y'know. Always get it with this sort of old property."

That no doubt, so odiously, was true; so to put it to my embattled mother was tactless. It imposed upon him a handicap for future engagements. Experience did show that only total demolition and burning of all remnants could have stopped the appalling tenacity of bed bugs. 'A sure remedy for bed bugs' said the label on the sulphur candle. As directed by that label all windows and doors were sealed, the candle lit, the room left for twenty-four hours before unsealing. For many months thereafter that room, so treated, was only painfully habitable. After an interval, too brief, the bugs re-emerged not in the least less virile.

So smothering a fact of life was the sewage farm that only by degrees did another smell become discernible. My mother, at once alertly suspicious, soon hardened to certainty. She perceived a connection; why, so chronically, were we suffering sore throats? As though declaring an outbreak of plague, she enunciated - Drains! Was this not her most constant dread? Bad Drains!

When next Monday brought Carter to the door she hurled it at him. "Mr Carter - this place has bad drains! Our health is endangered. What do you propose doing?"

"No, can't be," he bawled softly, "no possibility. No nasty things like that while I'm about. Very fussy about those things I am. Change in the air - blowing in from the country most likely."

That should have been enough - always had been. But my mother's teeth were in. Each rent day they bit harder. As persistently Carter boomed denial.

"He's had his chance," my mother said; she sent for the Sanitary Inspector. His diagnosis was positive. The drains of No. 20 Aylett Road and of all the rest of Aylett Road were an immediate danger to health, beyond hope of tinkering. Carter's defeat was catastrophic. The order was for total renewal forthwith of the entire drainage.

Muddy chaos came; it ran through every house. In each one floors were taken up, trenches driven through, fouled and broken drain-pipes removed, new ones laid. Through more trenches they were to join the main sewers in their great trenches running the street's length. For the prolonged period of the work all comings, all goings, were precariously on muddy planks over the trenches. It was to Carter's credit that in such draconian defeat he was not bitter. The clangour of his engagements with my mother was unsoured.

My hold on the chronology of that time is now insecure. I cannot remember which came first, the Battle of the Drains or the outbreak of the Great War. To my seven-year-old mind their impact did not much differ. In those few months between our coming to South Norwood and that day in August 1914 there must surely have been some premonitory unease as to what impended.

But of that day of August I remember a few minutes of its morning. My parents are looking at the newspaper; their voices are hushed. I catch their mood, half excited, half foreboding. War has been declared they tell us. We are at war with Germany. I feel through them a sense of something monstrous. On the front page, under the headline is a photograph. German soldiers with spiked helmets peer from under bushes, a machine gun between them. The picture imparts a sense of threat so strong that it fascinates and frightens. That is all my memory of the step over the brink. It was from an old world of peace and certainties. The new world was of War, unknown. So far it was dreamlike because my parents had so strange a seeming.

Now every day a half excitement hung on the air, vaguely frightening. Every day the newspapers raged. 'The Huns are coming' screamed captions to pictures of German masses trampling the crops of Belgian fields. 'Poor little Belgium.' 'The Hun jackboot on the face of little Belgium.' So on, day by day. "Poor little Belgium - poor little pawn between the competitive interests of both sides," said my father. Only within our own four walls was it safe so to speak. Nor, as in maturity I have perceived was that judgement entirely true though not without truth.

Outside there could be no dissent. On every hoarding that

famous poster browbeat all who passed - Lord Kitchener, fiercely Marshall, pointed an imperious finger, YOUR COUNTRY NEEDS YOU. All high and low competed to denounce 'The Hun' in rhetoric that should have embarrassed all but the culpably naïve. Huns in the trenches, the papers told us, sang the Hymn of Hate seeking to intimidate 'Our Gallant Boys'. No doubt they did. The German and Allied contexts were largely similar - though I think the common man of Britain would have found his sense of humour an obstacle to the singing of the Hymn of Hate. But in whatever terms, hate, either way, was the mode. My father quoted a verse:

> "*God hear the embattled nations shout,*
> *Gott straffe England, God save the king.*
> *God this, God that, God the other thing.*
> *Good God said God, I've got my work cut out.*"

Whether this was indeed a quote or of my father's devising, I cannot say. It was his style.

Nothing now must be German, nothing so tainted. A German sausage it had been; breakfast sausage now it must be. King George V, worthy man, blameless in his patriotism, but solidly of German blood, perforce must change his family name from Guelf to Mountbatten. His cousin, the German Kaiser is shown in the cartoons drenched with blood of victims as he tramples Belgian women and babes. On a corner in Portland Road there stood a baker's shop. So it had stood for many years, as established as sunrise. Edwards was the name it bore, British enough. But the baker was German. He was a mild man, a little tubby. His pale blue eyes, short-sighted behind his glasses, looked kindly on his neighbours. In the rooms above the shop his two daughters had been born, and had served their time at Portland Road School just round the corner. He was known for his small generosities to needy people roundabout. A gentle and respectable man, Mr Edwards.

Quite early in the war his neighbours came to the shop; they came as a mob. They smashed the windows; into the street they threw his sacks of flour. They wrecked the shop. So well those neighbours knew the Edwards family, they knew that the two daughters, coming from work, would arrive at Norwood Junction station at the usual time. They waited for the girls, engulfed them, mobbed them.

The lust to hurt was freed from normal decencies. Nice young ladies secure within Britain's safe shores, found fulfilment in the giving of the white feather. How warmly patriotic these young ladies could feel when, in the street, they could present the white feather to any man not in uniform, they could watch the wound. The white feather declared its recipient to be a coward, not 'doing his bit'.

The introduction of conscription ended these pleasures for young ladies. Progressively through the age groups all men were summoned to medical examination for possible induction into the army; among them was my father. Men were graded downwards from the fully-fit at A1 down to impossibly unfit at C3. My father was graded C3. It did not save him from lingering white feathers.

Inevitably but slowly the bursting of jingoism dispersed from the public gut. Where it remained it was usually coincident with the war proving less painful than profitable. In the earlier part of the war women were adjured 'Give your sons', 'Give your husbands'. They gave them. But by grim progression men so 'given' had less probability of return. They died, gloriously the women were told. Glory lost its lustre as it came to be known that the death's glory came so often with a man's spilled guts churned with mud feeding the fattening rats.

In Aylett Road the vanishing of men progressed inexorably. By halfway through the war the clouds of reality hung low. To me return two fragments of memory. I am in a train from Norwood Junction to East Croydon. There are three of us - another boy with me, and a soldier. The soldier is in full kit and has his rifle. From his waist to his feet he is encrusted with yellow mud; it cracks and falls with his movements. "Flanders mud," he says. The other memory is of an empty classroom at school, emptied by playtime. I, a monitor, remain legitimately. My teacher, who is young and pretty, is crumpled over her desk. She weeps desperately. Yesterday she was married; today her husband is snatched from her arms to the trenches of the Western Front. His return is not probable. All my life since then I have retained my anxiety as to his survival or not.

For much of the war's earlier part its visual evidence in South Norwood was slight, though once for several hours an immense column of troops, four abreast, passed through Portland Road, from whence or to where none knew. The slogan 'Business as usual' was much repeated - and indeed, were there not many profits to be made from the war? Outcry against profiteers was loud but did not lessen the profitable patriotism.

Then, of deepest interest to me, there were air raids. By the standard of what the then unimagined future was to show, the raids were mild, almost absurd, lethal as nevertheless they were. But they did shake some safe complacencies. The brutal realities of war had, so comfortably been 'over there'. England had been inviolate.

First there was the Zeppelin, a sinister monster by night. Astoundingly so soon it was proved vulnerable. It dropped a few small bombs, demolished a few houses, killed a few citizens. Then a fighter aircraft pumped bullets into its gross target; it and its crew fell blazing spectacularly to earth. Zeppelins came no more. Then onwards the sky of every night was lit with a trellis of searchlights. Now it was aeroplanes that came, small and hard to find in so much sky however lit, so hard for guns to hit. More bombs were dropped in more places; at last in London there was fear. England's sea-girt island was inviolate no more. On nights lovely with a gentle balm of moonlight the bombers came. As surely as moonrise, came also the air raid warning. By every street on his bicycle came the policeman, on his chest a placard. TAKE COVER it said. Also as his breath served he blew his whistle.

But I was a small boy; how could I but be delighted by excitements so strange? There came an evening when the policeman's amble found me a mile or more from home. Now I had the freedom of it; now no compulsions to cover should deny me. Spellbound and slowly I went towards home. The whole night was fragmented by searchlights, the celestial bursting of anti-aircraft shells. It was as dreams are; no sense of danger touched me; I wandered as though freed from fear and invulnerable. Shell fragments that slapped into the pavements told me nothing of risk. I came at last to home in a ravished trance. My truancy seemed not to have been noticed by my parents.

I was in bed on first hearing an anti-aircraft gun, unaware of its close presence. I had no conception of what could so gargantuanly rend the night. Its sound was as of a vast fall of planks, as vast as never before.

In a terrace of small working-class houses I first saw the effect of a bomb. It had, in the neatest possible fashion nipped out one house, as though unnoticed by the rest of the row. There until one moment in one night a family had had its being; now was nothing but a quite small heap of rubble. So strange it seemed that a house, so permanent a thing, so abruptly could be deleted.

To the air raids was owed a new phrase of unhappy permanence; then, and forever more, 'black-out' has had its place in the language. Blackouts at first were of apprentice kind, not of that black totality which was to sweep the world. The shine of careless chinks was common, and as common was the ritual cry - "Put that light out!" - little more than a cliché. Street lamps, still allowed their lights, were dimmed by a black smearing of the glass. The raids, a small salutary suggestion that danger need not be only for soldiers, really were little more than irrelevancies in the war's vast horror. The casualty lists from the trenches were a drain into which the lives of men guttered away endlessly.

At home through the days of winter, the food queues became patient straggles a mile or more long. Often the wait of many hours failed to reach the shop before the exhaustion of its stock. Potatoes, it must be assumed, still grew in England; we saw none. Basic foods became thin on the shelves of shops; their prices soared. Sporadically, briefly, coal could be had - often only by those who, catching the news on the wind, went quickly to the coal wharfs with such transport as they had - barrows, perambulators, often mere determination of arm and shoulder. Sometimes on winter days I walked the four or five miles into the countryside with a sack, there to pack it with fallen wood almost beyond my power to lift. The way was with the burden to stagger a few yards, drop it, sit on it and pant, repeat and gasp again. When, too long delayed, rationing did come, it brought more equitable sharing, abolishing the monstrous queues. As invariably it is in wars, it was urban dwellers for whom was worst privation; in rural places the soil remains fertile, so emphasising the essential unreality of urbanism. The tables of those engaged in profitable patriotism were of course not unkindly served throughout.

Supply of bread remained constant though few could guess what went into its making. It was mysterious in texture, often unmanageably loose; it contained anonymous blackish lumps. Its looseness often disallowed spreading of the rancid ration of margarine. My father, dourly in protest ate it with a spoon.

He before the war had been underpaid, posed on poverty's edge. As with the war's advance, prices rose, but no comparable rise touched his weekly portion of £2.10.0. My mother, though for her time enlightened on nutritional values, was the vaguest of managers and, more distressfully, a worse cook. She lacked the flair to draw the best from the worst. We were close to serious hunger. She urged my father, imploring that he should ask for a rise. He shrank from what he thought the certainty of rebuff. One Saturday she refused to take the minute housekeeping money. She did no shopping; we were without food.

"Till you ask for a rise I'll do no more shopping. This is the end of my tether," she said.

On Monday my father asked. The rise was given without demur. It was small but we could survive.

That my parents were desperate I can now perceive. Briefly - and soon disillusionedly - I was a member of the Wolf Cubs, those under-age scouts. The time was winter; on an evening when snow slush lay thickly we were taken on a march. I, that night, was in first wearing of new boots; by what racking struggles my father had achieved them I must guess. They were painful, almost beyond bearing, and not of leather but, in the wartime way, of some compression possibly of paper. In the icy slush they disintegrated. My father was close to tears; my mother attacked me fiercely. I burnt with the hot sense of injustice. Now I understand.

Within my perspective war was now normality; peace had softened to mist, remembered but not of today's life. Thought of war's end had no conviction, only for adults was poignant longing for peace; for them it must have become weak. Even into 1918 the end seemed no less bloodily distant. Presumably there were foreshadowings, but unaware as I was the end was inexplicable; suddenly, unreasonably it was there. How could life so known, cease suddenly to be? Nor do I understand how, on that November morning, we knew. No radio was there then, no instant news. But, at 11 o'clock, we knew. The strange fact of peace had fallen upon us.

Its first defining token for me was brother Bert. He said nothing. He took a bucket of water, a pair of steps and a cloth. He went to the lamppost in the street, mounted the steps, cleaned the black from the glass. He came back, restored bucket and steps to their places. He said no word. Peace had come to Bert. I, now eleven, was usually leader and games inventor among my peers. On this November morning I appointed some of them to be German sailors; the dustbin within our gateway I appointed to be the conning tower of a British submarine. I, its Commander, from within lifted the lid, hailed the German mariners. "Ahoy," I called, "don't be afraid. The war's over. We're all friends now."

As early dark fell on Norwood the flood tide of release burst restraint. All that evening I wandered alone seeing such things as never had I seen before. In every street huge fires were stacked almost to the road's width, infernos eating the recklessly thrown fuelling of anything combustible dragged from houses. Much furniture that night was given to sacrificial pyres in the hysteria of joy. It was over. Over. No more dying, no more weeping, no more dread. Round each inferno they danced red, demoniac; they sang, were demented. Dotards, grandmothers, all those younger, half mad in their joy. Drunks fell, lay as they fell, still singing. Towards midnight in Holland Road which is in the pit of Norwood, the fire had burnt to its embers, a red Hades from kerb to kerb. A man, scrawny, elderly, shabby, shouting hoarsely with cracking voice, was somersaulting through the incandescent heart of the fire;

again, again. His clothes began to burn. I came away, going home because he frightened me. Peace had come.

In the war's last complete year, 1917, there had come an event which, by the inference of my parents' emotional response, reduced to littleness the war's enormity. It came as the war had come, suddenly one morning, given by my parents a sense of unguessable significance, vastly looming, formless. To Russia had come revolution, as it seemed to me a miasma of blood and chaos. Her oppressed masses had risen in vengeful violence. In Moscow, in St Petersburg there was fighting in the streets. Soldiers and sailors, bidden to the suppression of the mob, had joined it. It was not riotous eruption, not a flame to burn briefly then die. It was an erasing of an old order, a change of totality. The Tsar, monarch and symbol was deposed. It was, I was led to guess, a titanic event.

Though to the world at large no doubt world-shaking, its scale as it came to me probably was dramatised. For the length of their adult lives my parents had anticipated it, prayed that it might be. My father did not live long enough for disillusion.

My knowledge of the outer world at ten was sparse; but, relatively, I knew a lot about Russia. I could not have failed so to do. I had heard about a decadent ruling class living parasitically upon the suppression of hungry serfs. I knew on occasions their suppression was maintained by onslaught of sabre-swinging Cossacks. I knew of the 'mad monk' Rasputin; the evil rottenness of his domination was flourished by my parents as a symbol. The Day would come they said; the Russian masses would rise from their hovels, they would sweep away that which lay upon them. So I had heard for all the length of my brief life.

Now I was to learn of Mensheviks and Bolsheviks - how the former were in their short first dominance not true deliverers but misleaders of The People; how the latter were noble saviours of The People. I learned too that there were 'white Russians' a term of deep contempt for all Russians who were not Bolsheviks. As time was to show, though not to my deeply sincere parents, this term, so amorphous, included not only the upper layers; in it too were the anonymous innocence of middle class people going their little ways. Bitter suffering came to them. That it was an historical inevitability did not make that more bearable.

It was a time direly of black-and-white in which objective vision was almost impossible. My parents saw through the eyes of passionate idealism.

Chapter IV

Lodge Lane led to Biggin Hill

HAVE I conveyed that those woeful years of war were a parenthesis, taken out of the gathering flow of childhood? Not at all was it so; the two were welded. The effects of war left too profound a print on the pattern of life at large; all was inseparable. The mind of childhood does not anyway make separations; all is normality because it is happening. The war was over; now other things were happening. It is the way of war that its demands throw up technical advances that give a forward lurch to life in material matters, and these in turn modify emotional consciousness in ways unrealised at the time. Such changes, infinitesimal as they must appear to eyes of the century's closing years, started a progression which has become manic at least and probably finally destructive.

But for that I could spare no attention; for it I had not the least cognisance. My absorptions were exclusive. In June of 1915 my sister Marian was born, but that salient fact, though interesting and somewhat startling, did not impinge intrinsically on what was central to my expanding being. Enlarging consciousness was woven obsessionally of many things. The wholly possessing delight in the having of life, its textures, scents and sounds. But of life there were two parts; one was that bounded by Aylett Road and its hinterland, and must be endured. The other was that in which the entranced senses were awakened, and, in that far time, no more than a walk away. Ecstasy was to be had by the walking of but five miles. There lay open country. Under sun-tangled hedges on days of summer there were secrecies that hummed and rustled with a myriad little lives, tiny burnished beetles and caterpillars soft to the touch as fairy's suede. In summer sinking of the light, great downy moths were out in fumbling flight, and it was then that I first discovered night. Night was not of the world of day; it had no shared part. Its entrance was through the half-world of twilight, that also was of itself alone, acknowledging not day nor night. Then day was done and gone, hardly remembered. Now was the huge murmuring world of night where sight lay in the feather-touch of the other senses. Hardly comprehensibly to people of this latter degraded world, I then, with no real anxiety for my parents, could wander solitary in the country till night sank upon it and the vast darkness whispered and pulsed with its unnumbered lives. How could so much shabby change come even in as many as the eighty-five years that have passed since then? But eighty-five years - is that so many in the span of history? Is the virtue of living to be accepted as being so fragile?

Memory so distantly recalled, more easily dredges what was of summer, but all seasons were of delights no less. In winter there were lost unpeopled lanes where the muscular twist of roots of ash trees gripped banks of deep-piled emerald moss. Other roots, oak and field maple and holly, held the banks as often, but those of ash were so smoothly moulded, often so satined to the touch that I must stroke them, with fingers following their flexions. I could sense the year-long movements of their growth. Winter was naked but with no sense of barrenness; I could feel in the trees their sleeping; instinctively I was worshipful of them and so have remained for all my life. Childhood accepts its responses without analysis, but it may be seen from this distance that without thought I had accepted worshipfully that I was of earth and that was my delight, and that the glory of trees was its expression.

Passionately as I was moved by nature, almost with a separate intensity, I was engaged by the sense of living water. That so haunted the imagination as to be a mysticism, and had no need for first meeting for arousal. The sense of it had been constant in instinctive thought from first awareness. When at Ham Street there at last, tangibly, it was found, I was - yes, mystically - entirely enslaved. There it lay, still, reserved and mysterious. The bewitched imagination was trapped in conjecture as to what gliding creatures could be within it. That first state of innocent, ecstatic discovery, however piercing, is by its nature fragile. An innocence once breached is not subject to repair. To this day, eighty-five years on, my mind, my being, are held still in lovely thrall by water and the slipping shadowed life that is elusive in it; but that first poignancy, that is not recoverable.

I think it to have been no chance, nothing at all of coincidence, that something else was creeping into consciousness to share obsessional space. I was held in fascination by shapes and textures and colour, by bulk and flow of form. I fell into the drawing of what I saw, as spontaneously as I used my hands for any other purpose, but finding in it a pleasure curiously compulsive.

Addington in its valley lay five miles from home. It was quiet and of such delight to me that as often as there was freedom for it, we two, Gyp and I, would set off as soon as breakfast had been snatched (or, as sometimes it was, forgotten to be had). Out of Norwood and through Addiscombe and passing the leaning fence where the ancient horse asked for company, and there town ended and country began. It was the point, always, where excitement began to rise, quickening by the step - not less for Gyp than for me.

Then Shirley Church Road, then there the woods, the tall fronded lovely smelling bracken. Then, anticipate, again here was Spout Hill, falling in its steep tumble to the valley. Under us in the valley was Addington. Here began exultancy. On the left down the fall was the time-lichened wall of Addington Palace. But on the left - ah there, not forgotten, unforgettable, the glory of the woods, a dropping mantle of forest, a solitary paradise, a sanctity. Probably this ecstatic place was not as we thought unknown; sometimes perhaps others worshipfully quiet entered too. We saw none, heard none. In May's time of darling buds the fragrance floating of bluebell's blossoming was a celestial drug; the blue sea of blossoming floored the wood, standing to my knees. The singing of blackbirds, full-throated, sounded temple-like in that place.

Deeply in the wood was a tree, a beech, which stood more majestically tall than all others. Always, ritualistically, I would climb through its mighty twist of limbs to reach the slender finality of its top. There I could cling, swaying in even the gentlest summer wind; Gyp, knowing all, waited patiently below.

At the bottom of Spout Hill's fall to Addington village there was a T-junction. So clearly I see it still. To the right, a row of flint and brick cottages lay back from the road, the ends of their long gardens always, in season, sprawling-bright with blossom. Beyond them was the church.

Addington Church

It too was of flint. Inside it was hushed; of that odour peculiar to ancient country churches, accumulated of time, of moist earth-textured air. I, in its spell, would fall into a dream of those generations who had trodden there in their seasons, gone, remembered by none. They had trod where I, soft-footed, now trod. Upon a tomb lay an effigy in ruff and armour. What breathing sentient man, passionate in his time, did that commemorate? There was his name; but who was the living man, warm in his living mind? What had been his thoughts when he stood where now I stood? How could he imagine that now I should see his tomb in such inconceivable future? Over the tomb hung a helmet; perhaps that had shielded the head that had been his and had thought as I thought. Coming from the church the brief shadow of the porch did not give time enough for transition to the world of today's daylight.

On Spout Hill's other corner, that on the left - was it the school that stood there? How odd that I cannot be more certain about that so well remembered village; it is so I seem to see it - and yes, so it was, brick and flint too, with a small playground. But recalling vision flickers. Beyond and a little way, vision strengthens to certainty; there the small smithy is unforgettable, a place of wonderful fascination. It was low ceilinged, cavernous, with sights and sounds and smells that held me in addiction. With time unremembered I must lean on the half-door to watch the shoeing of fat-flanked horses brought from cart and plough. The huge bellows, massively wood and leather, creaked to the smith's slow pull, soughing the furnace from ashy black to incandescence. The iron for the shoe, inert and dull, thrust into the furnace began to glow, turned red then almost white. Under the hammer's beating on the anvil it became magically plastic as flaming flakes of iron flew from it. Now it moulded easily, took horseshoe shape, allowing soft punching through of holes for nails, throwing off a waxy feathering of sparks. Then the shoe's plunging into water quenched its scarlet, filled the dusky recesses with billowing steam. Still hot it was put to the hoof in the grip of the smith's knees; the rich organic smell, thickly in the nose, was hypnotic. Every time the driving of the nails filled me with alarm. But the horse, stoic and dreaming, dreamed its private dreams, showing no fear, no impatience.

I remember at Addington an occurrence of the phenomenon of ecstasy - that state never with premonition. It was a day of a kind that comes in summer, warm with a suffused sky, a soft bustle of wind. I lay on my back on the top of a bank under the loom of an elm, between the hedge and the standing wheat. It was quiet, poultry gossiped distantly; I could smell soil and growing grass. I could see the stout flexions of the elm's bole and thrust of limbs. Light flickered in the green jostle of leaves and wind. A bliss came upon the moments, narrowing infinity to those few feet.

Three miles from home lay Shirley Hills; there I discovered fossils. It was a curious place of hummocky hills and loose patches of woodland of a kind that a little repelled me - silver birch and depressed-seeming little pines. The hills were heather-clad, with falling scarps of loose pebbles. Idly tossing pebbles, splitting them one against another, utterly I was arrested by finding in one a little shell, a mollusc, imbedded, of the stone. It threw me into fascinated conjecture. There it was, a creature of the sea; but it was of stone, imperishable, on these dry hills. Had the sea once washed over this most unwatered place? Wonder thus started grew, was insatiable. It led me by degrees to awareness of vast vistas of time receded from this little evidence. It was of those things that at this time began to fill my amazed mind with a sense of wonder that is with me still. It made of me an impassioned collector of fossils. So greatly was my imagination stirred that, briefly, hopelessly, I tried to light in another boy what so irradiated me. He told his mother but she scolded; he was not to listen to such silliness; living things turned to stone indeed!

The deep beguilement of fossils is inseparable from the heaven that was Biggin Hill. The path to Biggin Hill lay in my parents' friendship with the Edwards/Essen clan. There was old Mrs Essen and there was old Mr and Mrs Edwards. Of Essen and Edwards there was to each a son and a daughter. May Edwards married Alfred Essen; Kathleen Essen married Toby Edwards. Than this outcome nothing could have been more felicitous. They were people of such treasurable niceness that perhaps it was inevitable that they should be welded. May was small and cosily round; Alfred was tall, lean as wire, and spectacled. Toby was as warmly round as May; Kathleen was as tall and lean and spectacled as Alfred.

These were of those early days of the 20th century when a wishful idealism, much romanticised, about country living fell upon many urban people, particularly those who were socialists as were both my parents and the Edwards/Essens. H.G Wells' book, *The Wheels of Chance* had been an influence, and there were such socialist organisations as The Woodcraft Folk. It was that that had sent my parents abortively to Ham Street. It sent May and Alfred Essen to Biggin Hill.

Perhaps appearances were deceptive; perhaps in May and Alfred there did glow a streak of romanticism. It did not show. But they brought to their migration an unromantic earthy practicalness. Biggin Hill then was country as innocent of convenience as it might be, apart from a most rudimentary bus service. Who now could credit that, so close as it was to London? But the country movement had come to Biggin Hill, throwing a first faint shadow of the urban tide which was to overwhelm all that country round London till then inviolate.

Biggin Hill had slept in its valley under chalk heights unnoticed and peaceful; nature held the place undisturbed. Plots were offered, plots on which homes could be made by those able to surmount the absence of piped water, sanitation, gas, electricity, or indeed any conceivable convenience.

Of those ready - and passionate to do so - were May and Alfred. Of those no less passionate to help them were Kathleen and Toby and old Mr Edwards; all entirely practical people.

The plots were very long, very narrow, more strips than plots; May and Alfred bought three to make one roomy plot. It was clutched to the steep fall of the hillside, clothed with a thin and hungry quilt of soil over virgin chalk. On that they were to make a home; they were settlers.

At the top of the plot they gouged deeply into the solidity of the chalk. On the shelf so made they perched the rear of the house they were to make, floating out the rest stilted above the drop thus making a most commodious cellar - a place of great pleasure to me, so endearingly was it scented with earthiness, bicycle oil, and chicken food.

The house that grew, stage by stage as there was money and their labour, did so with no regard for recognised principles of domestic architecture, but it was cosy, very original and adaptive. To me it was the purest delight; it was pioneering, all its parts personal, contrived. Everything was of their love and their labour.

For water they dug a well (by what unguessable labour); they lined it, made it watertight. By rainwater guttered from the roof they fed it, and by hand-pump drew it in the kitchen. In that slip of kitchen under the pitch of the corrugated iron roof they installed a stoneware filter. The water that emerged from that, cleansed and one had to suppose, innocuous, was not entirely sweet and gratifying, but loveable for its context; that was as well because every drop of water for drinking and cooking was so had. Also in that little kitchen there was a Primus stove, a Beatrice stove, a paraffin oven. Paraffin was mistress (lighting was by paraffin and candles). The smell of an active Primus stove, unmistakable, penetrative, is for me forever that of May's Hut. I can be astonished to hear others declare it a stink. It is the scent embalmed in nostalgia.

May's Hut and its garden were well established, all stark labour over, when first I saw them. The steep fall of the land had been terraced out, with fruit trees, blowsy tumbles of flowers, warmed with gossip of hens in their enclosure. By what accommodation my parents slept on that first visit I have no memory, or of that for sisters, but of that for Bert and me, memory is imperishable.

"You boys," said May comfortably, "will sleep in the attic."

"But there aren't any stairs," we said.

Alfred, long nose as always wind-reddened, pale blue eyes kind and smiling behind spectacles, pulled open a narrow panel in the wall to reveal a vertical ladder of tubular metal rungs.

"That's the way up," he said. "See the trap door in the ceiling? That's the way in."

The attic was under the pitch of the iron roof which came down to floor level. On the floor lay our bed; it was a mattress roughly made, stuffed with hay. It proved to be prickly to lie upon because that is the nature of hay; but in the close air its scent was saturating. Never since has a bedroom made sleep more sweet than there it was.

In the meeting of the iron roof and the floor there was a gap wide enough for the passage of a hand. The exploring fingers of a hand so passed found the gutter densely populated. Nests were packed in, starlings' nests, and by no means to be crowded out, house sparrows' too. In their breeding season, which for those two is so much of the year, morning's awakening for us was by the dawn outcry under those iron eaves. Our fingers, irresistibly exploratory, found the downy linings and, according to occasion, the eggs or the small bodies, soft palpitant and naked. By all the latter-day precepts we should by this have scared off the parents from eggs and young; these were of a tougher kind. They seemed entirely unworried.

Life at May's Hut was closely dependent on the bicycle; for any journey up to ten miles or so, that was for walking; then came the bicycle. Thus each day Alfred plied to the railhead at Hayes, then still with no hint of London's suburbs, so that he might entrain for London Bridge. In cellar and waste heap the years had accumulated the residues of retired bicycles, and so for me they would have remained. But Bert was ingenious; he had intrinsic understanding of what was mechanical. To him kind Alfred gave freedom of the spoil. And Bert was erudite about cotter pins, cranks, and all the things that constitute a bicycle.

Patiently he probed; finding an item here, another there, till all things essential to the being of a bicycle were found. He brought them together, amalgamated them. Then for my astonished beholding there was a complete bicycle. It was inelegant, very heavy, not always reliable. But, uneasily, it functioned. For a number of years it served us both. At either side of the rear hub Bert mounted a step; on these I stood clutching Bert's shoulders as he pedalled the united weight of us and the dreadnought bike. For many miles - as I see now, very hazardous miles - so we travelled.

But Bert first must learn to ride, and doggedly he did so. For fifty yards the road below had a downward slope, then bifurcated sharply left and right. At the fork was an extensive bed of nettles. Leaning against a tree Bert mounted the bike; then launched it and himself, giving both to the will of the slope. Gravity accelerated them. At the fork Bert attempted the left turn. He plunged unseated into the nettles. But, it must be repeated, Bert was dogged. He continued. Finally, much stung, he had the way of it. For me, riding had to wait for growth of leg to reach the pedals.

Biggin Hill would anyway have enflamed my lust for fossils; Alfred ignited it. Though London had given him birth, country and all that was of it had his soul. It was inevitable that at some times fossils should engage him. He showed me his pocket fossil-hunting compact. Never had I been more burningly covetous, more scalded by envy - though loving him for showing me. This magic thing was in a most neat and tactile leather case; it contained a jointed geological hammer and a small cold chisel. Alfred had bought it from Watkins & Doncaster, suppliers of material needs of naturalists. I was in somewhat later years to find them at their enchanting little shop on the first floor in the Strand by Charing Cross. From there they have been gone these many years; rents in the Strand long ago soared beyond the reach of anything so loveably good.

Alfred had another spoil heap, one mostly of stone and rubble oddments. In it, Alfred said, artfully casual, I might find fossils; I could have any I found. My attack on the heap was furious, careless of broken nails and was rewarded. With the commoner fossils of the local chalk I was by now fairly familiar. I had carried my geological education that small stage further that I knew the chalk was of the Cretaceous period; I knew that there were other periods most fascinatingly named, and that all of them were earlier and by that even more compulsively fascinating. The heap yielded to me Cretaceous fossils - sea urchins, various bivalves, sponges - but also others not of the Cretaceous. My small erudition, very tantalisingly, could take me no further.

The treasures of the spoil heap were not all; at the top of the hill into which May's Hut had been inserted it wore a crown of woodland. In the skirt of the wood there was a chalk pit. Here, would I excavate for fossils, abundant, not as it were second-hand, but virginally in their matrix. A junk shop had for a penny or two provided a tool, one side hammer, the other a claw. Given a handle it served me well. It and I spent many completely blissful days alone in the chalk pit. It was small, with a lonely privacy, not easily noticed under the wood's overhang, its silence felted with the rustle and whisper of a million little lives.

Biggin Hill's profound happiness, so long gone, cannot now be recalled in sequence. Its memory is of a pervasive exhalation of the scent of wild thyme, of butterflies and of those two day-flying moths of such hardly bearable beauty - six spot burnet and cinnabar. On picnic days, in the reaching shade of beech boughs, they were always there in the sun's dazzle beyond, they and the butterflies - meadow brown, everywhere dipping and pausing, chalk hill blue and common blue, small tortoiseshell, and, hardly believable to my wondering self of then, the imperial loveliness of peacock and red admiral. I knew that in other places there were butterflies; but could they be as they were in that sun-cherished valley?

Could wild flowers indeed be elsewhere as there they were? Each day to fetch the milk we must go to the farm beyond the hill, and in the bee-drowsed hum of afternoon the track climbed the hill against the jungly hedge rampantly thicketed with honeysuckle and travellers' joy. Grasshoppers sang among the flowers, the high grasses. Memory cannot separate from that valley the flowers that grew there - harebell, bladder campion, scabious, the rich purple of great knapweed, toadflax, the yellows of St John's Wort and ragwort. As always on the chalk there was the wayfaring tree, no tree at all but a shrub; but what other shrub could be more beguilingly loveable? Its leaves are large and comely, palely felted on their backs; the flat heads of berries are lacquered vermilion until, in August, they begin their turn to final lacquered black.

Through the wood that capped the hill, ran a thread of footpath, then a stile and there were the meadows of the farm to which each day we went for the milk. It was a farm of a kind nowhere now to be found. Its buildings were as if they had risen unbidden mushroom-fashion from the ground, brick and flint, mossed and anciently established. It had about it that old kindly smell of farms - of scent of cows, of milk warm from the udder, cow dung - dearly memorably mingled.

In the meadow, by the rutted track, there was a pond, an unobtrusive little pond as then farm ponds were, but spellbinding for the life that throbbed and thrived in and about it. Its newts were so largely splendid that I have not known the like of them for so many despoiling years. Where now could I find such newts - if indeed I could find newts at all in this time when they and so many enchanting creatures are being nudged towards extinction? That was in the halcyon time before abuse of land had become eulogised as efficient farming.

So happily right as were the sun-basked slopes of Biggin Hill for so much life, they were no less for adders. Adders were common, often to be found coiled and drowsing in the sun's embrace. Often they were of the commonest kind, light silvery grey with the strong black zigzag that ran the length of their backs. But there were those that puzzled me, so richly dark brown that the black zigzag was hardly discernible; only later was I to know them as males. Male or female all, adder-fashion, were short, stumpy, distinguishing them from the grass snakes which, hardly less common, were lissomely long, elegant, slender-tailed.

Perhaps Biggin Hill and all that was of it might not be of such precious nostalgia had there been no association of water. But, unforgettably, there was. Quite early in the time of Biggin Hill Alfred took Vi walking and, quite soon, I went too. We tramped long idling days in country still hardly stirred from inherited ruralness - something that only longest memories could now accept. All that is, and for many years has been, Green Belt suburb, London suburb. Horse and cart then more often stirred the chalk dust than did cars. There were ancient churches by the villages, so settled in peace and silence that the souls commemorated by the headstones under the yew trees seemed more true presences than we. The stone of tomb and headstone was often wrought into garlands and

Bernard's eldest sister, Vi.

cherubs of the 17th and 18th centuries; if moss and lichen were not too obscuring epitaphs might just be deciphered.

'Here she lies
Deprived of life
Which was a verteous and a loving wife.'

So they went, these wraith-like echoes of lives long gone and remembered by none. They put me into a semi-trance of imagining, seeking to grasp what had been when they were sentient.

To Westerham we went often, and so dearly did Westerham engage me that for succeeding years I would walk the thirteen or fourteen miles from home to stay for a little while in its enfolding atmosphere before walking back. Changed it must be now and hardly could it be for the better. Near the church there was a footpath; it ran narrowly between the houses to cross a crinkling and crystalline small stream. Beyond lay Squerries Park, with the big house distantly standing over its acres. Little attention I had for that; that same little stream threaded down the gentle decline of the land. It was so clear, so cleanly rippling over its pebbly bed as to seem no denser than the air above. Though unknown to me, this paradisic tiny water was the headwaters of the River Darenth, as true a chalkstream as ever held trout. Pools, each with its ruined mill, punctuated it. The pools were shallow, so clear under the high reflecting trees that each leaf and stem of water plant seemed possible to be counted. As clearly I could see fish, large, just sub-surface, a sight that thrilled through me almost painfully. So small as was my experience of fish that I could not with certainty name them - never had I seen fish so big. So clearly to be seen. But the vision of them still is clear; I think they were trout.

Above the pools the stream, here a wisp of water, a mere yard between the banks, ran glistening over gravel, inviting paddling feet. Bare footed, slowly, I went upstream searching under stones, becoming deft-handed. In deep wonder and delight I caught small creatures swift as shadows - bullheads, those queer great-headed tiny fish, crayfish like little green-brown lobsters. There, substantiated, were such things as had searched my imagination since birth first gave me breath.

Out from Westerham, past the church and down past the cottages low-hooded under their thatch, embowered by garden, past that corner house where was born General Wolfe, victor of Quebec, the road ambled by the meadows to Brasted, charming and broad-streeted but remembered sharply not for that but again for the little Darenth, small still but growing. From the open meadow it ran into a green tunnel so closely arched with tree and hazel bush that an enchanted privacy came upon it. Paddling in the green-filtered half light, the water was caressive, the air soft with the dank bank's mossy scent. So long ago, such a mist of years, but still how poignantly clear is that memory.

What was to come to Biggin Hill must have been clear to eyes less bewitched than mine. Already rather sordid little bungalows had begun to rise, first eruptions of an incipient rash. They were to spread.

Our earliest years of Biggin Hill were those too of the first Great War. To Biggin Hill it brought that aerodrome which was to be so much a part of two great wars. To Bert and to me it brought many spellbound days.

On many days there we went after a hurried breakfast, there to ensconce ourselves day-long in the boundary hedge. From there quite closely, very clearly, we saw the parked aircraft, being by that overwhelmed by so magical a sight. How little we guessed what that fortended. Those wondrous machines were biplanes, strung into being out of wire and stretched fabric, strutted of wood. Their noise, deep-throated nearby heard, were awesome, so nobly inspiring. How could it be that they, in that same century - in my one lifetime - could evolve to the monstrous things of the air that, relatively, are commonplace?

For us in our hedge there was spine-searing thrill enough. Planes taking off came over the hedge, over us, so closely that we could see the supra-being who was the pilot. From that take-off they were at once high because there the land fell abruptly into the deep valley, to Donkey Lane.

I, once walking in Donkey Lane found my way blocked. Strewn all about was what had been an aeroplane, its aluminium pipes melted into nuggets. So had one demi-god been brought to earth.

CHAPTER V

War and Peace

RETROSPECT tends often to treat the past too much with kindness. It calls up what was happy, thus that lived-out unhappiness may not be revived. But those old years were not all of Biggin Hill and kindred delights - they were basking intervals of respite from the heavy skies of day to day life. Of that the dark heart was school.

School was not invariably bad; better or worse, it was confinement. On mornings of November when the sky hung low and factory sirens summoned their captives, the school bell sounded its summons of unbearable melancholy. School closed its door upon me so that my soul died. With fifty-nine others so I must stay through the musty hours in air clotted by the whispered hum of prisoned voices.

But summer brought its mornings to school as to all else. In the big hall at morning assembly the sun peered through the high windows, too high for sight of a free world beyond. Its beams hung trapped in the hang of dust motes, and outside the birds sang of freedom. On such mornings often we sang the hymn which begins

'Summer suns are glowing over land and sea'.

Then a wistful trance would fall upon me; almost I would forget that indeed prisoner still I was. Then the dream over, disconsolate to the classroom I must go.

The pattern of schooling for such as I, then started with elementary school: undeniable as were its faults (and which were probably hardly less dreary for the teachers), much of the fault was also mine. Inherently I could not adapt to enclosure. The passing of the war years had not yet returned many men to their civilian niches; a majority of teachers still were women. Many were sensitive to what seed might be found in our rough soil, if any there was. As far as they were able they gave freedom and encouragement to my compulsive drawing and loving interest in words. I was encouraged to write, often bidden to read to the class that which I had written. So it was that my legend of the despatch rider found birth.

We had been put to the writing of an actual experience. I, disdaining truth, told of an army despatch rider, of his adventures. Since none was true I had much scope. The class, most attentive, heard how my rider astride his bike, rode by night through war-shattered Flanders. He passed the ghosts of great houses 'that once had been the haunt of superfluous wealth'. I, reading aloud, pronounced that word 'super-fluous'. The saga, growing in its episodes, almost persuaded me of its truth. I assumed my teacher gave it belief: perhaps I was wrong.

So the burden of captivity was lightened. Perhaps even, reluctantly, there was stimulus. But captivity remained. Not all my devices of sore throats and other deceptions could give me more than brief respites. Last day of term, hardly believable glory, released an inner knot. Were it the start for the summer holiday, that whole month, it was too long a time to conceive its end. Freedom's gain seemed perpetual. To that bitter heir was the black despair of school's restarting. But, withall, elementary school was not without mitigations. Secondary school which followed had almost none.

When first I made my ascent it was called the Croydon Borough

School. It was a war-time makeshift sited in the shadow and scent of a brewery. There it was I laid the foundations of my hatred. Hindsight shows that its first footing was put down on the first morning: its occasioning was first sight of the assistant headmaster. In the playground under the mantle of the brewery's redolence, we were paraded, there to wait for a solemnising interval. Then, as a Coming, he appeared. He wore a mortarboard, his tread was measured, his feet were large; as by a garment he was hung with sanctimony. He surveyed us conscripts: cold rectitude oozed from his every pore. His lightless eyes were set closely by his nose; his chin was raised a little as though to lift it above our taint. He wore brown boots, very unctuously polished; their soles very thick, seemed to push the toes into an upward curve. I see them clearly now. Only by degrees did I realise that they were smug. So traitorous can be the fall of fate that almost upon my coming he was to succeed to the headmastership.

Though so soon hatred of that school found root, its bitter blossoming was to come gradually. Meanwhile we left the brewery's kindly shade. We became the Selhurst Grammar School, housed again in the buildings that through the war had been a hospital for war casualties. Even I, least inclined to any acceptance of what was of school, was stirred to transitory excitement. There were two buildings, one for boys, one for girls, it then being an accepted certainty that to allow the two within reach of each other must have unspeakable moral consequences. Our old building had been plain, no better than basic; now here was this new containment to touch even in me a little pride, however temporary. In the assembly hall there was much pomp of panelling and a dais and, above, a gallery. There was a gymnasium elaborate with appliances, a chemistry lab and a physics lab. It was impressive; but still it was confinement, not as had been elementary school, largely benign. The teachers now were men, survivors mostly of the war, bearing still spiritual scars of the trenches. There was he, normally quiet, but occasionally, bursting into strange rages - so once felling a boy with a blow round the head with a Latin grammar. The headmaster, too old for that, tattered by many years of boys, a straggle of moustache and gown, soon wandered off into retirement, pausing only long enough to cane me in an absent flurry. Now, ill exchange, the assistant headmaster had ascended.

Very early I was embroiled with the less lovable of the masters: and, least lovable, or worse, was 'Sammy'. He taught maths as if to scarify. He was a man harsh to the eye, his pebble eyes inset in a stony head. For Sammy mathematics was a faith of bitter bigotry. 'Ma'ma'dics' he called it. "You're no good," he told me. "Can't do ma'ma'dics. S'pose can't expect any more from you, coming from the slums of South Norwood. Finish in the gutter." Those of us least susceptible to ma'ma'dics he would take by the scruff and scrub the chalk on the blackboard with our noses. That increased neither my aptitude nor my sympathy for ma'ma'dics. It left no love for Sammy.

He was a man of Northern Ireland: there for the summer holiday he went. From there returning for the autumn term he came with no right hand. It, so lusting rumour suggested, had been lost in the troubles there. Pious joy filled us; clearly here was benign intervention. He never learned to do it with his left hand.

There was also Barlow. His face was modified for the better sneering, and a sneering master is of the abominations. His nose, sharply beaked, had on one side a nostril able to lift narrowly into an upward twist. For him and for Sammy I bore the taint of being known to be 'artistic'.

"Venables," said Sammy to me. "Mr Scott tells me you're artistic, probably like poetry, like him. Silly nonsense. Fools. Need ma'ma'dics. Finish in the gutter." The therapy needed for my stupidity, laziness, artisticness was clear to Sammy and to Barlow. Very firmly they had the co-operation of the headmaster. To his task he came with dedicated unction. His chin was raised the better to bend down his corrective eye, his mouth tightly drawn. So for a time he stood, regarding me. "Come here," he said, pointing as if to the block.

Slowly he detached the suction of his gelid eye, as slowly he turned to a cupboard. Its opening revealed a rack of canes. Again he turned his eye to fix me; from the rack took a cane. Meditatively he flexed it, made an aerial cut, shook his head. He replaced the cane. As studiously, slowly, took another, flexed it, replaced it. The third he accepted. "Bend down," he said. I bent "Further," he said. I bent further.

He put his hand on my head, pressed to a point of strain. With finger tips he turned back one coat tail then the other. He threw back his gown from right arm and shoulder, made several aerial cuts. He paused as though invoking. The first blow was orgasmic, its pain ineffable. Again he paused, rhythmically flexing the cane, then accelerating into the next harrowing cut. When all were done he seemed to deflate. That first therapeutic encounter; its repetitions induced in me no cure.

But, also, there was Mr Scott. He was gentle, amiable and perceptive, never with a need to assert authority: he shared with us his sense of humour. Teaching English and music, in both was quick to discern potential. In me finding enough to give encouragement and dilute the corrosion of Sammy and Barlow. Even from the not hopeful raw material he did conjure some quite acceptable singing of Schubert's songs. By Mr Scott was made tolerable what would have been intolerable.

And there was Mr Drew; quaintly lovable Mr Drew; he also a good and encouraging man, so perfectly, entirely a gentleman in the conventional sense as to make his presence there bizarre. Always in a slightly old fashioned way he was impeccable, always of a magical cleanliness. His hair, his close-clipped moustache, were shining white. He was precise of manner and speech, a little clipped, and hanging by a black silken cord he wore a monocle. Mr Drew was the Art Master, and so being was induced in the manner of the time to impose the sterilities of copying white cubes and cones. But having perceived in me a passion for drawing he nurtured it so far as he was able.Years later I, then an art student, met him in the street with his wife. Eager to show some fruit for his past help, I showed him the pocket sketch book which always I carried. "Yes, yes, my dear fellow," he said, "you'll do, you'll do. You will find yourself exposed to many temptations. But I'm sure you will conduct yourself honourably."

Dear Mr Drew. I am entirely sure that never in his life did he conduct himself otherwise than honourably.

Though school had those never to be minimalised graces, they were not such as to melt prison walls: they were blessed mitigants, no more. On summer days still the birds beyond in their freedom sang; it was of freedom they sang. Sometimes in the month-long hours of afternoon there came to the street outside the railings a man who, in the way of that time, played a piano organ. It drew my soul most poignantly - not for its musical sound, but because where it was playing trees stood over pavements dappled by their shade, where those who would walked under the trees. They were free, they were free. I was in class: the voice of Sammy was upbraiding: "Venables," it was saying, "you come from the slums of South Norwood, that's why you haven't got the brains to do ma'ma'dics."

From affliction there was no respite but to seek to convince myself truly a time would come when I should leave school. Meanwhile potentially another affliction threatened. I had abundant curly black hair, large blue eyes. Undoubtedly I must have worn the look of easy prey. I had a friend, a Jewish boy, by that obvious prey. His father was a tailor who spoke the most delightful fractured English.

"Svanky vellers," he said to me, "alvays vant their coats very tight in at the vaist."

Any school, any mixed community has those who must try to appease their inadequacy by tyranny. Some become famous rulers of nations. Most just remain the common bully. To Maurice and to me came early notice. Bullying began. I found it intolerable not only for its pain but as much for an unwillingness to pander to crippled minds. Maurice was no less unwilling. We must do something: we must make ourselves formidable. We would teach ourselves to box.

By Maurice's parents was donated a cheap set of boxing gloves. We each stuffed a sack, hung it from a beam to be a punchbag. It was fortuitously, at this time that the great but tiny Jimmy Wilde became World Flyweight Champion. Into the cinemas came a film of his victorious engagement. Very assiduously, analytically we watched it. As assiduously we shadow-boxed, we sparred, we punished the punchbag. From the public library we borrowed books on boxing. Meanwhile we studied to avoid embroilment until we were ready.

The time came. Wearing innocence like a garment, openly we went into exposure, knowing well its provocation.

"Dirty Jew," said one in innocence to Maurice. His swinging right hook reached the astonished countenance.

"Want a fight pretty boy?" said another to me. "Yes," I said. My right hook caused pain and dismay. We had rather polished our right hooks; they were really quite pretty.

Our path for a time was one of salutary conquest; but we became known to be best avoided; now with a taste for the aesthetic of combat we found ourselves with an absence of combatants. The principle having been established that aggression unresisted grows in vice, made inevitable though unsought, another combat. In Aylett Road lived Ron. Ron was legendary, a bully of awful fame. He maintained a rough-knuckled intimidation which none had felt ready to withstand. But Ron was not the true bully of craven spirit; he subdued not from ill intent but from an exuberance. He was strong, his punches ponderous; he had simple pleasure in deploying them. Having been, with his family, absent from Aylett Road for a while, he returned not doubting that he would resume his throne. It was in that interval I had assumed resistance as a principle. A decisive clash could not but be.

But, was this, that Ron of legend, invincible? Then who was this whose punches lumbered so predictably, so long on the way? Such ample time they left me, feinting and slipping, to hit as I chose. He fought on until utterly defeated. We became great friends.

Often we walked, long days of country wandering. On such a day we walked thirty-nine miles, on beyond Westerham, into country where never before had we trodden. At the slanting of the sun, climbing the thyme-scented downs, still we were about fourteen miles from home. "Weary and worn the poor boy came, up to the farmer's door," quoted Ron, chanting. The day's end came in a twilight fog of exhaustion.

On a day before that time of secondary school, when I probably was eight, I was with my mother when she, meeting a neighbour fell interminably into gossip. Waiting, I became gripped by stomach-knotting pain. An acrid upgush of fluid filled, scalded my mouth. Half fainting I retched it into the gutter. My mother did not notice; I said nothing.

So heralded began what was to be recurrent and worsening, for many years. Attacks, sometimes for days, as often for weeks, assailed with scarifying pain so constantly recurring that I came to accept that as a normality that, oddly, did not affect other people. When pain gnawed, temporary appeasement could be had by eating; I became importunate with crazed pleas for food. My mother at last taking me to the local medical practice, he whom we consulted listened absently, pushed me in the stomach.

"Stomach trouble," he said. Perhaps he gave us a bottle of something; I cannot recall it.

By the age of twelve, as subsequent knowledge has shown, I had the clear symptoms of duodenal ulcers. They were not diagnosed. The pain sometimes was devastating, as almost to prevent activity, of very little help in living with Sammy and Barlow and the therapies of the headmaster. Nevertheless there were intervals in the constancy of the bad times, sometimes prolonged.

Once in every week, on Wednesday, there was a half holiday; officially its purpose was for games. I put it to better purpose. Often on fine Wednesdays of summer I walked the ten miles to Biggin Hill, from Addington making the long climb of Lodge Lane. Then always as though suddenly, there was the crest of Skid Hill. From it fell the narrow twist of road, steeply forested on the right. Beyond, under the mantling loom of bole and bough, there lay Donkey Lane in its honeyed light of afternoon. Then, out from the shade, a host of butterflies dipped and faltered over the fields.

But in winter afternoons of Wednesday also I climbed the rise of Lodge Lane to Skid Hill's drop, now leanly leafless, threading Donkey Lane and through the valley's length again to find the chalkpit, there to quarry for fossils till the light sank to early wintry dark.

Now no warm and mothy twilight for return: at once relentlessly the fall of night. Along the valley, along Donkey Lane, where all was dark, no interfering light to thwart growth of night sight, the going often was half mystically a pleasure of solitude. But from that into the engulfing black of Skid Hill where, sight lost, a multitude of voices, half heard, sighing of things strange, sibilant mutterings, sudden cracks. Darkness pressed as though weighted, interminable. Then, suddenly, there was the top, darkness now luminously of openness.

Fishing, as was its chance, had some share of Wednesdays but how spare indeed was chance in an area so blankly arid.

Of games, only cross country running had for me any pleasure - unlike a game, not played on ordered pitch or court, unconfined, of countryside, individual. I detested cricket.

After all respites, pressures of school and, it must be said, home, led back to torments of that which afflicted me. Constantly my parents were in their whirl of reformative campaigning. My mother particularly was always quickly to be of anything advanced in thought. The name of William Morris was heard often in the home. A bust of Keir Hardy stood upon the mantelpiece; she was an earnest reader of the works of Havelock Ellis. There were many other symbols of high advancement in politics, nutrition, clothing, social philosophy. Though of such irrational purity in sexual matters in her personal life, for the world at large she had a genuine breadth of thought. She had kindly tolerance for prostitutes and the bearers of bastard babies. And of course she was a suffragette though not of those who chose martyrdom. For her groceries she was exclusively loyal to the Co-op; she founded a local branch of the Women's Co-operative Guild, and was its secretary. "Those women respect me, you know," she used to say. I think they did, if a little bewilderedly. In so doing they had to absorb shocks rather close to the nerve.

"You," she told them, "are in no position to pass judgement on prostitutes. Most of you got married for a living." Her multiple causes involved her nearly exclusively. They made her a not very close observer of the things of home and family. In those she was idiosyncratic rather than practical. Her management, always high in principle, was inconstant. She was strong about nutrition, passionately and spasmodically a vegetarian. The basis of much of her cooking was pulses and beans, unappetisingly, variably supporting the soundest principles. In justice it must be recorded that we very properly loved her apple pies and puddings; in season her summer puddings lavishly overblown with all the summer soft fruits. Day to day the tenor of our eating was depressive

Often in out-of-school times I went for long solitary wanderings in the country; sometimes I forgot breakfast. I was not reminded nor given food to take, my mother's rapt mind being elsewhere. By midday hunger drove me pillaging into fields for turnips or over hedges for apples; or in season to strip the thin flesh layer from dog rose hips. Probably nutritional deficiencies were partnered by emotional stresses; though of things so long past, certainty is difficult. That there were distresses I remember with unhappy conviction; as certainly they were coincident with physical torments that were to be mine for so many years. Often in the long winter evenings my parents were out in pursuit of their causes, not returning until 11 o'clock. Sometimes then I was alone; how that came to be I cannot remember. But so it was and each minute of every hour had its separate passage in a silence made drear by the singing of the gas mantle. The hours so interminable with listening, lagged till at last I recognised my mother's approaching footsteps, with my father's - three steps and a heel scrape - three steps and a heel scrape.

My mother abhorred the common tasks. Very early we children were coerced into the sharing of them. I was an accustomed cleaner of windows and could darn my socks not much more badly than did my mother. It was of course salutary training, but left to my mother a major part of what must be done. Her bitter loathing of it corroded her life; that by contagion doing the same for my father's and for us. She nagged. My father, burdened no less, was drawn into a futility of quarrelling. More damagingly she talked of him pejoratively to us: it may be seen now how deep was the distress of that for us less conscious than otherwise. Their discord, seeming often so sharp, essentially was superficial: that did not diminish its effect upon us, nor of her denigration of him. We, but children, could not perceive that theirs was a devoted union.

At evening of summer weekends when the weather was fair, it was sometimes my father's way to take solitary walks in the country, returning only after the fall of soft summer darkness. So one night he came, his arms filled with flowers. We had not seen their kinds before, musk mallow, vipers bugloss vividly blue, frosted over on leaves and stems with a silver hairiness.

So it was that first I heard of Farleigh; there it was my father had picked his flowers. Often thereafter I went to Farleigh, often so caught in its spell as not to have free ease of leaving. There I saw light of day seep away, saw the huge summer moon lift until it sent milky shafts of light into the tunnelled secrecy of the lane. In the dew-soft air fragrant with moss and earth and dog roses, barn owls drifted so closely that a reaching arm could have touched them. Once in recent years I came again through Farleigh. Not one trace of that enchanted solitude was there. All was lost: the busy sweep of road and shops and trim pink housing had left no trace.

Another memory of summer night is so poignant still after most of eighty years, as to make an injustice of the final forgetfulness of mortality. Surely there should be something after, so that a memory so properly immortal can live on. It was a night of late summer; where I had been I cannot remember. In the velvet night, without sense of time, of home, of anything but the bewitched moment. I was high up Lodge Lane. The moon hung hugely, the air was drowsed with the fumbling flight of moths; it seemed that I could hear each least sighing breath of every smallest creature of the night. I wandered out of past, out of future, through hedges, over fields. I came to wakefulness in Addington; the church clock stood at midnight. I ran the five miles to home.

My father had been raking the streets; my mother was distraught, but, as in later years she told me, they saw me still so transfigured that anger died. But never now shall I or any other find summer moonlight ecstasy there. All has gone, all extinct under the barren wastes of New Addington, one more place of air and sweetness devoured by sordid urban jaws. The common fate; Farleigh, Lodge

Lane and Addington, the happy fields of West Wickham, gone from all but longest memories.

There we went blackberrying, returning in twilights of late summer with laden baskets. In idling hours sometimes we found a hayrick partly cut, from its shelves of hay to jump to make soft landings on heaped hay beneath. Now, inexorably, clanking machines make their impeccable bales. In those old days hayricks in fields of summer were placid to see. At midday in the sun the big hay knives cut blocks of hay from the ricks like cake, making the senses sway for the delight of its fragrance.

My father, so inept a man in things material, as a gardener was immaculate, patiently perfectionist. In these same days of summer, with gardening imperatives accomplished, came his reward of dalliance. Still he came with tools as token of intent: they, duty done, stayed in the barrow. Into the insect-humming shadow of the hawthorn hedge my father retired, there with back against a tree trunk, straw hat tilted over his eyes, he dawdled out the gentle hours with his pipe, his book, his flask of cold tea. His dalliant hours nevertheless did not prevent his providing us with fresh vegetables, otherwise not to be had in those war years.

That these memories are so much of summer is because for summer I lived. Winter was endured. Evenings of winter as then they were, surely are hard to conceive as being of this same century. Of piped entertainment there was none; no radio, no television, not any of the wonders that blanket our minds today. Some people had gramophones. Second-hand-living had still then not invaded the home: people then were still living their own real lives not knowing how much they were missing in not seeing other people living unreal lives.Whatever entertainments there were in the gas-lit parlours were home produced. It was the time of the 'musical evening'.

My parents were loving practitioners. They shared a love of music that, if naive, was passionate. Then, if you of today can imagine so grotesque a state, there was no voice from the speaker, no face on the screen. There was no such thing as broadcasting. History awaited its coming for its mass effect on musical taste, good or bad.

For their solos, their duets, my parents were much in demand: inseparably music of their kind was a part of our lives. My father played the piano, by ear, with great facility; but not I believe without sensitivity. It was his way on winter evening homecomings to go immediately to the parlour, there in darkness to play the piano.

Often we being summarily to bed, candles out, stone china hot water bottle clutched against the cold, we would hear them practising below. There was a song my mother sang: till death ends all I must remember it. To it she brought a finality of feeling of her brimming soul. Its name I cannot remember: 'When all was young' it began, hardly bearable for its searing yearning, then ended 'Three hundred weary years ago'. In the dark, I heard the depthless melancholy, I lived every minute of those three hundred years. Their burden lies upon me yet.

Perhaps never otherwise has an event historically so vast come upon the common life so modestly. The coming of broadcasting fore-ran social changes that were to penetrate every crevice of life; contemporary vision, at large, could not grasp implication now so obvious.

I noted only that my brother Bert had fallen into a detachment. Bert, never superfluous in speech, now brooded silently. He became obscurely busy with spools of hair-fine copper wire which he wound on to other spools. This and other arcane activities beyond my grasp were conducted in our tiny kitchen, using its entire length between spools; thus it was that my sister Vi, making her legitimate way across the kitchen walked through the nearly invisible wire. This, as we saw, was a calamity drawing from Bert a cry of anguish:

"Oh corks," cried Bert, "Oh corks."

First agony passed, he began again. He made a wireless set. It was a crystal set, and of constant anxiety. The cat's whisker, Bert explained, must retain its contact on the crystal; and that was hypersensitive. Our least footstep, forgetfully heavy, caused disconnection. But in its more secure intervals it worked: though often all was lost in banshee howls, into our kitchen there did speak an elegant voice. It was that of the British Broadcasting Corporation.

That I have made no more mention of Gyp is false to true chronicling. Wherever I in times of freedom went so too went Gyp. Between Gyp and me was a great love. It did not occur to me that life would ever be without Gyp.

When I was fourteen Gyp sickened. His legs would not bear him, he lay in the kitchen on his side. A yellow trickle oozed from his mouth. He had been poisoned my parents said. Inexplicably, terribly, they did nothing. Still I had to go to school, wrenched from him; running home on release, going on my knees to speak to him. He, otherwise quite helpless, just stirred the tip of his responsive tail. So it was for three days; then he died. Never again in all my life has such grief come upon me. After fall of darkness my father dug a grave at the end of the garden. He made me go with him for the burial; I cannot know why. We put Gyp in his grave. One leg rigid in death would not fit in the ill-dug hole. My father stamped on it. I heard the cracking of the bone. As long as I live I am condemned to remember it. My relationship with my father did not recover.

A year later in March when I was fifteen, the weather was bitter. My mother and father were to sing at a concert. Waiting in the wings my father shivered. Next morning his temperature was soaring. He had pneumonia. For a week or more he lay visibly sinking, but he passed the crisis. Then his heart failed. The end came on a Tuesday. A woman acquaintance was standing in by the bedside; about 12 o'clock she summoned us. Queer sounds were rasping frighteningly from my father's throat. Then they stopped. My mother flung herself upon him. "Daddy, Daddy! oh Daddy!" she screamed.

It was time for the midday meal; it was stew. That I know because it was Tuesday. My mother, blindly weeping, stood to serve us. "Daddy, oh Daddy!" she moaned. Unseeing she ladled the stew on to the tablecloth.

CHAPTER VI

I an art student!

I WONDER, having come so far, if I have conveyed any sense of what was so dominant a factor in my living, and, as far as I know, in that of many others of similar bent. It was that enthralled fascination imposed by life in water. For those of us who, in youth were so inclined, all nature was lovely; but in water, mysteriously, it is intensified.

But for such as I, secret delights of water had little chance; no rivers flowed nearby, no lakes lay, nothing but quite minor ponds. But where often I went, there was Miller's Farm. After so great a toll of years it returns to me as does a vividly remembered dream. So comes back to me one of those timeless afternoons of summer when quietness lies tangibly. It was as if no wind had ever blown there, as if no event had ever trespassed there or ever would. A rapture of loneliness wrapped everything - the mossed and lichened roofs, the brick and flint walls. There was no movement, no sound but the pure white turkeys that came softly gobbling to inspect me.

The pond could hardly have been more than half an acre, but its still green water was bewitching; willows leaned over it, rotting timbers and rooty tree stumps held the oozy bank. My red-topped float stood so still from the water that it fixed my eye, seeming to stir and dip until I must blink to see it still unmoving. For the hours of that immortal afternoon so my float remained, not in the least diminishing my faith. There are other fragmentary memory prints of Miller's Farm, of occasions when, miraculously, the float did dip, when a small force unseen within the green mystery did pulse to set my hand to trembling. So, seldomly, shining slips of roach, stout little crucian carp were yielded to me.

But there came the death of my father. Delights of fish in green ponds, visions of being an artist were submerged; survival was the immediacy. I must leave school; I must be an earner. But dark as were the circumstances, last day of school was a sublimity.

At last, at last, the hated thing was done; no more, not ever again was I to be school's prisoner. I walked out of the school, free.

But now there must be a job; a job was found. I became a book collector, but to say so is deceptive. All my life from then till now I have collected books; but not as then I collected them. I was employed by the Workers' Educational Association: I was paid one pound a week. Each day, bearing a dark blue gaberdine sack I went on a round of the trade counters of publishers to collect books which had been ordered by members. Each evening so laden, I returned for the packing and posting of the books.

The office was at 10 Harpur Street, a cavernous turning from Theobold's Road where Bloomsbury felt some touch of the main world. With my eye of now I can see that Harpur Street had had in its 18th century beginning a retired elegance. Its houses faced each other narrowly across the street, tall, close-fronted over their deep basements. The original reticent charm of the bricks now made largely anonymous in the universal London grime. Subsequent change has swept away the greater part of that area, substituting building sharing the grime but never having had the elegance.

At No. 10 offices had the ground floor and those above. My place was the basement; it had a musty smell entwined with that of the gas ring, cocoa, packing materials and a cling of the mice that nested therein. Presiding there was a little old cockney, frisky as a sparrow. His hair was white, so was his wiry straggle of moustache. During the persistent recurrences of cocoa he told me his ancient reminiscences, of his growing up; sometimes rather luridly illuminating. All those days of his childhood had been on the infamous Ratcliffe Highway, these many years swept away, its ill fame having been too strident. It had taught much about survival to this crinkled little nut of a man.

The Ratcliffe Highway lay in the most intestinal dockland labyrinth of the East End. To it came seamen of all nations. They, ashore and avid, were lured into houses by prostitutes that swarmed out of the crannies. When the men were thrown out they had lost the money and were in the minimum of underwear. At the time of his telling, he, well into his seventies, gave me intimate vision of that foetid life of mid-19th century London.

The basement's close smell, the bird-beady blue of those ancient eyes, returns to me sharply.

The world of publishing as then it was is as remote as all else. Then still it was intimate, still, so to speak, organic. A book ordered one day could be in the hands of its buyer the following day. The humble means for that were such as I, the book collectors. At Amen Corner, almost under the shadow of St Pauls, facing the canyon of Paternoster Row, as then it was - who then could have imagined the bombs? - were the premises of Simpkin Marshall, Hamilton & Kent. They were the book trade wholesalers. Almost it could have been said that at Amen Corner beat the hidden heart of the book trade. The trade counter at Amen Corner was virtually the book collectors' club.

About 4 o'clock each day was the time to start the packing of books for the post. Under the packing tutelage of the old man I learned the small skills of packing that would survive the hazards of the post. To this day I blanch at the innocent optimism of many who commit parcels to the Christmas post. Approaching 6 o'clock I would begin the carrying of parcels to the post office in Red Lion Street, load after load, sometimes hardly able to stagger under their weight. At any time after 7 o'clock I would reach home. On Saturdays I worked till 1 o'clock. My weekly pound was paid into my mother's housekeeping.

It was a routine that allowed for little else. Only quite rarely were there chances to fish; drawing I continued by the carrying of a pocket sketchbook. On those days, scarce and treasured when I had the twopence which would buy me a cup of tea, in a Lyons' tea shop, I drew those about me. At 10 Harpur Street they called me the 'Michelangelo of the nethermost region'. But I was transferred from the nethermost region.

At the London School of Economics the WEA had a bookshop for the service of students and staff. There now attached, I continued book collecting, but freed from packing and posting, had some time in the bookshop. There in my deeply humble station daily I met some who, unguessed by me, were to become the stuff of history. Of those were Sir William Beveridge, who then was Director of the LSE. But it was he who was to be the author of the Beveridge Report, thus the father of the Welfare State. As so often it was with men of historic stature he was small, of slight structure. His head was fine, aquiline.

But not for long was I at the LSE. To the WEA came a new head in whom I raised no approval: he sacked me promptly.

I was unemployed; it was soon clear that society was well able to do without any service of mine - or of a great many others; so many irrelevances. Now for fishing and drawing, time was abundant but fishing within walking range scarce. Drawing was obsessional. I could not believe that such passion as was mine would not some time find fulfilment.

That charmed belief was not all I had. There was also my mother; she saw me predestined. I was to be an artist; I was to inherit the mantle of her father. She was not prepared to allow unfulfilment. In Croydon there was the Croydon School of Art. It was a minor school, half hidden behind the Public Hall; but it was a school of art. There I must go.

She took me with my drawings to see the principal, Oswald Crompton, a gentle kindly man. It must be supposed that at least to some extent my work impressed him. Astonishingly, immediately he offered me an evening free studentship. Never has sun dawned with such sudden glory as on that grey day.

That very next evening I was there, I an art student! From 6 till 9 nothing asked of me but that I should draw, wonderfully just that. I was put to the drawing of the 'antique' - the plaster casts of the great Greek sculptures. In an abandonment of happiness I drew the eye, the nose, all the features of Michelangelo's magnificent David. The meaning of each day now was waiting for its evening.

For three blissful weeks so it went. Then Mr Crompton sent for me.

"I - er - have seen your er work," he said. "Yes, er, satisfactory - I um - have decided to offer you a full-time free studentship. Would you - er - care to accept that?"

For four years I was a student at the Croydon School of Art: never could there have been a more ardent student. Each weekday the school was open morning, afternoon and evening; Saturday morning it was open till 1 o'clock. At every time it was open I was there. Deprived on Sunday I went sketching in the countryside that still nudged Norwood. For all other purposes the afternoon of Saturday had to serve. Mainly that was fishing and in season cross-country running.

Then, in the 1920s, as in all centuries past, it was unquestioned that whatever might be the inspiration potential of an artist, he must have a tradesman's skills. An art student's need for professional training was as great as that of a plumbing apprentice. The difference lay in the fact that plumbing remained a craft; an artist, has he the potential, can find wings to soar creatively. Of the essential, still the first, the basis, the key to all, is draughtmanship, drawing; from its gracious art springs all else. An artist must be as good a draughtsman as in him lies.

I was fortunate in my generation. Croydon School of Art gave me a training which has served me well. The more I see of what is still called art education, the more I am grateful for that.

Croydon admittedly was nannified if comparison must be made with such as the Slade School of Art to which most dearly I would

The young artist.

Above and right: Bernard as a young man.

have liked to have gone. We were not encouraged to stray beyond the codes of suburban usage of that time; and, at least openly nor did we. But I was too passionately busy to have much thought for straying - and too poor, too ill-fed.

A majority of the students were girls. They were nicely brought up girls, marriage culminated the careers of most of them. A few qualified to teach 'Art', probably in schools, and a very few did become working artists of some sort. I suspect that only I of my time did become a fully professional artist.

To that end there were difficulties; I had no money. The time of realistic grants for students was still in the far future. I did win a grant, one of £3; I cannot remember if that was for the term or the year. Materials for work were hard to get, and I could not have the course books for, for example, anatomy. Similarly I must make do on the minimum of food, mostly fasting out the interval between breakfast and a meal between afternoons and evening sessions.

Occasionally I had money enough for bus fares - a penny for half the journey or twopence for the whole journey. More usually each morning I walked the three miles, walking it back after the afternoon session, back for the evening session, then finally home.

These difficulties might seem to have been more depressive than indeed they were. I lived in so pervasive a happiness of work, so joyful for each new day, that these material factors were not very important.

Life class at Croydon was taught by Percy Rendell; he was a gentle man, a quiet man. He was olive-dark, Gallic-looking. Sometimes he, a man of steady sobriety of dress would wear a scarf of clearest lemon yellow in singing contrast. Never did I see in him the least trace of a sense of humour; it greatly enhanced his impression of vulnerability. He always bore with him strongly a smell, presumably, of an unguent. Sometimes on Saturday morning when he taught me oil painting he talked to me very modestly about his own work. He was a landscape painter of subdued passion - though I think of fairly minor talent. Fairly regularly he exhibited at the Royal Academy. Shyly one Saturday he said, "I've just heard, just this morning, my picture in this year's RA has been sold. I'm very pleased - I put on it what I thought was a very high price - I rather liked it you see. I would have been quite happy to keep it. Well - it's been sold. It is nice."

Others of the few male students were sometimes there for painting on a Saturday; sometimes they were more playful than painterly. "Ah," said Percy Rendell, "they're not keen like you and I." He dwelt on the word 'keen', prolonging it.

From time to time Oswald Crompton, owlish and vague, emerged to do a round of the life class. On such a day, having discussed my drawing of the model, he spoke illuminatingly on the foreshortened drawing of one arm, so for a lifetime improving my understanding of form, so excellent a teacher as he was. "Yes," he said, beginning to ease away. "I, er - think - yes - um, those are the main points."

His wife was Rebecca. She was young, younger than he, ebullient, joyous. The smiling curves of her torso were closely held in a luscious brilliance of what she wore, as lavishly embroidered as lichen on an ash tree. It was an outburst of her happy kind - and indeed she was a very distinguished authority on embroidery. She was voluble as a brook.

And there was Miss Bradford, clear-voiced, loquacious and in her fifties. She taught watercolour, and in that I suppose it should be said, was robustly nannifying, most able to lead her subjects through the most stainless orthodoxies of watercolour. Till death she would stand by the purity of the 'high light' preserved by leaving the paper's whiteness to sparkle from the painted surface surrounding it. Not for her should there be any of the diversive tricks of many of the masters of watercolour: never would she have countenanced 'scratching'. To me she would say, "Deah boy, remembar those hay layts, more precious than jewells."

But within her self-set limits she was a most dashing, most competent performer, of great bravura. Miss Bradford, immaculate, with her glisten of white hair, impulsive blue eyes, was youthful.

As chance came, Oswald Crompton passed to me small opportunities to earn a little money. The Carl Rosa Opera Company came on its round to Croydon; to the art school they came seeking someone to paint a prop portrait to use in Verdi's *The Masked Ball.* What they paid me I cannot remember; but I loved them.

Then there came a signwriter. His need was for an artist who could paint the figures in a big sign to be erected in Piccadilly, in London. It was February, the weather bitter, each morning the day dawning ice-hard. The sign, so big, must be painted outdoors; I must work on a narrow plank some ten feet above the ground. So for a week I worked, freezing, trying not to fall.

When, the job done, it was taken away, erected, I came seeking payment. But, improbably, the man really was as unpleasant as his face suggested.

"What's all this 'urry," he said, "cummin' 'ere arstin' for money?"

"An' you be careful," he went on when I, timidly, questioned his honesty, "I got a witness, see." He never did pay me.

Also to the art school came an important city firm of estate agents; they too wanted an artist. By appointment I met them in a drear working-class South London suburb. By the great boss himself they were led. He was short, imperiously, unctuously he looked expensive. His Homburg hat was wide-brimmed, his fur collar cossetted his ears. His attendant clot of subordinates were deferential. With the mighty man we went to a little house crouched in a mean street. I knew nothing of what was to be my function.

Then we were on the doorstep, the upholstered chief, his genuflecting tail, and I. A lean woman opened the door. The chief, unbidden, walked in; we followed, into the forlorn little room, filling it. It smelt of damp and stale usage. The chief stood in its centre not removing his hat.

"Come to see this wall of yours, Mrs Er-um." I saw the wall. A large flap of wallpaper hung from the dingy plaster.

"Brought this artist - he's going to paint that bare patch - make it look like the rest."

The woman, hands on hips, leaned her head to one side. "You think that do you? Well listen. All these years I've paid rent for this hovel, and now you come and say funny things like that. You can put on that hat you haven't taken off, and you can leave as soon as you like. I shall still be expecting you to re-paper this room and no more skinflints about it."

She held open the door.

How odd, I thought, this little mightiness and his troop to this mean little end. What, I wondered, had he been expecting to pay me?

Passionate as was my addiction to my work, I was no less passionately aware of earthy, airy delights of having life in a world where trees were worshipful and flowers blossomed in hedgy banks and meadows. It came to May and the sun had the first soft warmth of late spring. Happily though I worked, I thought of trees just gaining shade before June should thicken that to canopy. In that still dappled shade I thought of pink campions and bluebells. I thought of brimstone butterflies remnant from April. I must be out, I must go to the fields. I went with my sketch book but it was a pretext, I must go.

The air was warm with the caress specially of that season; the meadow grass was in its first lush tallness. I had walked without direction, almost without thought; just ecstasy.

Then there was a girl, from where, by what means I do not remember knowing. She was about my age, faintly smiling. I think we talked a little, but not much. We wandered, smiling at each other, knowing nothing of time or anything beyond. Uncaringly the afternoon declined and I must go because I must be at art school for evening. I suppose she went as she must have come. I never saw her again. I never knew her name. I have never known anything about her.

Looking down that distant past I still see the remote glow of that afternoon. I suppose that now it would be said that was a profound initiative sexual experience. Its fragrant innocence is probably not possible for adolescence today. The honesties of today are admirable, not possible in my youth. But there are wounding losses.

1926 was the last year of my studentship, and was anyhow memorable. The deadly disenchantment which was a legacy of the Great War had been straining the seams of society each year more strictly; now they ripped apart. 1926 was the year of the General Strike. It seemed cataclysmic; never again could there be the familiar world that had drowsed from day to day. So it must be supposed, and indeed that old world was ended, but not in the seismic way that had appeared imminent. Social separations became suddenly militant. Working class people found themselves suddenly common in cause rather than warily guarding their minuscule social separations. Young men of the middle classes rushed enthusiastically to the untrained manning of public transport; going in the challenging dress of school and college scarves and blazers. They brought some havoc to public transport.

At the strike's height, confrontations of police, strikers and the blazered young, boded direfully. Wives of strikers paraded singing, "My old man's a striker, so what d'you think of that? So what d'you think of that," and so on in parody of the old popular song - 'My old man's a dustman'. But it all ended; the world returned apparently to that placidity which is so endemically English.

But also, in 1926, transcendentally, I for the first time went outside my native country. That now, when from any high street agent you may be whisked almost anywhere in the world, may seem quite ordinary. But not then did aeroplanes minimise continents. Travel then was only half to be believable; it was magical, romantic. Only by ship and train could travel be then. In foreign places could air be the same, could sight and sound and substance be of familiar kind? But beyond England! To traverse frontiers of ocean? Could even soil underfoot be of such kind I knew?

I was to go to Italy! To Italy - beyond the sea, beyond France, even beyond the towering Alps. It had been benignly thought that such a thing might enlarge the vision of an artist just budding into small leaf. At Arona in Northern Italy, at the southern end of Lago Maggiore there was a base for the Workers' Travel Association. There, for the length of the art school's summer vacation I was to go as temporary assistant to the resident hostess.

That I was to go by night crossing, from England to France, heightened the sense of departure. At Newhaven in the shrouding dark of a wild night we went aboard - aboard ship! Already, still at our mooring the deck had a slightly infirm movement. It confirmed that adventure had begun. The ship was crowded to its last inch, below deck and above. The night cried and blew. Then we edged out of harbour, out of England. Wind and sea took us; the deck became as though jellified; we rolled and we pitched and I was exultant. Only by degrees did I perceive that I was not part of a general jubilation. Much of the rest of the ship's company retched in vile distress. It was a long passage to France, the longer for the night's black wildness. But for all the hours on the rioting deck I was in a glory that the queasy context could not defeat.

Then in the pitching dark a deeper dark solidified. It was France, foreign France; it was Dieppe, in France. As we edged in it was visible that the half-seen quay was thronged with unquestionable foreigners. They shouted in their foreign way. It was almost intolerably exciting.

In the lift of dawn a train bore us onward to Paris. I, standing in the corridor saw the passing panorama of the foreign fields. Though the night had been sleepless, now there was no seat for me, I felt no fatigue. No moment of such experience could be spared for fatigue. Nor when we reached Paris did that give respite; we must be whisked immediately to another station for another train which carried us on; never can the carrying be forgotten. We went south-east, deeper, deeper into enchanted strangeness, across the golden smile of the Burgundy country to Dijon, all the way through vineyards. I who had never seen a vineyard must stare and stare to convince myself of reality.

Now we rose into the Jura; the sun-spilt plain dropped beneath us. Never since have I seen the Jura, its endless vistas in the tilted meadows, clinging airily high and higher towards Switzerland. Then there was the frontier, my first land frontier; I discovering the curious fascination that frontiers have. I who have crossed so many frontiers since still feel some remnant of that first delighted fascination. In the evening of that day that had dawned at Dieppe we came to Montreux on Lac Leman under the astonishing soaring of the Alps. How was I to believe, I who had been in South Norwood the day before? Such difficulty of belief may be hardly to be grasped by those today who are flying-conditioned.

In the morning the air was limpid; it had a clarity which was not of England, not of France. It had to do with the aloof white peaks remotely against the sky. We again in a train soon were seeing the Rhone almost newly from its source. Threading under the naked peaks it was a river of milk, with no bush, no tree, no flower that I could see, a wild bare skyscape. So from the austere wildness we came to the Simplon Tunnel. It runs its twenty-odd miles and is a frontier.

All frontiers are significant; some touch drama. This frontier, under the Alps, out of the stark natal reaches of the Rhone into Italy has drama that is sublimity. First that lunar loneliness, then the Stygian interlude. Then the astonishing emergence. Suddenly at Domodossala without preamble, the exuberant fall from the heights to sunny valleys, slender *campanili*, nestling villages, an arcady, all smiling in a gentleness of sun. Then falling again, down to the valley. The train stops at Baveno, Baveno is on the shores of Lago Maggiore. There it lay, opal-blue to far transparencies. On the platform at Baveno the porter was small and roundly smiling. "Baveno," he called and it was melodious as a song. Beside the lake then on to Stresa; then to Arona, journey's end.

Arona lay serenely, its piazza facing on to the water. At its end was the *Albergo e Ristorante el Giardino;* it was our base. A great clamber of vine roofed its dining room and made its outer walls. I thought that romantic; what else could so wonderfully demonstrate removal from Norwood.

Miss Catherine Dawson was WTA hostess at Arona; she was sun-bleached blonde and very healthy, slightly aggressively free from nonsense. Her mother was of the pioneer feminists: I think she had bequeathed to her daughter a dubiety about men. She was only twenty-five and, in her nordic fashion, handsome. Her rather splendid blonde and independent vigour must have made the clearest targets for the young men of Arona for whom anyway blondeness is halfway to beauty. Her job was probably exciting. The young men of Arona I perceived to be robustly and overtly devoted to the pursuit of women.

Also, I believe, Catherine Dawson was a socialist. This was 1926, three years after the coming to power of Mussolini. It was the strident peak of that time of bludgeonings, dastardly dosings of castor oil, shots from dark corners. There was no wall space in the public places without its stencilled portrait of Mussolini. His aggressively armed blackshirt thugs strutted in every street and piazza. No time was free from the brass bands that stopped by every café to play the fascist anthem, *'Giovinezzo, Giovinezzo'*. Each time its drear banality was pumped out everyone must stand and cease all else until it was done. And these were musically passionate people.

With the ease of youth quite quickly I gathered a rudimentary basis of Italian, quite free of grammar, but adequate for common occasions. Of those was the occasional escorting of parties on trips. Of which was the conducting of middle-aged women up the lake to Stresa. Public transport in the lovely local mode was, by paddle steamer, to make of it a dream voyage. The day was ecstatic, with the fineness of heaven as we started up the vistas of Lago Maggiore. But Maggiore is a capricious lake. The sun did not lessen its gentle lustre, the air was diamond-clear. With no warning a wind arose, of such violence that the lake erupted mountainously. The little ship breasted bravely into the seas; I in the foremost peak of the bows was enraptured.

But at Stresa I discovered the state of my charges. They were not enraptured; they were poorly. I had to get them ashore and their state was unfavourable. The ship could not ride quietly at the quay; it bucketed erratically. I could see that my party blanched more palely at the frantic see-sawing of quay and ship. There could be no gentleness. A crewman, seizing a second's levelling, got ashore. Imperatively I seized the first of my ladies. At the next level instant I projected her, the crewman snatched her. She was ashore; so one by one my nine ladies were roughed to solid land. There providentially, was a café that could brew strong tea; soon my ladies were restored. Concurrently rage fell from the wind; the lake became again a placid plain of blue silk.

But my party had lost its taste for voyaging. I took them back by train.

Bernard, aged about nineteen.

Sometimes in siesta time I took a boat and rowed over the lake to where Angera dozed in the sun. Strident tourism which even so distantly had put its hand on Stresa, was unknown in Angera. In the still afternoon I would climb the rocks, sit timeless in the sun and watch the foot-long green lizards. They moved toy-like in flashes - a flash of movement, a stop as though painted, a flash again. Their eyes' jewelled flicker betrayed the having of life.

In the vignettes of memory of a long life of travel, those of Italy shine with a distant glow not matched by any other. Perhaps the tranquil bliss of Angera's afternoons stays most dearly. When I hear Debussey's '*L'apres midi d'un faun*' I recall Angera.

CHAPTER VII

The Path to Professionalism

I, RETURNING from Italy, had one more term as a student. My student days then were done. I must launch myself as a professional artist in a world which showed no discernible interest. Here was I, in January 1927, emergent into the wider world, there, eagerly, to begin a career. With proper modesty but with no serious doubt I looked forward to its unfolding. I was to learn that between student and practising professional artist there is a third state.

The function of an art school training is not to make of its students fully rounded-out artists; it is to give them that essential solidity of craftsmanship from which later flowering may come. So it was and had been for all foregoing centuries, that same purpose having been served by apprenticeship in the studios of artists. In our irrational time the training of artists has been abolished. Of art schools, art colleges, now there is excess - so to accommodate those many deemed worthy but lacking nature's gift of talent.

Now I, starting in bouyant innocence, had to suffer a cool

douche; I had till now been foundation laying; now must come that second state, I must pass through the door which is called 'Experience'. Before me was a nebulous world in which I hoped were those with a potential need for my services as an artist. Somewhere I must begin, somewhere find a place of entrance. I must start 'going round'.

Persistently, dogged, bearing a folio of my work I must make an attritional round of places possibly of potential. London's geography became marked for me by publishers, advertising agents, printers, editorial offices of magazines and newspapers. Publishers then were largely settled in clots; in Ludgate Hill's hinterland dimly close in the shadow of St Pauls was the intestinal environs of Paternoster Row giving lodgement to publishers uncounted - all wiped away by fire and bomb these fifty years and more.

By Covent Garden too there they were, publishers jostling cheek by jowl within the pervasive embrace of the smell of the fruit market: publishers and their authors, and I, picked a way through a gutter litter of mashed oranges and greens. How there, too, change has swept since in the twenties so well I knew it. It was noisy then, the air close-filled by shouting of market porters, of steely clatter of horses' vast feet iron-shod on cobbles. It was gutsily, commonly, organically real.

And now how changed. Where now the hollering, where now the hot breath, the sweating hides of horses? No sweating now is there; all now is *prinkct oot* to serve the endless need of tourism - and indeed very prettily it is done, pedestrianised, carefully spontaneous with café chairs and tables in continental fashion. Whatever it may do for tourism it must be gladdening for those office-freed at lunchtime. It is, hardly questionably, pleasant, even a little gay; but for those who remember not quite convincing.

Outwards from Paternoster Row and Covent Garden publishers thinned rapidly, cropping up randomly. Westward, nearly to the bottom of St Martin's Lane there was Chatto and Windus; further a few hundred yards, Constable hid in a back street behind the National Gallery, and to this day continue faithfully so to do. Far away, opposite the Law Courts in the Strand, a street dived down nearly to the river, and in its ultimate corner, there inserted was Methuen.

But wherever its being, there was no publisher escaped me; as doggedly I pressed all of any possible promise. Response varied only in its words of use: I was but raw material yet to be moulded by experience, too newly from art school. That realised, the need was for stamina and witless optimism; both with passage of time, difficult to sustain. When again and again Art Director, Studio Manager or any other passed scanning eye over my specimens, with what deadly certainty I forsaw what I was to be told.

"Hm, not bad," he or she would say. "But you need experience. Come and see me again when you've had some experience."

They were right, so right. Sometimes one would say, "Mm, yes, promising. But your stuff's art schooly."

There then dilemma; to get work I must have experience; to get experience I must have work. In some way, not visible in its happening, a solution comes - slowly, slowly - mainly as by an osmosis, an unconscious seepage into the mind.

One day quite early in this process I called upon the manager of a commercial studio. He, good man, received me kindly.

"Your stuff's not bad lad. Need experience though; smells of the art school. Come back to me when you've scratched up a bit of experience. You're promising right enough. You'll come out all right. Some day you'll be driving your own Ford car."

The flavour of that is not to be tasted by anyone not of that time. This was the era of the Model T Ford, the 'flying bedstead'. Wide ownership of cars then was only haltingly on its way. Its precarious prophet was the Model T Ford. It was unpredictable; it was eccentric, rich in material for humour. But it was one that came before. Much quoted was a re-writing of the 23rd Psalm which ran thus: 'My car is a Ford. I shall not want another. It annointeth my head with oil. It maketh me to lie down in wet places,' and so on.

The Model T was not very fast: it ran rattling with a certain stateliness high on its wheels. So too its occupants, sitting high, very upright. On an occasion I saw a rear wheel detach itself and, emancipated, bound ahead, outpacing the limping parent vehicle. The butt end of the rear axle warped over to run on the road. As so the car ran, three-legged, the passengers strove bravely to appear that they too thought it funny.

Latterly as a student I had acquired a girlfriend; it was my way to go with her on the bus to see her to her door. Having no futher fare for a bus I walked the five miles home. One such night of winter I overtook a young man. He weaved as he walked; he was stooped, hollow-faced, very thin. He was unemployed: he had walked from the north of England. In Brighton, so he had heard, jobs were to be found. To Brighton from there was fifty-five more miles. Not one penny had I that I could give him: I felt bitterly guilty. I waved down a lorry going that way.

"Come on mate," the driver said, "Give me yer 'and, up yer come."

I saw him last, small, hunched beside the driver. I hope the driver found him food. I have never known what happened to that one starving vagrant young man. He was one of so many in that harsh obscene society.

For two years and more I trod my round with little sign that ever I should do anything but that. The pangs of the still undiagnosed duodenal ulcer tormented recurrently; food was chronically short but never entirely absent. Because the soles of my shoes wore to holes, I must before going out on winter mornings of cold or wet, pack them with brown paper packed hard. But I do not recall that ever I fell into despair: optimism's small flame flickered on - though occasionally falling faint. And, so slugging on, there were compensations. I loved and was fascinated by the British Museum, was constant at the National Gallery, sometimes venturing into the museum of the Royal College of Surgeons in Lincoln's Inn Fields there to see the very good anatomical collection. And, half stunning in their temples of delight there were the fishing tackle shops of London. I must assume that the tackle shops of today have very great attraction for current fishing generations. But, can it be possible that those of today, being as it seems to me, of a somewhat severe efficiency, have the wondrous allurement of those I remember? A fishing tackle shop now is multiply crammed with all the devices for going fishing, but surely those black inorganic things cannot stir the lusting imagination as did those of the past.

Those old shops were not all of a kind. Some were temples. Some were intimate caverns of delight and that word is appropriate: they tended to shadowy retirements saturated with scents of tackle and groundbait and maggots - though they then, more pleasantly, were called gentles. They were brotherly places. The tackle they sold was of nature - rods of Spanish reed, Tonkin cane, landing nets whose meshes were so unforgettably aromatically impregnated with linseed oil. Bait cans for live bait were honest solid things of zinc, becoming easily objects of love: love for a plastic bait can is not attainable.

Those old sequestered places, earthily ancient with association, filled with echoes of anglers gone, just beyond hearing, were of the coarse fishermen. Westward were the temples; in rarer air, more lordly they received those who came drawn by the spell; in Pall Mall the House of Hardy; round the corner and up St James's Street, Ogden Smith. Before both those hallowed windows many times I stood drunk with lust for delights unattainable, as then for me they were. How slenderly supple those rods, split cane so softly amber, luscious varnished. I ventured in sometimes to savour air so sanctified. I begged catalogues, and in the understanding kindliness proper there, was never refused. Farlows lay then in a huddle of streets just under Leicester Square; there on a corner of Panton Street and another, a place almost of excruciating magnetism because more than any other that small slightly muddled shop was solidly intense, in absent-minded way, with the mysticism of angling. Once through its unassuming slightly shabby door, all other worlds were forgotten.

Meanwhile the constantly trodden round went on. It is improbable that any possibility was so obscure that I did not find it. Forum Publicity surely was obscure but I found it. Forum Publicity was so hidden in Great Queen Street as, it might have been supposed, to be secure from finding. But by the climbing of many narrow stairs it was to be found high in a narrow-fronted 18th century house. One day I climbed the narrow pitch of staircase to the company's two rooms. The front and larger one was the main office; behind, small and dark, was that of the Managing

Director. By the climbing of a few more stairs, narrower, steeper, an attic was reached which had been made to be a photographic studio. It was conducted by an excitable middle-aged single lady.

The Managing Director had an ordinary look. He was short, thickly short, his face large, unresilient, declining in its lower areas to jowls. His eyes were of that very brown kind, the pupils underhung by the whites above pouched lids. He made me a proposal.

I was astonished: long since I had forgotten to expect proposals. I was to have a place in the larger room; there I could do whatever work I had (if I had any). I would have no salary, but when there came a need for artwork, as a freelance I should do it. Optimism in its foolish fashion leaped. Undeniably these people were in business; they were prepared to regard my presence as being practical if not worth the gamble of a salary. My foot was on the ladder. Now I could acquire that magic garment of experience. Even I should get some money.

I did gain some experience, though rough in kind. Some accounts they had, for motor bikes, one for drums, another for cosmetics: I remember nothing very clearly but that a very attractive German girl worked opposite me on much the same basis as myself. How I ceased to be there is lost in the mist of years.

It was by chance and later that I learned of the Managing Director's discovery; it was no less than that he was Jesus. Being thus on a Second Coming, very properly he gathered about him disciples. How his destiny was culminated I never knew, whether ever he achieved his Calvary.

The short stay with Forum Publicity must have made my work look a little less larval because on another day when I was about twenty-two I climbed another narrow flight of stairs. It took me to the premises of Maxwell Foster Artists. At a salary of five pounds a week I became a Maxwell Foster Artist. I was to be a 'figure man'. In the main studio with me there was a 'lettering man', a 'still-life man', and two girls who did 'women's stuff'. There was also Jim Hart and Ateo Cassadio.

Jim Hart was tall, willowy, twig-thin: he wore his incandescent red hair in a tossed swag. His shirts were turquoise, his ties of yellow silk unconstrained. He was conspicuous, wrote poetry constantly, often declaimed it. It was bad poetry, but superior to most declared today to be poetry.

Ateo was Italian, ebullient and small; he fermented with his chronic rediscovery of the delight of life. He was aquiline with a pallid delicacy suggestive of Leonardo da Vinci; and indeed to the yearning discomfort of us all, his sister had that almost insubstantial beauty of Leonardo's Virgin of the Rocks.

Jim and Ateo were designers: in me they awakened a first small sense of design. It was a bud that, tentatively, put out small leaf. They and their circle dissolved the cling of suburbanism which my Croydon training had left upon me. In that then not fashionable area of Islington behind the Angel they had a studio; there first I met Charlie Watson. I think it was his studio: his presence filled it as to an extent it filled any place. Charlie was a Londoner; he was of that South London purlieu that encloses Brixton Hill. It seemed too cramped ever to have contained him.

The sense of Charlie was large; he dwarfed the sense of what was about him. Physically he was large, but it was his sense of size that was big. He stood six feet, possibly an inch more; from his feet he ascended past his huge chest to his head, set back as though to top off the monument that was Charlie. He appeared to peer over his shoulder mass to observe life beneath which, so often, was funny. His hair and beard, errantly curling, framed the slight back tilt of his face above his open-throated shirt, his loose flow of bow. Perhaps he was not entirely unconsciously Byronic; his short leg and surgical boot added to a romantic suggestion.

But Charlie, lustily aware of women though he was, was not romantic. He was earthy and extrovert and lovingly constant at the London Palladium where then the Crazy Gang and Flannagan and Allen were an institution. But Charlie was attractive to women; exceedingly so he was, as though by no intention and randomly among the social strata. There was she who, being rich, as a passing gift sent him an imperious Daimler car. It and him he had driven to the nearest garage there to sell it for the first offer.

Charlie was a painter: had he pursued nothing but painting he would have become outstanding. Exuberant talent ran from his pores. He was a fine, flowing draughtsman and an instinctive handler of any medium. He was good enough always to be in deep discontent with his work. Returning drunk to the studio, as sometimes was his way, he would throw at his work an eye of baleful frustration. "I want to paint like Manet," then he would shout while smashing his current work. There seemed strong promise that he would come to painting splendidly like Charlie Watson.

Then it came to Charlie that he perhaps should earn some money, it being obvious (as so blindingly it is now) that good, honest painting, genuine painting, had only the least likelihood of so doing. So, speculatively, he looked at commercial art. Almost instantly success snatched him up, bore him away. Quite casually he earned a great deal of money. Every week for *Woman's Own* magazine he painted the cover picture of a pretty girl; effortlessly they were brilliant, much praised. Charlie was not pleased.

"Well paid rubbish," he said, contemptuously, "I want to paint people with funny bottoms." He admired Rowlandson.

My period with Maxwell Foster Artists picked me up, shook out the tightness, started me anew; but as now I see, not as Maxwell Foster had anticipated. He had supposed of me that I would become a good steady 'figure man', unbothered by any cross-currents of creativeness, fully reliable for the marketing of beer, tobacco and all else.

But we talked, Jim, Ateo, and I, and those others at the studio behind the Angel. We made constant raids to the Tate Gallery, to the British Museum. My dawning perception of design induced self-discovery, stirrings of creativity. A stylistic excitement carried me off. Foster, alarmed, removed me from the disquieting company of the main studio. I was to share a room with Geoffrey Squire. He, good honest man, was the very pattern to which the rising 'figure man' should aspire. For all from beer to bikes he used himself as a model with the aid of a mirror. From many hoardings familiarly he looked down. His work was solidly competent, ugly, entirely untouched by humour or aesthetic feeling. He was to be my good influence; alas, a good and decent man though he was he had no colour sense, his soul was never tempted into flight.

A yeast of new awareness stimulated me, to painting, to design at large, but, very specifically at that time to poster design. This was a golden age of the poster - though, very painfully, very bad poster design abused the eye on every side; so bad indeed that it was a catalyst to the urgent movement to a delightfulness of good design. It appeared, through the 1920s and 30s that a classic period of the poster was arising - as truly it was. How beautifully it might have flowered. But there came the blight of the camera: it spread its cold inorganic wrap over the warm living body of design, suffocating it. In more recent years photographic poster design has much improved but has not and cannot recover the warm humanity of the past. The designer of that good time was an individual artist, lovingly working: the modern photographic poster is a collective job, therefore lifeless. Art by committee is an emptiness.

With reverence I must genuflect to the memory of historic poster designers of the golden age, to Austin Cooper, McKnight Kauffer, Sep Scott. It seemed their work inaugurated that which could unite common commerce with the common life for a common acceptance of beauty. It was a concept of great appeal to young designers such as I then was.

But meanwhile it was obvious that I was not profitable to Maxwell Foster. The spectre of return to the bitter round began to walk with me. Sooner rather than later Maxwell Foster must sack me. I went to see Fred Phillips who was, rather famously, Managing Director of the Baynard Press, which in his hands was among leaders of good design in advertising. He was well enough impressed by what I showed him to give me several small freelance jobs: then, on the evidence of those, offered me a staff job if I could wait a short time. It was precarious, too precarious. I was summoned by Maxwell Foster. He, not of stern kind, had no taste for the wielding of axes. He was distraught, trembling; I felt painfully sorry for him. "You've been freelancing," he said. It was better for both of us that he sacked me.

For me it was joyful release: now, at once I was free to join the Baynard Press. But at the heart of that fruit so happily seized there

Above and below left: Poster designs for a series of spice promotions.

Book jacket illustration.

was a maggot. The Baynard Press had taken over a company called the Lochend Printing Company; to see why that company should have been so vulnerable needed no very acute perspicacity. Mainly their business lay in the design and printing of confectionery packaging: their designing was a desolation, a weary flaccid echo of the 1890s. A mind less innocent than mine would have noted that of the two designers one was the son of the Managing Director.

Because so prematurely I had come, Fred Phillips fitted me into the studio of the Lochend Printing Company, so making there a design staff of three. It was immediately visible that thus I should be imposed was painfully not to the pleasure of the Managing Director. He was a man of slinking mien, regarding one obliquely rather than directly. His general air was of detesting all he saw; I never saw him smile.

The general practice for any job was that all three of us should produce a design, all three being submitted - an arrangement at once uneasy. In every case, as the jobs came, my design was chosen. Again how deep my innocence: I saw no danger. Then, oddly, I ceased to be chosen.

Fred Phillips sent for me. He must give me notice. Recently my designs had not been chosen. Yes, I told him, just that morning I had found those unsuccessful designs hidden at the back of a drawer. They had not been submitted. Phillips, obviously in discomfort, avoided my eye: it probably burned with outraged innocence. Phillips, an honest man trapped in dishonesty, said, eyes downcast, "I expect you've been riding the high horse or something." I was fired.

But in the Baynard Press I retained friends. One, a large rambling amiable man, was endearingly cockney. Of his accounts one was the Orient Line shipping company. He asked me, now compulsorily freelance, to submit a design for a poster for Orient Line cruises to Norway. It was to be competitive.

To my vast surprise, only half belief, mine was the chosen design. To my further and most happy astonishment when later the Victoria and Albert Museum put on an exhibition of international poster design, this same poster was one of those few chosen to represent Britain.

Painting, 'The Day is Coming', 1926.

Theatre poster.

Book jacket illustration.

Could it be then, at last, that I was on the road to success? Was this a straw in the wind? Another soon followed. The year was 1933; in that year was held the great Advertising Exhibition at Olympia. Of the exhibitors one was the advertising agency, Mather & Crowther; of them was the Eat More Fruit campaign. It was to be the theme of their stand. To me came the design and execution of its decoration.

The stand was triangular; to cover its three sides I must produce murals expressing the theme. I was given a free hand: I used it freely, with joy. The abundance of joy was qualified by a small anxiety - from first conceptual sketches to delivery of the complete work I had three weeks. It was formidable.

For the frontally-facing panel I used a sweeping design of piled fruit; for the other two panels the designs were of the harvesting of exotic fruits. For seven days a week I worked furiously against the onrush of the deadline, The price for the work, astronomical as then it seemed to me, was £95; of that 20% must go to my agent.

For the delivery of the work on the appointed day I had engaged a Chelsea art carrier. The day came: the carrier did not. I telephoned: they had forgotten. They declared themselves sorry; at once they would send a vehicle. It began to rain; a sense of disaster began to nudge me. The rain augmented. Tardily the van arrived; the rain rose to deluge. But there the van was, agony of doubt dispelled. The respite was short, as was the van. Not nearly was it long enough. "Tell them to go to hell," my mother advised loudly. But I must get the panels to Olympia; hell must wait.

I forced an unreal calm. Suppose I were to perch on the tailboard. Suppose then the projecting ends were draped with at least partially rain proof material? So it was that the van set out from Norwood to Olympia in Kensington, I on its tailboard striving so to remain and prevent destruction of the panels in their whipping and lash of the downpour.

The journey to Olympia would be better forgotten, could that be. But arrival came: it came to the delivery yard at Olympia and it was flooded. But with some wading the panels were delivered. Tribulations at last were done; I saw the panels safely into the hands of the stand's constructors. Now in nervous need, I went to the bar to knit up my ravelled strands. There soon I was joined by the Managing Director of Mather & Crowther: he was distraught. "The bloody oaf," he cried. An aperture was needed through which to project a light. He who must do it had cut it in the middle of one of my designs. By some coincidental luck I had with me the means for repair.

All now at last was peace, and happily, success. The Art Critic of *The Times* declared in his review that my panels were the best decoration in the exhibition.

Fragilely I had begun to build a reputation. The magazine, *Commercial Art And Industry* published a piece about my work. It even seemed that a reliable living might be imminent. But art buyers, peering from their ruts, were askance.

"Hm, yes," they said of my work, "Yes, very beautiful, very beautiful, but oh not practical though, not for our needs."

Occasionally I designed posters for what then was the Southern Railway. Occasionally too I was called upon by my friend at the Baynard Press for travel designs.

Then there came to me a call from a well-known printing and poster company. They invited me to design six double-crown posters: of those though so much is unforgettable, I have no shred of memory as to what was their subject. The whole six were to be done in one week. The clear impossibility of so doing did not prevent my being asked, or my determination to strive to it. My family was away on holiday; I was alone. Of that lonely week I made one extended day: without stop I worked six times sleeplessly round the clock. I paused only to brew strong coffee. Food was what I could grab and eat left-handedly while working. The work of course was bad; it was turned down. I received no payment.

But, creeping in small steps, the road to the future could be discerned. Inconspicuously I had begun to move into journalism. When *Time And Tide* accepted a piece from me it was well received. I had nature pieces accepted by the *Christian Science Monitor*; they too were well received. Here and there I sold a few pieces illustrated by my own line drawings. For *Lilliput*'s happy pages I did line drawing illustrations, which I did most lovingly, and for which I received a guinea and a half. I did remark to she who was Art Editor that it was worth doing because the magazine was so good a shop window for the artist. Never again did I receive a commission from *Lilliput*. *The Radio Times* for whom too I did drawing did not pay well, but so much better than *Lilliput's* pittance.

One day for a cup of tea I went into a Lyons' tea shop. I became aware that opposite me was a small oriental. He engaged my eye and held it.

"The name," he said out of no context, "is Tunga. I am from Ceylon. What are you?" He spoke in the rather barking fashion which is of Singhalese of Sri Lankans as now they are. So caught I could not but confess that I was an artist.

"Then we must work together." And, odd as it seems, we did. I think I was very easy to capture; a kind of weakness. And it was interesting; many things he told me about being Singhalese, and a lot of it was scandalous. Not the least so was what he told me of goings-on in the temples. Women in trouble with their husbands for failing to conceive would come by night to the temple, there to wait in darkness for the coming of the god who would bless them with pregnancy: much of the time so it transpired. Otherwise the priests' erotic needs were met by the temple's boy acolytes.

He conceived, and together we carried out, a series of features for the *Star*, the London evening sister paper of the *News Chronicle*, sadly both now extinct. 'The Stranger In Your Midst' the series was called. Its subjects were the foreigners, mostly oriental, living in London. While my partner conducted his interview I drew the subject, afterwards doing the finished drawing. Thus we covered a Chinese resident of Limehouse in London's dockland; we did a Burmese and a Japanese and an Indian. We did a Singhalese lady and an Arab. We also did he who, as I was told, was an Hungarian Gypsy. He was a band leader in the Tottenham Court Road. Of him I had great dubiety; it was much easier to suppose him a native of Whitechapel. Our series was successful.

But my old duodenal enemy was still with me, active and deeply hostile. I was not often out of pain; it gnawed almost constantly, grindingly, demoralisingly. The only relief was to eat something, any morsel, anything, desperately. Constantly I must dose myself with bicarbonate of soda. The church of St Bernard The Bicarbonate a friend called me.

At last, after many years, there was diagnosis. I had very maturely established duodenal ulcers. Short of operation there were many treatments, and I had them all. None was successful.

There was the remaining option. I must be operated upon. My mother in her anxiety could find one consoling factor. "A duodenal ulcer," she said, savouring the words; "it's called the king of ulcers you know." She also pointed out how big an operation it was to be, and in that she had some pride. I lacked her dramatic sense for appreciating that aspect. I was to have a gastric enterostomy - a short circuiting of the duodenum, an operation now extinct these many years.

CHAPTER VIII

Skirmish with Eternity

IN JANUARY 1935 I entered the Royal Cancer Hospital which, long since, became the Royal Marsden Hospital. I was twenty-seven. I was not as might be supposed cancerous: the hospital accepted such cases as mine. It was a world away from other worlds, a seclusion.

I entered towards evening; upon the passing of the door all sense and texture of previous things became distant. Perhaps that was premonitory. My bed was Number Twelve, and that now was my identity. For the duration I had no other name.

I was in a rectangular offset of the main ward. On my right was an elderly man about whom hung a curtain of evil smell, as of malignant decay. That was to become familiar.

He introduced himself. "I got cancer, see, in me guts. But they made a bit of a slip - pricked me bleedin' bladder."

On my left was a man who had been a petty officer in the Royal Navy until cancer of the lung demobilised him. Beyond him, round the wall, was he who had been a marine. Now here he was with distorted utterance because part of his cancerous tongue had been removed. Every day in the last hours before evening dosing time he paced the ward, gripping his face to stifle pain. Maximum pain-killing drugs could not see him round until the next relief.

I cannot recall now who was there with whom: they were shuffled constantly. Some, treatment over, went home. Death, always lurking, took its pickings. An elderly and enormous former Lifeguards trooper, erect in dressing gown and slippers, marched every morning in the hospital garden. And there was Bill who had been a fireman. The little stick-fragile man, a wispy straggle of limbs and moustache, had been a bus driver. "'E won't drive no more buses," they said, and indeed he did not. He died quite soon.

Newly to the ward one day there came another naval petty officer. He was in uniform, in that context debonair. "Look at 'im," said my naval neighbour, "in uniform an' all. Very smart. I 'ad a uniform like that." He turned his face to the wall; his future was to be short and out of uniform.

There was an Italian, and I do not remember the going of him. Until then he was ebulliently present; very numerously visited. They swarmed about him, always very abundant with the fruit they brought him.

"Ha," he said, "you tella me I am lucky - so many loving family bringa me the fruit. Not so bloody lucky - they bringa me all the stock of my shop."

For a few probationary days I awaited that which was to come. On its eve they told me that I was to be first up to the theatre in the morning. "Get it over early. Isn't that nice?" I did not think anything of what was to be could be nice. And because of my privilege I must have no supper. Five o'clock was ward wakening time; but no need had I for wakening. Before the uncaring January light seeped in, the trussing-up of me for the theatre had begun; the thigh-length woollen stockings, the ballooning gown: then the barber for nether shaving. He waved his open razor with carefree confidence and the morning jollity of one who is not going to the theatre. "'Ave to be careful like wiv the razor, 'ad'n I mate? Would'n want me to 'ave a slip, would yer?"

I was ready, trussed and hungry. But my priority? They did not come for me. The morning passed; lunchtime came and I watched others eat. Afternoon passed, and when settling to evening routine began they came for me. I was given a morphia injection that was to dull my sensibilities. It made me very queasy and uneasily alert. As I was taken to the theatre I hoped the long day had not made the surgeon tired, impaired his skill. Then the mask and the ether's awful reek carried me away.

My eyes opened slowly. There was unreal light and no form. Images grew slowly. I was in the ward; that was my first awareness. Then the nauseous wave engulfed me, retching at my emptiness. I vomited for fourteen hours, stifled by the regurgitated stench of ether. I was wedged as nearly vertical as aggression of pillows could make me. I was immeasurably weak, so without strength to support my head that it wilted over on to my right shoulder. Sister, with that appalling cheerfulness to which sisters are prone, called me the Drooping Lily.

"How are you Number Twelve?" they asked me, obviously confident that I felt well. I did not: but when it came realisation that the vomiting was not to be permanent I did begin to perceive that there were acceptable alternatives to death. But now I knew, not for life's length would I be able to bear the smell of ether.

Faintly I began to feel a wan cheerfulness: I had had the operation and was alive. I had stopped vomiting, begun to tolerate sister's jolliness. And, had they not promised me that quite soon, perhaps two weeks, I should be able to leave hospital, go home without a duodenal ulcer, without pain?

The night nurse was small and looked fragile. Her pretty brown eyes were in a doll-like pretty face. I had no premonition that she was cast to be the instrument of my survival.

The pyjama jacket was thin; vertically propped as I was, it was my only covering above the waist. January's cold night air came through a window's open top to play about my chest, and so again for a second night. The third night my breathing began to rasp, became hard, short and shallow. Thus it was that night nurse entered my destiny. She was the girlfriend of the RMO; when she called he came: he was promptly to my rescue. He gave me oxygen.

It gave me easement: but in the next days there came pain that I guessed to be essentially no different from having a bayonet pushed slowly through my left side, slowly out, in slow repetition. The houseman came.

"You've got a bit of pleurisy old boy. Have to aspirate you." He told me as if bringing news of a treat.

I guessed that aspiration, whatever it was, would not be enjoyable; it was not. A large bore needle trailing a tube was pushed through my left side, between my ribs, into the lung cavity. From the tube into a dish came a stream of straw-coloured liquid. Could that really be coming out of me, so much of it? Nasty as it was, it was rather fascinating.

As the days followed, so did the aspirations, and never did the source seem ready to dry up. The houseman one day, pushing hard to go through my ribs said, "Have to be careful," grunt, "before you know where you are," grunt, "you could perforate the lung."

My grasp of sequence weakened as days slipped into weeks. I was drifting, into a miasma that became a nightmare of incoherence. The routine of the ward continued about me, sometimes with my awareness, sometimes not; its routine was dull horror.

Deep radiation patients had vessels to receive the appalling disgorgements of clotted viscous mucus. Opposite me an old man waiting for death cried continually, day and night, "The pain, the pain, oh the pain." Each night I must be given heroin for brief respite. Cancer's rotting smell hung often in the air. Death was constantly attendant.

Sometimes it was noisy, rasping away the remnants of diseased life. For the rest of us concern was for how long that should be - there was a small broken shard of a man who for two unforgiving days and nights made the ward raucous with his death rattle. Another man whom death was cheating had no face left. Death evaded his dire need. One night a lethal haemorrhage came upon him. The RMO, being called, walked the long way round the hospital. "Let the poor fellow have his chance." So later I was told by night nurse.

Nurses are people and so of many kinds. But I, having known them in what may be called extreme circumstances, cannot believe there are many exceptions to their all but divine vocation. To be a nurse in such places as I was in demands qualities not given to the majority. In that hospital some nurses were flighty, some flirtatious, some merry, some moody, but in the constancy of every day they performed duties of such dreadful intimacy as could not be thought tolerable. That there was the odd exception was the more noticeable by contrast.

I cannot forget Nurse Jones, a little lame lean undoubted saint. She was drably inconspicuous and beyond mere goodness. A nurse whose name I have forgotten was bounteously formed; her lovely eye was always ready to be caught. She was a girl of voluptuous promise. But she was a nurse in a cancer hospital: she must do things of appalling disgust for people beyond self help. This was of course a very long time ago, no doubt in medical terms the Dark Ages. But whatever change there may have been, cancer is still cancer.

The parson did not lessen our discontent: he came with his mission of spiritual balm regularly if infrequently. It was easily to be seen that he would have preferred other assignments, and we would have preferred him to have them. His assessment of the ward's spiritual quality was low.

"The only Christian among them," he said (as I was to hear), "is Number Twelve." That was odd, I being an agnostic.

As the weeks passed and by degrees I sank, my spirit's support was the window. There was little it showed me, but just discernible beyond the recession of roofs, distantly there were trees. It was an affirmation that beyond the ward there was a world under the sky where breezes sighed, birds sang, cattle were placid in meadows. Above all, obsessionally, it suggested that still there were rivers, that weirpools had their water scent at evening, that fish hung in the current on flexing fins. If I could live, if I could feel again the pulse through the rod. I must live; I must live to fish again. In my times of lucidity that was my beseeching all.

To all but me that was daily less of a probability. Pneumonia succeeded pleurisy. Each evening high temperature raged; each morning I was cold. I could no longer eat. I grew thin, then almost skeletal with a distended belly. I floated in and out of consciousness. "Like a famine specimen, old boy," said the houseman, seeking to rally me.

As I was to learn later from night nurse, I had become a focus of disagreement; the consultant physician who examined me pronounced acute TB: he gave a maximum of two further weeks of life. The RMO had another opinion.

Something should be said of him. But for him, through night nurse, I would not be here for the saying of it. His name was Levy; he was a South African Jew. He was young, probably under thirty, small and with dark eyes of great gentleness; and, as I am the evidence, of great capability. He had come to inspect me on that particular visiting day.

I remember it, the last visit of my family before final crisis swept me up. Visiting days had become intolerable; a nightmare agitation. I drifted out of consciousness, returning to some sort of awareness, cloud drift that consolidated, became my family: they were talking but I could not understand. Then again I slid out of consciousness again. When I returned they had gone; the ward was peaceful again.

It was a day about that time that Levy came to me in the afternoon, he and others. It was one of my times of lucidity. They took me to the theatre: it was the first time I had been conscious in the theatre; I was alert and interested. How good a studio it would make I thought, and told them so.

"I hope you don't mind," Levy said, "I'm going to do a little operation - not too big a thing. Make you feel better. I'm going to give you a few whiffs of gas and oxygen to pass you out for a little while." Then the mask was over my face, and from a great distance as though through cotton wool, I heard, "Have you gone yet?" and, faintly, heard myself, "Not quite." When I opened my eyes I was still in the theatre, but stitched up. Levy was washing down.

"I'll tell you what I've been doing," he said, "You had aseptic peritonitis - aseptic mind you; just caught it in time. An abscess on the peritoneum, but it hadn't broken. If we'd left it till tomorrow it would have broken. But, well it's all right now. I've cleaned you up."

Then back to the ward. Did I feel better? How was I to know in all that haze? I could think of nothing but those distant trees beyond the window; I must live for the promise of those. What was left of my body lay in Number Twelve: my mind could smell the evening river smell, see the meadows.

Until evening so I lay. The ward had tea and evening dressings and doses, and then it was 8 o'clock and lights out. They came for me again. I began to shake as always I must now at the sight of a white coat at the ward door. What could they want of me now? Why could I not be left to think of the satin current sliding under the hollow bank? There was night nurse and others and some sort of trolley. They pushed that under the bed, cranked it up, lifting bed and me. They were wheeling me out of the ward, into the lift, up to the theatre again.

"I must do another little operation, but sorry, can't put you under this time."

On the table again. No peace. And there was the river, still running sweetly under the bank. I was packed up with pillows to lie half on my right side. I was injected, I guessed that was local anaesthetic. On my right, night nurse was holding my hands. Behind on my left I heard Levy, "You're going to feel a scratch, just a scratch."

There it was, along my left side. After that there is confusion - what I remember, what later was told me by night nurse. There was a soft gripping at my left side, I remember that, a crunching sound. Something had bitten out a section of rib.

Now in the theatre's haze of brilliance I did feel a sense of climax; night nurse's hands tightened on mine. I was to know that then an abrupt cut was made through the pleura. I cannot remember if I heard spurting; perhaps I was told.

Something was inside my chest. Something was searching, insistently, not stopping. All was timeless nightmare under the white relentless blaze. There was a low ululating and I began to wonder what it was. It was I; I was shocked, I heard my whispered apology. I concentrated on the sound to stop it. Night nurse had a mirror; she was tilting it. I knew what that was, she was tilting it to show Levy my face. I guessed why; my eyes had been turning up under the upper lids. I must concentrate to stop that too.

There was no time or shape now of anything; the ceaseless drawing in my chest seemed to be sucking away my sap's last drop as if never to stop. But stop at last it did, and I, limply lifted, was back on the bed; and now I saw all those who had been behind me. They, from head to foot, were densely spattered, yellow and red.

In the ward they were busy about me. A large bore hollow needle, inserted into a vein in my arm was strapped there: it was fed by a tube from a vessel above. A saline drip they told me. All else was haze. I suppose they injected me to induce sleep; I did until morning.

Then, that next morning, they were about me again. The many-tail bandage and gauze and lint were heavy with blood, tinctured pus because there was a drainage tube in my side. The tube was taken out to be cleaned; the pain of that is fresh in memory. By another tube the lung cavity was irrigated, washing out pus and, to my unbelieving eyes, large pieces of fungus like grey army blanket. The irrigating fluid had a smell like that of a much-used domestic cleanser. When that is used I must go elsewhere.

Later Levy, gently commiserate, returned to explain. He had not accepted the diagnosis of acute TB. His prognosis was that I was dually affected - I had peritonitis, not as yet septic, and empyema. Empyema, of which till then I had never heard, is an abscess in the lung cavity. So completely had it filled that with pus that the lung had collapsed. When he made his releasing cut it had burst in a jet. Nowadays I suppose nobody hears of empyema: antibiotics have relegated it to medical history - for the time being anyway. The rest I heard from night nurse. A time had come when it was accepted that I could not live more than another day or two. Levy had the freedom to act upon his diagnosis.

For a time I continued to be Number Twelve, continuing a routine of dressings and drainings and irrigations, almost a sort of peace. But my lung was flattened; it must be reflated. For that my union to Number Twelve must be dissolved.

My new union was to a bed by a radiator. By that conjunction I was inserted into the water cycle, so in effect to create a suction pump. From the radiator came a tube to a large water-filled glass jar set upon a chair against the bed. From that came a tube that passed through the hole in my side to enter the lung cavity, there to exert its suction.

This device, simple, excellently effective, had a flaw. Each morning there came the ward maid and her broom, She was merry, happy, also mentally retarded. She was jolly with her broom, jostling, very energetic under the chair on which stood the large water-filled jar. Under attack it wobbled perilously: I was conscious of its attachment to the hole in my side. As chair and jar rocked, and I, a little desperately strove to steady them, she was amused; the almost daily recurrence becoming a daily recurrence. This nearly daily recurrence sent her into chesty laughter.

A series of weeks on the suction pump achieved its purpose; my lung was restored. It was time for a test healing. The tube was taken out; nature invited to intercede. The hole healed. But, almost promptly came evidence of refilling. I must be re-opened. Again the white coat must come round the door of the ward; again I must shake. But so it was the way with post-operational empyema - repetitional experimental healings until re-filling came no more.

The constant drainage imposed another factor. I was directed to eat as abundantly as possible: I found an urgent zest for that. The good Levy also prescribed champagne, and I did once receive a glass, a token I suppose. The rest of it caused merry sessions in the ward kitchen.

The feeding, unaided by champagne, was effective; most noticeably my face re-inflated. Brother Bert, visiting, considered me seriously for a few minutes. "Is that," he asked, "going to be your permanent face?"

Recovery now was on the march: tentatively launched from bed, I must learn to walk: it was very suprisingly difficult. My feet seemed unbelonging, dithering, undetectable. By a nurse either side I was held danglingly, encouragingly vertical to help my puppet legs and feet rediscover walking. After first venturing, feet did find some sense of purpose, but painfully unable fully to take the weight above - they buckled. But improvement did come to the point of my achieving an independent hobble. "Flannel-feet," said Sister, and she stuck to that.

There were more test healings; each time I re-filled. But now I had been four months in that hospital, in cancer's appalling presence. I had been to nudging distance of death and clawed a way back. Day by day I had seen the sights, heard the same hospital sounds, smelt the smells of illness. My inner eye, my whole being were filled with other things, I saw sky-rumpled vistas in which sweet rivers ran and fish lurked in green weed trails. So driven, so obsessed, I dismissed myself from hospital. Still with a tube in my side, still with the daily need for removal and cleaning, I left the hospital. As on my flannel feet I reached the door to the outer world, I met the shaving-barber.

"Blimey, mate," he said. "I fort you was goin' out feet first."

CHAPTER IX

Through Suffolk Back to Life

I RETURNED home but not to life's normalities. A probationary pause was imposed by the daily need for attendance upon the local doctor for wound dressing and tube cleaning. My lead was short, and better so: I was weak, my feet painful and disassociated.

The year was 1935; that of the Silver Jubilee of King George V and Queen Mary, and of much national festivity. Of that one bit, unforgettably, most memorably, fell to me; a first post-hospital after-dark outing, I was taken on a slow hobble to see the local High Street clock tower in its glory of coloured lights. I was greatly thrilled.

Spring melted into summer; strength seeped back into me. At last the wound healed without refilling; almost now I was off the lead. There came a time when I could venture to London, there to re-activate the earning of a living.

During my hospital interval the *Star* had published our joint series, 'The Stranger In Your Midst'. So to the paper's office I went, there, I hoped, to collect my share of the fee.

I was too late. My (late) partner had collected the money, all of it. The deeply regretful Features Editor, Robert Sinclair, told me of it.

By chance a little later I met my late partner emergent from the office having been told by Robert Sinclair that he would have no more work from the paper. He was in a state of highest moral outrage. The ill service I had done him, he said, was entirely beyond forgiveness.

The loss was of money and undoubtedly distressful, an economic blow; it was not spiritual. I who had been so nearly dead was alive: overwhelmingly the world was lovely. I went for a time to Suffolk to walk and wander among drowsing villages still then not smothered by a plague of cars. Still then the innocence of their pubs knew nothing of weekenders striving for hyper-ruralism. Never since then have I returned to that area so lovingly remembered. Perhaps I should not.

It was quiet country; it spoke modestly of itself. Under its mild sky its roads, often with wide verges, went their way as if ruminating, through cornfields in which bloomed chicory and corncockle. Its air had the clarity of heaven.

There was a small river which went inconspicuously in its oozy valley, rushily beautiful. There might have been great fish there for all I discovered; but I was but tentatively making first returning steps fishing, seeking immersion again in its incomparable balm. I caught a few inconsequent perch; though they indeed were of such poignant consequence. As much there the urge to paint swept upon me

I cannot remember the year of my first exhibiting at the Royal Academy: but I remember the picture. There had been snow; from the window I painted it. Having no canvas, I used the unprimed plywood bottom of a budgerigar cage using the side which had on it no droppings. The picture was not sold, but thereafter I exhibited often, and often my pictures were sold.

The Royal Academy of that time, the Thirties, so vastly big as it was, could not but have in it much work that plodded but did not sing. But some worthy painters there were. Richard Eurich, James

Fitton, others. But that was at a time when competence, vision, aerial spirit, had not become disreputable, anachronistic. In the force of fashion those good men of the Thirties, in their late days had taken upon themselves a feigned naivety, a fashionable littleness.

As memory recalls the later Thirties, it is as an oddity, a brief period entirely and only itself. Its retrospect is of an uneasiness, an unreality. Though the shadow of the Great War shrouded memory of what had been before; though Hitler was spreading his pestilence, Mussolini going a corpse-strewn way through Abyssinia, and prancing black-shirted blackguards were at large in London's East End, there was concurrently a sense of a mellowness.

This was the heyday of the sports coat and flannel bags, the time of the ordinary chap, the every-day amiable ordinary blokes. There was a sort of sanctity of ordinariness; time seemed to jog from day to day. I suppose to that was attached instinctively a preciousness because, unacknowledged, there was a sense that the world we had known was about to plunge into horrid disintegration. It seemed to say how heavenly was ordinariness.

I in the later Thirties drifted into the circle of R.O. Dunlop, then ARA, later to be RA. On the Ridgeway at Wimbledon he had a studio: it may be said that gave Wimbledon contrast. Wimbledon was tidy; it was nice, a respectable suburban place. Ronnie Dunlop was not at all like that. By ascent of a dark and narrow staircase the private world of R.O. Dunlop could be reached. I never fully mastered its confused geography, so intricately stocked was it with the detritus of years. In it Dunlop had all his being; in a conglomerate of canvasses, crippled furniture and bottles he slept, fed, and painted. In the hours of darkness candles in beer bottles gave him light. Sometimes he had some money; sometimes he had not. Within his beard he smiled hazily and was not bothered. Every day he painted a picture. Every day with his ramshackle gear he went out and painted directly from nature. His easel was decrepit, his palette any odd piece of cardboard. He painted not with brushes but with a painting knife, thickly, often brilliantly. He floated placidly about the margins of normal acceptances, mildly smiling under his greenly mouldering hat.

His pictures once painted he was careless of them; easily acceptant often of very demeaning offers, not looking far beyond the security of the next pint. Coming one evening to his studio I found him giggling. That day a dealer had offered him forty-odd pounds for a group of pictures. So he was drunk.

That was a Tuesday evening. Every Tuesday evening I and others went there. Several were as yet unsuccessful writers, one was an artist-actress, former girlfriend, another a large pallid Russian woman of dubious texture topped with straight yellow hair: she was hugely earnest, dwelling in an astral cloud. She talked constantly and quotingly in a mist of psychology. "According to Jung," she would say, falling into dogged quotation. I, having once interjected, she asked according to whom was what I had said. Lamely I said, "Well, according to me." The Russian lady fell silent and appeared thoughtful.

One evening, privily, Dunlop and I were in a pub; he had a new girlfriend he told me. She was, he said, very delightingly nice: how courageous as well as nice I thought, to move into that studio.

At the studio I met her, and indeed simply, directly, she was as nice as was his claim. She, an actress, was Rosalind Iden: her lovely name was happily right.

They were married later. When with the RSC, she was working at Stratford, he went with her, painting in the area.

"Who is that dirty painter who's always hanging about?" someone asked Rosalind. "That is my husband," she answered, and my guess is that that was demurely said. She, telling me of it, found it funny.

But life, moving on, found another way for Rosalind. She left Dunlop. She left him to go to Sir Donald Wolfit and, later, married him. Mrs R.O. Dunlop into Lady Wolfit. Dunlop could not understand how such a thing could be.

"My little girl," he lamented, "My little girl."

The years passed; the war came and then was over, and Dunlop was living in Sussex; in Sussex another marriage, with a child of that marriage, and in money difficulty. It was not just his old perennial difficulty. Now with new dependencies his prolific past had come to betray him. For so long he had produced so many pictures and undiminishedly still was doing so. But, now, those of the past being resold clogged his market. He had become his own very formidable competitor.

He came to me. Would I be agreeable to his painting my portrait for £20? For his coming on the appointed day I had prepared as I knew to be appropriate. I bought six bottles of Guinness.

Through the morning he painted as was his way - laying in the main colour and structure with brush and turps-thinned paint. On this he would work with finishing paint after lunch.

At lunch he was placidly happy; gently he proceeded through the six bottles of Guinness. And, in the afternoon he seemed to be working well, knife-painting with strong impasto. The portrait was not good: I had misjudged the Guinness.

So long ago, all that; all past and over. Long since Ronnie Dunlop died: so, a few years ago did Rosalind, she then an old woman. All now of their crises is over, all done, all joy, all pain. All now is nothing.

I cannot disentangle the latter half of the Thirties. The world at large was in headlong stagger down the disintegrating slope of peace: but I was in an enchantment, my world renewed. Now again there was fishing, and I was painting. But particularly in fishing astounding revelation had come upon me: I had discovered the Wye.

The pleasures of fishing had hitherto been much more of imagined joys than of ones made substance; only in waters of very minor virtue had I fished, where fish mostly were meagre. Now I discovered the Wye.

Just downstream of the little grey town of Hay-on-Wye, just in England, just out of Wales, Dansy Price and Mrs Price lived at Glan Wye. There they were as cosily set as imagination of fisherman could desire. Comfortably they were in their stone house fronted on to the road that runs with the river all the way down from Hay to Hereford. Unforgettably on those Glan Wye mornings one would go out of the door by Mrs Price's kitchen; down stone steps against the wall, then to be in the yard. There were the pig sties, amply occupied by a jolliness of pigs snuffling, grunting conversationally, their queer half-hooded eyes, pale, white-lashed, quizzically sharing a joke about eating. Nature who made all sorts of animals, never surpassed her pigs.

After that obligatory passage with the pigs there was the shippon and through it to the field beyond; down that, and there was the level-crossing. It gave crossing of that dosing little branch line that, hand-holding with the river, pottered up from Hereford. Down another field then there was the river, wonderfully, besottingly, lovely Wye. So, at first glimpse was set upon me the spell of the Wye. It remains unbroken.

As I have told elsewhere how,* nearly sixty years later, I returned to Glan Wye. Now Dansy, Mrs Price, the girls, all that was of the Prices were memories of old inhabitants. Not now were there pigs in the sties, nor were there sties; the shippon was not its old utilitarian self but was decorous. The level-crossing no longer was there, nor any trace of that loved little ambling railway. By the river

* *A Rise To The Fly,* Robert Hale, 2000

the fishing hut had gone and, going upstream, the meadow by the river where uncle Davy Jenkins used to have his pedigree Hereford cattle, now had upon its space a Co-Op supermarket. I had no wish to fish the Glan Wye water; I had no wish to intrude upon its ghosts.

But my long-gone self was of them, an episode of life apart, as it were with them preserved in amber. In every mood and season of its cycle I knew the river, the towering floods, summer water so low that the very stones of the bottom parched in the sun. So often, so many unrecorded times I made the journey to Hay as to confer upon Paddington a nymbus excluding all but its promise of Hay. From its floating vaultings, themselves so uplifting, I was borne away to Hereford whereupon fell a peace. There, gently puffing waiting in its bay, was the little train. Soon in a bliss of leisureliness it began its idling up to Hay, all the way going with the river. The river sometimes one side, sometimes the other and I must change sides that I might miss not one of its vistas.

Then there was Hay, Hay again; there again the Prices; Dansy, wiry-lean, eyes dancing-brown behind his spectacles, invariably in breeches and gaiters because he was a horse-wise man. And Mrs Price, amply comely, pink and snowy-haired and smiling. Daughters Doris and Patty too in their country fashion, round and fresh and ample.

For me enchantment lay on all that was of Glan Wye. Not any one thing could be so separately loved as to have preference: all was within one consecrated entity. How may be given the sense of the bewitchment of all there? I, whose fishing before had been but meanly served, had here this river, which had a sense almost of being as a sentient creature; never static, of moods, of tremulous response to weather - itself there so sensitively changing.

Such fishing the river had as till then had been of my dreaming, rosy vapours of what might be. Here it was proven, made visionary truth. In the pools deep, eddying reclusions under the banks had reticent promise. When wind stirred the overhang of alder and willow, peering sun shafts revealed dusky hordes of chub, sepia tails just fanning. They, on the bank in the willows' dappling were of such beauty as could be only of such a vision made real. Their heads were big, boldly sculpted, as of agate; over the scales a soft patina of brassiness.

Under the far bank of one pool where the sheep pastures of Radnor rose away, within a secrecy of gnarled old willows there was a deep hole much knotted about with roots, out of the push of the current. On an afternoon of October, of the tranquil maturity which is of October, I took the punt over. In the bland light, away from surface shine, all in an aqueous twilight could be seen. There in flaunting parade were the perch, in aggressive swagger patrolling the hole, imperiously prickling. Of such things was the delight of that, for me, hallowed water. Where a great ash leaned from the bank, under its clutch of roots a cavernous darkness of water, it could be guessed that there in surly ambush lay a pike. Idyllically so often it proved to be.

Were I to go back would the ghost of Dansy return to tell me again those stories of the river? Would he tell me again of how Miss Doreen Davy caught that monstrous salmon that, at 53lb, is still the record for England and Wales? Perhaps he would tell me again that story of the old man who hooked a mammoth salmon. He could make no impression on it, for the unconquerable strength of it. It made run after run, and the power of them had no sign of weakening. When an hour had passed, the old man, exhausted, called a gamekeeper who chanced to pass. He was husky and full of youth. Take the rod, the old man implored him: he could fight no more. The young man was reluctant; no fisherman was he. Take the rod, the old man told him; he would tell him what he must do. So for a time the keeper did, under direction playing the salmon which did not lessen in strength. The old man, too tired, fell asleep. The keeper, seeing his chance to be done with such tiresomeness, held the fish hard. It broke, and that, it seemed, was the end.

A week later a river keeper going his round near Hereford, saw under the bank such a salmon as he had never seen before. It was direly sick; he gaffed it out. It weighed 75lb. It was estimated that its weight at the time of hooking had been 80lb. The old man's minnow was still in its mouth.

CHAPTER X

Walking Down Fleet Street

I WAS gardening that day: an ordinary day. In the afternoon my vision began to sway; I became faint. I collapsed.

A massive gastric haemorrhage had fallen upon me. There had been warning, had I been able to perceive it. Return of pain had declared the failure of the operation. Now for six weeks I was prone in a darkened room, spoon-fed with glucose and water. I lay with confused consciousness, a headache of pounding violence, unable to speak above a whisper. My survival was given a poor rating. I did survive, that tendency being nature's gift to me.

I recovered, and appeared then to be normal. It was illusory. There came another haemorrhage; being detected earlier it was not so nearly lethal. More haemorrhages followed, so repetitive as almost to be habitual. As I must, I adapted, learning to recognise earliest symptoms, then to retire to bed.

"The vay you go," my doctor who was not English said to me, "soon you shpit it up and carry on."

Carry on I did, precariously. I strove to live and work normally, but was regularly punctuated by crises. Those crises were variably embarrassing. I was at Hay, far from home, when again there came the knell. I telephoned, asking that a car should meet me at Paddington. Moving as smoothly as I could in the carrying of my baggage, that I should not aggravate the bleeding, I took the ambling train to Hereford, there to take the train to Paddington. The car was waiting. Again was the worst evaded.

It was an uneasy mode of life; that it was not insupportable was because my urgency for living could not be denied. How could it be otherwise when spring blossomed by the river, summer mornings were ecstatic? And could sadness dwell long with the incomparable joy of work which so nearly had been lost? At about this time music was putting upon me a strengthening hold, its tardiness in so doing being part of an oddity of failure to mature evenly.

Intermittently now I frequented concerts, of those sometimes the Proms - then still at the old Queens Hall, and then so long since, still under the baton of Sir Henry Wood. Once, just once, I went to a Last Night. My pleasure in music has always been one of a privacy: the flood of its sound bears me away in an isolation. The pleasure of that Last Night was surrender to the warm bath of mass emotion, communal, impersonal. It induced in me a chilling recoil; I felt lonely. At the concert's end the hysteria - which could have said to have been pent - burst out swirling on to the pavement. Manic hands tied ropes to the car of the embarrassed Sir Henry and Lady Wood. With much feverishly jolly cheering the car was towed. So much throwing of identity into the common pot caused in me a disturbed embarrassment. I suppose it was my loss. Perhaps I should suppose myself to have been a stuffy prig. Probably I would have been so regarded. But my fullest sympathy was with that clamour; they had had their glorious immersion. They were tipsied in gratitude.

As Munich came and went, as the decade, as I stumbled into a marriage of no hope, so by contrast did that decade show its homely face. As history ran its dreadful way, so the more plainly was the last of the sports-coats-and-flannel-bags-chaps era to be seen.

"Don't you feel," said a chap to brother Bert, "that you

could never trust a man who wears corduroy trousers?"

Very easily it could be thought that in these falling years it was no accident that the Crystal Palace came to its unforgettable end, that that wonderful and endeared pot-pourri of memory and atmosphere should have its monstrous funeral pyre. That magnificent relic was the very symbol of so much that, after the Thirties, was never to be again.

From its birth the Crystal Palace had splendour and was spectacular: as the years of its glory drifted away a wonderfully aromatic mellow came upon it. In my childhood still it wore a faded remnant of old grandeur; still at summer's end had its spectacle of fireworks; already they were loved ghosts rather than of current life. That I see now; but we, children then, were rapturously moved. How great a spectacle was its glass and iron self, though then so gently elderly. It was proper, even inevitable that its passing at last should be immensely spectacular. It was a conflagration greater than I ever saw, until then; I did not guess I was to see a greater.

The Crystal Palace stood upon its eminence at Upper Norwood in South London: the ground dropped from it on every side. So it had stood through our child lives. It was majestic, as familiar as a tea cosy. On this moonless night the news ran sibilantly, itself like a racing trail of fire.

'The Crystal Palace is on fire.'

It emptied the houses, emptied the pubs, snatched the sick from their beds, the old from their firesides. To every hill-top vantage people thronged. Some walked, many ran, some came on bicycles, some in cars. Cripples with flailing arms flogged their chairs to wild speeds. They came miraculously mobile on crutches. Having come, awe fell upon them. Never again such a sight could they see.

I cannot remember the date of the Crystal Palace fire; it was probably not very distant from the day in 1937 when I walked into a fishing tackle shop. I walked often into fishing tackle shops, but this time it was momentous. They told me of a man, as devoted as I to angling, who sometimes came in. A newspaper man he was they said, Art Editor of the the *Daily Express* they thought. His name was St John Cooper.

I left at once. I caught a bus to Fleet Street. In a call-box I introduced myself to the Art Editor's voice, not omitting the fact that, while being an artist I was also a fisherman with access to fishing on the Wye.

"Where are you?" asked the voice. "Round the corner - New Bridge Street." "Come along up can you? Now?"

It was so that I met Bobby Cooper. It was so that I joined the *Daily Express*. For nine years I stayed with the *Daily Express*. For the earlier of those years I was exclusively an artist about the place, a resident do-everything-as-it-comes-along artist. I illustrated short stories; I did caricatures, pictorial maps. At Christmas I designed and drew decorative festival pages. It was a sequence touched with excitement - this was the era of the great Arthur Christiansen. He, as Editor, exercised a rather dizzy inspiration. His flair flowed through all.

Whatever might be said - and was said - of the paper's political attitudes which reflected those of its owner, Lord Beaverbrook, and so were sometimes bizarre, the *Daily Express* of that time had technical brilliance. Its typography was succinct and clean: its features pages had fine dash and bravura. Its 'Woman's Pages' swaggered splendidly.

To recall Christiansen's *Express* is to observe how transitory is newspaper fame, like that of broadcasting. He, by nature, drew exceptionalism into his orbit: he made names that in their season rang loudly. There were few not now forgotten.

The phenomenon of Tom Driberg could probably have happened only in Christiansen's *Express*. It is a truism of newspaper journalism that the best jobs, of great success and reward, are self-made, not by appointment. Seldom do they settle workably on other shoulders. Thus was Tom Driberg's column, 'These Names Make New'. It was inimitable.

Among we who clustered about the ladder to hoped-for eminence was Winston Churchill's nephew, Giles Romilly. He at Oxford being asked to write about Russia, it being then in those quite early times after the Bolshevik revolution, wrote to Uncle Winston. Could he give helpful advice?

'Just say they eat their babies,' Uncle Winston wrote back.

Also expectantly among my contemporaries was Anthony Cotterel, as clearly marked as any for future distinction. We, he and I, had neighbouring desks; we shared our optimism, our tales of current adventure. It was then that that rather haunting song, 'And the Nightingale sang in Berkeley Square', was lodging itself in everyone's mind; Tony was telling me of his girlfriend who lived in Berkeley Square. The nostalgic little twist of that was to be immortal.

The war came: it snatched up Tony. Of him it made a War Correspondent, for the special practice of which he was made a parachutist. He was dropped into the hell of Arnhem - but, does anyone now remember Arnhem? Is it only those of us who lived then who do remember and cannot forget? Few of those with Tony lived to remember. Of Tony I knew no more until the Nuremburg War Crimes Trials. A German officer testified to the finding of a British officer at Arnhem who lay desperately wounded. To the German he whispered, "Don't touch me - I'm dying." That officer was identified as Major Anthony Cotterel. The song haunts me still, and will.

But all that was still to come. We lived from day to day, in that slight unreality which can forerun what is known to impend. We knew war was coming; we knew it though we worked on a paper which, with historic vacuousness, declared 'There will be no war, this year or next.' The year was 1938. It was a time for the watching of dawdling trivialities.

Sometimes on Saturday in this hiatus we went fishing. Bobby Cooper, Bernard Wicksteed and I, all three that day freed from Fleet Street. Bernard was later to wear a famous face, it and its inevitable pipe and its chirpy grin. It appeared so constantly in illustration of articles in his series, 'It's Fun Finding Out'. Bernard, for life spiritually a boy scout, game for all that might come. In his forties he volunteered to serve in Beaufighters, and, so doing, by night was shot down over the Bristol Channel. As with his aircraft he went to the bottom, he struggled to open his hood: it was jammed. On the bottom at last he succeeded. "The ascent to the surface," said Bernard, "seemed to take years. My lungs were about to burst as I broke surface." They gave him a DFC.

Bernard Wicksteed, as his many adventures showed was a survivor. But, soon after the war, he who had survived all, was seized by a mysterious brain disease: for two years he lay wasting. Then he died.

One fine morning in September, 1939, there I was again at Hay. I was wading upstream of a seductive eddy under the bank, trotting a bait down, so working it as to cajole it into the eddy. I was hailed from the bank. It was my wife.

"War has been declared," she called.

I saw the bite. The chub plunged for the entanglement of the roots but it was well hooked.

CHAPTER XI

Through the Valley of War

THE FIRST days were anticlimactic. Almost they were disappointing. Armageddon was to have come in, and here was placidity. The mild September mornings were as if no drama could touch them; the sparrows were as familiarly under eaves as ever. It was even a little deflating.

There had been an initial stir of excitement, then this benign ordinariness soothed each day. There were signs enough of war, but no distressful reality. Trenches were dug; in perfectly ordinary streets air raid shelters were erected and almost at once began to look sordid. Buildings grew sandbag ramparts. Powerful symbols all of them should have looked; but they had no conviction: a little fancy dress worn on the true ambling peacefulness.

Something nevertheless was afoot; rather startling small signs in the office. There was Robb, Robb who drew fashion drawings for Woman's Page; Robb, constantly about the place, not quite dapper, sparrow-chirpy. Now, overnight, here was this Scottish officer of

His Majesty's army, fully kilted and bonnetted. Then with that flourish Robb was gone.

Quietly evidence gathered; something was toward. Lately to the office there had come Osbert Lancaster, dropping in to do his Pocket Cartoon - not yet the Osbert of later fame. His smudge of moustache had still to evolve to sweeping splendour, though the Lancastrian eyes were the authentic protuberant cobalt orbs. So we knew Osbert; now here was he, shoulder-slung with steel helmet and insignia of civil defence.

All at once helmets burgeoned on the most unlikely heads. It showed what the least touch of uniform will do for the least gallant citizen. So far, not unpleasantly, we were playing at war. Mildly we strove to feel martial. It lightened such unpleasantnesses as were put upon us. The blackout had come and was very fully imposed; no least betraying chink was allowed. The fall of night was Stygian. Windows of the *Express* building were bricked up.

In the meantime there was fishing. The year 1940 is forever memorable for its awful events; for Bobby and for me there was epic reason for remembrance. On the last weekend of the coarse fishing season we went fishing. We went pike fishing on the lake at Aldermaston. Essential to the story was the rod. It had been mine, a little split cane wisp, by its nature for spinning for perch: I had given it to Bobby.

The day was fine, the fishing soon fair; by mid-morning I had had two modest fish. Then Bobby's two-inch spoon stopped; it stopped as dead as though fouled to a log. Tentatively he pulled; all was fast. He tugged. Up the line, through the rod, came a heavy throb: the 'log' surged into heavy life. The little rod bowed in dire labour. Bobby gave line, the reel shrilled. I perceived that if the fight were to end successfully it must be at length, not sooner. I looked at my watch.

The fight became attritional. A ferocious plunge; the rod a shivering arc; line torn from the reel; Bobby with desperate delicacy controlling the sullen plunging.

We both saw the knot; a shaggy knot, loose and large. We saw it snatched through the rings; large, loose. We did not speak of it,

each fearful for the other's nerve. Clearly Bobby's two small sons had been at the rod. Out and in went the knot, out and in. How was a knot so dubious to hold in such distress? The tortured minutes dropped away one by one, added and became five, ten, and fifteen. The deep surges showed no weakening. Then, hardly daring acknowledgement, I saw a change. Surely the line's angle to the water had changed. Surely the fish was lifting. The adding minutes had come to thirty. Still the fish was ponderously, stubbornly fighting. But the runs had shortened, now were shallower.

It was breaking surface, an unbelievable mottled green lunge of flank. Now it was staccato, jaggedly thrashing. Bobby was shortening line, mindful of the knot, sensitive to yielding line. I unclipped the gaff. The minutes had added to over forty. There must be no mistake: this was Bobby's fish to crown his life.

I would touch it, just touch it with the gaff to test its reserves. I touched it, but touched it. It snatched line in a smother of water. Bobby brought it back: under the chin the gaff took hold. Then there it lay, on the bank, lithely long, beautiful in its deadly symmetry; its green-flecked flank very deep, a most lovely pike. On that wisp of rod it had taken forty-five minutes to land.

Hugely it lay, on the path which was of the retaining dam of the lake. It gave passage to those coming down from Aldermaston Court, then a reception base for recruited ATS girls. Along the path there came two women of the establishment; they were talking, nodding heads turned each to the other. Coming upon the pike, crosswise before them, without glance or pause or break of talk, they continued noddingly till out of sight.

Then from the church there came the Vicar, a black straggle of lanky limbs and flapping coat. He stopped, ecstatic.

"Oh my dear chaps. How utterly splendid. How perfectly marvellous. Oh, but chaps, how are you going to get it down to the village?"

We, not yet normal, had not thought of that.

"Ah, dear boys. I know. I have the answer. Wait just a few minutes."

Leanly flapping he was gone. Soon returning, he carried a long roll.

"Here we are chaps. The underlay of the carpet of the aisle. Roll it up in that. Take it back in an odour of sanctity, what?"

So it was we carried the hallowed body to the village, to the shop for weighing. But, there, when all the weights had been used, still the noble weight of the pike was unmatched. To the weights were added two pound-cartons of sugar. Thus it was settled that the weight was 30¼lb. Only later was it realised that no allowance had been made for the weight of the cartons. The true weight of Bobby's pike was never known.

Festival came to the pub that night. At the falling of the final hour all the, now merry, celebrants transferred to Bobby's house for ritual viewing and further celebration.

By next morning which was Sunday, the news had spread. From all about they came, knocking at the door, wishing to see the now famous fish. In the afternoon we cased it about with wood and, next morning, with keen help from the guard of the train conveyed it to Paddington, thence to Fleet Street - there to disturb the routines of the *Daily Express*. Then properly in classic fashion we took it to Coopers there to be set up. That of course they did very handsomely indeed, with white-painted case, fine with gold lettering, all that at Bobby's special wish. I wonder where rests that trophy now? How greatly I would like to find and have it. Bobby, my old friend, is dead these few years past. As I write now, that day of 1940 is more than fifty-nine years gone. Somewhere there is its monument perhaps possessed by someone not then born.

Anglers' ways have changed since that old time: then it was unquestionable that such a fish should go for eternity into a glass case. Now so to do is all but blasphemous. Admirable as is the urge to conservation, true biological understanding of its processes is uncommon.

Meanwhile the war continued its unwarlike way. Inexorably men seeped away, out of their civilian niches for recasting as soldiers, sailors, or airmen. But war's reality did come.

It came with grim absurdity. What, it was said, if the Germans should at last attack, was there not the the Maginot Line, impregnable for the length of the French-German frontier? But the Germans, with so little respect for walls, walked round the end of this one. The war that now was upon us had lost nothing by keeping.

That year of 1940 the summer was glorious. Reliably day by day the news was disastrous: the weather was lovely. Seldom are summers so unbrokenly lovely.

Still in basking immunity we waited: until August. I, on the vantage of a hill looking south over Croydon, saw a flock, a crowd, of aeroplanes. In that beaming light of summer, from their bellies they were spilling what looked like little beans. They were bombs: these were German planes.

A few idyllic days later from afar came a multiple throbbing, soon to be seen as an aerial horde. It was traversing our sacrosanct sky, our own blue vault. It ploughed on with deadly phlegm, weaved about by the wasps of fighter escort. It went as by right, sullen, unhindered. The docks of the Port of London were its destination. It left them under a flame-shot pall high as heaven.

So began the Battle of Britain. Through that celestial August and into September what was to be our fate was enacted over our heads. That now we know: few grasped it then. In our English way, in our island, it was too improbable for belief then. We watched the aerial dots weaving in combat, not conceiving that what we saw was the holding back of the Nazi hordes. Towards the end of September it was over. As time has told us, it was a decisive victory.

One tender evening in that beautiful summer I was in a railway station bar. One other person was there, and he was young. He was in the uniform of an RAF officer; eagerly he told me, he was newly commissioned, newly and proudly having won his wings, now on his way to join his Spitfire squadron. I guessed him to be nineteen. Often over the many years since, I have thought of him and his young life. Spitfire pilots in the Battle of Britain had a low level of survival.

As autumn sank to winter there came the Blitz. Considerably I was involved in it. Each evening with dire dependability, fall of darkness brought the sirens' wail. Never can have been heard a sound more doom-laden. As dependably, within minutes, the guns, at first distant, then nearer till the heaven-splitting bursts merged in hellish chorus and shell fragments hissed like hail. The scarifying reliability became in time a sort of normality to blunt the edge of fear. And still there were the pubs, still prompt at opening time, still Fleet Street's social focus.

The Olde Bell was quaint and cosy, modestly at the end of a passage from Fleet Street. Ivy behind the bar was probably forty, competent, firm, calm as St Pauls. She was an aboriginal Londoner, and also a cousin of Charlie Chaplin. Several of us were as reliably there as the sirens' lament; Victor Taylor, Claud Saywell, and I, in our nicely cramped little corner of the bar. Outside each night the world was outrageous cacophony: we talked of philosophical things, of poetry and peace and half-remembered things. We talked of fishing too because nothing could more signify the sweetest face of peace. We could not always exclude that which raged outside. Victor Taylor was speaking one night of Herrick; the bomb that fell was stupendously close, with the customary aftermath of disintegration and cascades of glass. The lights went out; the Olde Bell rocked giddily. In the blackness, fume and dust, Ivy's voice was calm.

"I'm sorry about the interruption gentlemen. Be patient for a moment."

A brief rustling, and Ivy's steady hand was lighting candles.

The Olde Bell was insecure but was sanctuary, a transient healing while the Blitz had possession of the night. But, each night, the awaiting problem was how to get home, or at least be ingenious in attempting it. Many made no attempt, night camping in the office. But I was urgent in it: if a bomb were to find me I wished that it should find me at home.

Some blessed nights a train might be found running out of Victoria, sometimes London Bridge, chances to be gambled on. Often it was neither: but very slightly there was hope of an adventurous taxi driver willing to risk part of the way - that sometimes sharing the cab with up to a dozen strangers.

If (and often) none of these, then which was the most hopeful route for the ten-mile walk, free of bomb diversion? As was essential for night walkers in the Blitz I became adept in diving for shelter when the bomb's falling scream was close - a bomb crater, a gutter, too often the naked pavement. One night, as I walked up Victoria Street, the shrapnel's fall became such a deluge that I must plunge for a deep doorway. There soon I was joined by a very large young guardsman in acute fear. He trembled violently. Probably he had had no acclimatisation, perhaps was too abruptly tossed into the Blitz.

Often the journey was a chance jumble - of policemen and wardens seeking to cajole or coerce me into the claustrophobia of shelters, of unexploded bombs, of blocked roads. One night at London Bridge a bomb on the line had closed the station: a policeman compelled me to a sort of subterranean box, rough concrete of floor, sides, and ceiling. Accepting the inevitable, I composed myself prone on the concrete. I believe I slept a little before morning's release.

On a night resigned to walking I came upon a bus. Its destination, if achieved, was Crystal Palace Parade which, if indeed attainable, was well on my way home. In the uproariously deserted world empty of all else there was this empty bus, it and a driver, a conductor and I. The driver and the conductor were laconic men.

"Take a chance mate? See if we can get frew?"

Feeling down through the southern suburbs the going was fair; then across the road we were confronted. There was a barrier; it bore a familiar notice - 'Unexploded Bomb'. We got out, regarded the notice; driver and conductor looked at each other. The driver sniffed. Unhurriedly the conductor removed the barrier; after the driver had driven through he put it back. When through the ghostly interval of abandoned houses, we came to the other barrier; that we passed in the same fashion. With no more event we came unscathed to the Crystal Palace Parade.

"All right, Mate?" they said to me.

Now there were only four or five familiar miles to go; I walked down from the Parade, past Low Level Station. There I was joined by a man in nervous need of company. It was an average to bad Blitz night, noisy, shell fragments smacking into the asphalt. Intermittently, near or far, bombs crumped.

"Bloody horrible, isn't it?" the man said. He shivered, ducking his head into his shoulders.

"Don't mind if I walk with you?"

Distantly a wavering glare fanned up the sky; after seconds the muffled roar reached us.

"Bloody land mine, that one. Y'know," he went on, "I was in the trenches all through the fourteen-eighteen lot. Bloody bad too. Bloody sight worse this is."

I think healing time must have covered the worst of his scarred memory.

Land mine he called it, as people did then; though really they were parachute mines. So softly they wafted to earth they made no crater to lessen their spread of blast. In Norwood there was a small boy often to be seen, six perhaps, plain but prepossessing, going stumpily about his business. A parachute mine fell in the vicinity of his home. I saw him no more.

At a crossroads in Norwood one night I was stopped by a man. He wore a bowler hat; he carried an umbrella neatly rolled. He was slight, a little stooped, his way mild and courteous.

"Please forgive me for bothering you Sir," he said. "Could you be so kind as to direct me to Herne Hill?"

Absently, as I directed him, I was conscious that high above an aircraft droned. There came the scream of falling bombs, rising to that hell's crescendo that indicated that they headed for us. We flung to the pavement, seeking as one did, to grovel into it. There were two bombs; we were between them. After the inconceivable double detonation we must wait: what had gone up must, perilously, come down. About us, flattened on the pavement, it fell. A shattered chimney pot lay between us. A hundred or so yards up the road a gas main inferno roared from the crater. Round the corner a little way a ruptured building was in leisurely collapse. We stood up.

"I am so sorry Sir," he said deprecatingly. "Could you be so kind as to repeat what you were saying - let me see, up this hill wasn't it, to the top - and then where?"

Cinemas, as disregardful as pubs, continued to function. One place was as unsafe as another. I knew a girl and she and her boyfriend were in a cinema. A quite small bomb piercing the roof, exploded in the auditorium. It was so awkward, she told me, in the dark and dust getting out from the clogging of injured and dead.

On a night when no trains ran, neither from Victoria nor from London Bridge, I set out southward in resignation: somewhere perhaps, beyond bomb damage, I might find a station still with running trains. My circuitous way brought me to Balham, but there to be balked. Spanning the road to its last inch either side was a crater awesomely deep, so deep that the double-decked bus that stood on its nose within it showed only a foot or so above the crater. In the pitchy blackness, scrambling and clutching, almost directionless, I did at last gain the far side. And, just beyond, wonderfully, there was Balham station; there was a train able to run.

Later I heard more of that bus-receiving crater. The Underground station there was shallow, 30 feet below the street. The bomb had penetrated, smashing water and sewage mains. The hundreds sheltering there were drowned.

Death's best potential for night wanderers in the Blitz were bombs and shells. Incendiaries were only secondary. When I one night walked in the Strand's total desertion I came upon a building blazing unmolested, I was not perturbed. It would not blast me into eternity. Dodge the bombs, dodge the shells' shower; get home. Comfortingly, irrationally, there for you was the sense of shelter. Get your fitful sleep on the mattress on the floor: with luck wake there in the morning. But I did know a man, thus securely in his own easy chair, when an unexploded shell came through the roof to take off his leg neatly.

I was comfortable in the belief that incendiaries were a lesser menace until the night of 29th December, 1940. That night I did not get home. The sirens were on time, the guns began their blasting; the dread-punctuated drone was over us. I, working, was prodded to awareness. All was not to pattern. There was no sound of bombs.

What was this insistent tattoo? It was incendiaries, a hail-showering of incendiaries, a deluge downpour rattling down on every surface, on street, on roof, to lay a blazing carpet. Already the city's sky was canopied with fire. I have no memory's trace of interval, but here I was on the roof of the *Express* building. All the floors below were empty; all from those were in the machine room two floors below ground level.

On the roof with me were two, perhaps three others. And Bernard Wicksteed, never able to resist adventure - this being before he winged away into the RAF. Fire had entirely possessed the night, filling it, a fire jungle. Shoe Lane, debouching into Fleet Street by the *Express* building, roared with fire lapping hungrily to reach us. St Pauls was a serene island in an engulfing sea of fire.

The incendiaries' confetti upon the roof sent us into an alpinism, monkey-scaling on a roof of which till then we had known nothing. In all the confusion it seemed to me an intricacy of levels. Constantly the most fiercely demanding clusters of incendiaries were upon any level but that where I was perched. I must go scrambling, swing up the sand bucket to the next level, then by fingers' clutch and legs' swing follow it. So, roof-high, I looked over Fleet Street to St Brides - 'the madrigal in stone'. On its roof lay one incendiary, seen I believe by none but I. There it burned, unreachable. Below, in Fleet Street, knitted with fire hoses which had run dry, who could be aware of that one fire bomb visible only from my eerie?

I saw its fire take hold, send flickering fingers for further holds, spread till that one small bomb made of St Brides a pile of fire.

Shoe Lane's inferno was licking nearer: we ran out a fire hose; we aimed it uselessly. It was dry. Between us and the fire's advance one roof's space still held. In that roof we saw a hole; an entering incendiary had made it. Below, as we knew, was a reel room - storage for the great paper reels.

The others left me: they must go to the reel room, trace that one incendiary if it were not too late. I, solitary on the roof, must with waving arm through the hole guide them. I must be alert to their coming; no less alert I watched the tossing fires of Shoe Lane. Their hot gusts fanned me: I could feel the singeing of hair and eyebrows. That vigil seemed little less than eternity. Of the others I saw no more.

When all was over, when the bombs fell no more, with the whole city a furnace, a vast ineffable peace seemed to fall. On the roof where now a few had come, we looked over the city. There, sublime survival, stood St Pauls, in that infinity of fire. Beside me a staff photographer made an exposure; that shot has become one of the most famous ever made. It has travelled far; history will know it.

There had been rumours of explosive incendiaries; even, it was said, some had been on the city that night. I saw none. I was to see them.

That was later. There was a night, and I at home, when HE bombs were all about: a stick of three straddled us. One, a mere 30 yards distant, fell in soft garden soil making so deep a crater that much of its blast was absorbed. But not all.

The three of us crouched in the only possible survival niche in a house that collapses; under the stairs there was a chance. We, so poised at calamity's edge, waited for the house to crumple upon us. Rather slowly the kitchen wall swayed inwards, then paused; it hung interminably, slowly returned. The house did stand, but decrepitly. For two weeks we must move out for essential first aid.

The sirens sounded on the first night back; we were not desperately anxious. In the protective irrationality of those times it was easily supposed that a hit or near miss gave a subsequent respite of immunity. It was invalidated; again that night they came upon us, not with HE. It was an incendiary night. They came upon us saturatingly, making colanders of roofs and ceilings. One bomb, passing through everything, came to fiery rest under the kitchen floorboards, in the foundations. I, frantically with a hatchet, strove to reach it.

Then, very queerly, I had no weight. Dream-like I floated, out of the kitchen, wafted spirit-like, then to be most softly dumped in a corner. They, under the stairs, saw my levitated passing. What had come upon me?

I had been blown up. It had been an explosive fire bomb that had been under the floor. The skirting boards were pushed up to the ceiling. The table, set for breakfast, was tossed, marmalade spread on the ceiling which also was perforated with metal fragments where I had been. I was unhurt.

For the houses both sides the night was full of terror. To one side there was father, mother, and two small daughters, abed and sleeping at the time of onset. Father, rushing to the children, found between them on the bed an incendiary just igniting. He saved the children, but fire snarled through the house. Then they, parents and children, stood mute on the pavement as the familiarity of home was consumed.

The other side of the house, semi-detached, was the home of an elderly couple; completely fire had invested them. They too were forlorn, mute on the pavement. Firemen were there, but they too helpless. The hoses were dry.

Our house was still unkindled. I remembered my dog, Boris. Boris was small, a mongrel half blind, and sixteen years old. He was wise with the wisdom of long life, and had fine plebeian intelligence. In these late times most of his living was with me, intimately in the studio. In the first alarm I had left him there with the light on within the blackout curtains.

I opened the door: still the light was on, but of visibility none. Smoke solid as a wall, seeped through from the burning house next door. I wedged my handkerchief over nose and mouth, belly-wriggled with out-thrust hands quartering to find him. My hands found him; he was unconscious.

Later consciousness returned: he, vomiting, declared himself ready to take up life again. It could not be.

CHAPTER XII

River Air Still is Sweet

AT THE summoning of my age group I attended the medical which was to filter all suitable candidates into the armed forces. Its main outcome - apart from my being rejected - was that I was officially 5 feet 7 inches and $^{7}/_{8}$ths of an inch tall*

The examining doctor, terminally bored by the endless passage of bodies, spoke no word. With vague passes of the hand he conveyed that I must put a foot on a chair, then, repeatedly, spring up the other foot to join the first, then to have pulse and chest checked. I suppose my routine of haemorrhages disqualified me.

Mine was a busy war made of many things apart from being a target. While still the Blitz hammered us nightly, Bobby Cooper left the *Daily Express* for Ealing Film Studios. There, for the Ministry of Food, he was to produce cartoon films for propaganda. Meanwhile on a vaguely undefined basis I was to take over his job art editing the *Express* - at least keeping it ticking over. But, soon, Bobby asked me to join him at Ealing: could I help him

*The passage of years has been very reductive. It has reduced me to 5 feet 4 inches.

make cartoon films? Without a pause, without previous knowledge, I found myself in full activity as 'Chief Animator'. At Ealing by day so I worked; by night at the *Express*. At Ealing they paid me eight pounds a week. I needed two jobs.

My function at Ealing was to initiate sequences of action. The work was done on celluloids - 'cells' mounted on a light box. I having drawn the key points through the sequence of action, the cells were passed to 'in-betweeners' who, on other cells, filled in the intervening parts of the action. The whole sequence, when photographed, produced flowing action.

So, as day by day, we worked in a rehearsal room, next door George Formby rehearsed on his ukulele under orders from his formidable wife Beryl. It is not entirely true that 'we' worked; Bobby did not. We seldom saw Bobby. This first film's purpose was to convince the public that the true road to glowing health and strength was by the eating of herrings. Sadly not one member of the public did we convince; not one member of the public saw our film. We did not finish our film. Indecisively, not quite visibly, it no longer had being. At Bobby's asking I cogitated a plot for a second film. It died of neglect after conception, it and all else. Bobby had been too fully occupied in socialising about the studio.

Without regret I returned full-time to the *Express*, just in time to make room for a returning Bobby. From under him, too, cartoon films had stolen away. So too had my art editing job.

"You see," said Bobby to me, "it's you or me."

The flawless logic of this, delivered entirely innocently was un-answerable. It was said of Bobby that he was unscrupulous. To that extent he was; but he was not a rogue. What he did was unconcealed, without intention of wrong-doing. We knew Bobby; we were fond of him.

From that brief sojourn at Ealing there did come something of great impact. It was then that first I met Jack Hargreaves, an occurrence not liable to forgetfulness, too entirely he was inimitable. There will be more to tell of him.

There was room for Bobby and for me. Diversely and fully I was occupied. James Agate, then at his cantankerous height, bestrode criticism of theatre and books. He was dogmatic, discerning, prejudiced and sometimes fair. Also he was readable, important, and influential for good or ill. Each Thursday I illustrated his page of book reviews. Now Agate was a square man, square and squat, square of head, minimal of neck, sparse of hair. He stumped, bowler on the back of his head, walking stick dictating to the ground. He was by nature so verging upon caricature that for me, who must caricature him each week, he was a boon: I had but to dwell upon him a little further - though I was often tempted into a little wildness beyond. Should his review relate to ballet I put him on his points and in ballet briefs, and on his carven countenance a coyness. Week by week he was many things from bullfighter to dairymaid. My most extreme nonsense seemed never to offend him.

Also this was the time of Mr Middleton. Mr Middleton? Thus is topical fame defined. Mr Middleton, gardener, in those years of war was as warmly loved a household name as any could be. Everyone knew and liked his fatherly ordinary voice giving his homilies of gardening wisdom on the 'wireless'. And each week he wrote on gardening in the *Express* and I illustrated him. My mode for that was affectionate caricature - his reliable grey Homburg, his mild ordinary eyes behind his spectacles - his monumentally reassuring ordinariness in that time of distressful rupture. I showed him in the garden as the inconspicuous definitive figure of down-to-earth wisdom. Who now knows Mr Middleton, Mr Middleton who was as famous as the Queen?

In those days of war I trod strange soils: I, least martial of men, was partner in the paper for a soldiering manual for Home Guards. Soldierly authority was supplied by a colonel whose name has long escaped me, but whose image is ineradicable - such caricatured authenticity he had: simple soldier, altogether rightly orientated, officer and a gentleman. His voice was of that kind singular to his vocation, a little high, slightly neighing, prone to cricketing allusions. I had the sense that behind his protective colouration he was a shy man, insecure beyond his regiment. I liked him.

I came perforce and without understanding into engineering.

The Spitfire, saviour in the Battle of Britain, was a national hero which almost attained to human status. So for all to see in the *Express* I must do a drawing of its cockpit; the drawing must be proof against the keenest technical eyes. The cockpit was appallingly complex, entirely beyond my understanding. I must, with minutest care, just copy what I saw before me.

The drawing was well received. It drew me more deeply into engineering's alien country. I must know all the current aircraft; I must show them and all their parts for the public interest, and all with not the least understanding.

Then from aircraft to tanks; I was thrust into an intimacy with tanks. I must know them all; I must explore and draw all the visceral facts of tanks. Everywhere that tanks were made, designed, used in training, their contributory parts made, to all those places I must go. I endured the skull-splitting noise of a tank factory in Leeds; at Chilwell in Nottinghamshire I attended upon the installation of guns in tanks' turrets. At another factory I saw the making of periscopes for tanks. At all these places I made my minutely painstaking drawings.

I went to Lulworth Tank Gunnery School, there to make drawings of the interior of the Matilda tank which was at that time Britain's leading infantry tank. It was designed to the last inch to accommodate its crew of three, the driver in the forward compartment, the gunner and the commander in the turret. I, to draw the whole, must contort myself into space not left for man: it was painful, it was claustrophobic. So for hours at a time I must stay, while drawing as painstakingly as was needed.

I was boarded in the Officers' Mess; it was friendly, welcoming. On my first evening I was offered friendly overtures by an officer who, most clearly, was out of the dizziest social drawer. He was tall, handsome as a not very cerebral god. In the evening his consummate ease of bearing was partnered by his enhancing uniform - the skin-adhering trousers broadly red-striped, the mess jacket; all was perfect. His nose was short, his mouth finely chiselled. He appeared to be taking me under his social wing.

One evening the barman, a 'common soldier', with an accent

obviously that of South London, revealed his coming from an area well known to me: we fell to the swapping of pubs there which we had known. My late sponsor evaporated.

An immediate outcome of my intimacy with tanks was a broadsheet published by the *Express* carrying my drawings displaying all aspects of the Matilda tank, inside and out. It had the blessing of the Ministry of Supply. Why, they suggested, should I not produce a small book about tanks for propaganda purposes? So came to birth my first book, a most modest paperback. No first book by me could have been more improbable; no less so was its publisher. It was published by *Country Life*. It was a great and pleasant surprise that it sold very well. Its title was *Tanks - Their Place in Modern Warfare.*

Brother Bert was an engineer; he was an engineer of repute. Out of his kindness he was tolerant of my failure also so to be. What pangs he must have suffered when a colleague, referring to my book, said of me, “A damn good engineer too.” To know less of engineering than I was not possible.

About this time I began, humbly, to write for the paper. On a day tender with new leaves and soft air I came into the office reluctantly. From the heart I wrote a piece and called it ‘My Spring Fever’. Next morning’s paper carried it. This was in that impatient eternity of the war’s middle years when all waited, edgily, for the Second Front. I drifted into writing pieces, suggesting that, unseen, vast events were toward, simmering silently towards their climactic end. I haunted Ministries, particularly that for war, I picking up this and that which, with a drawing, would dress up into encouraging pieces.

For a time in the Ministry of Information studio I had a staff job, doing my eight hours there by day, by night working at the *Express*. For the war’s length thereafter I worked as an artist freelance for the ministry. So it was I devised and drew a strip cartoon biography of Winston Churchill.

For its many purposes of propaganda the ministry set up exhibitions; often I was called upon to design the decoration and lettering of the exhibition stands.

People meanwhile continued to seep away into the war's labyrinths. Tony Baerlein, late of Eton College, and as *Express* colleague smallish, scruffy, quietly amiable, was sucked away to be reconditioned as a bomber pilot - he who was as warlike as an easy chair. And Bernard Wicksteed, as I have told, very quickly on his middle-aged way to his DFC. Bobby Cooper, as invalidated as I for active service, for a time had an assignment of a naval nature. Up and down Fleet Street he was splendidly nautical, bearded and uniformed.

Early in the war James Cameron had joined the *Daily Express* as a sub-editor: such talent could not long be so under deployed. He became a correspondent, then a foreign correspondent; soon most deservedly famously he was *the* James Cameron.

Before all that Jim was of our circle. At Pulborough in Sussex he took a house, rather fine and mellow, with a four-oven Aga in its kitchen, and a garden running down to the river Arun. Being down that way for the fishing Bernard Wicksteed and I used sometimes to drop in on Jim. For him there was to be little fishing more. The war, then other wars, other dramas, left him little chance.

Still from time to time I was able to punctuate other things with such fishing as I could reach. Just a little out of London, still entangled in the frayed-out wastes of London, there was the little River Colne by the A4 road at Colnebrook. Still there a fly could be cast for trout, though there it was no arcady. Great machines growled; with vast groanings, wrenching out gravel. Heavy traffic pounded the road, and though no doubt birds sang they could not be heard. But in that not too degenerated water trout lay, tilting to take fly that still could hatch there. Right under the road's concrete crossing of the river, beneath the beat of wheels, I took a trout.

In early June of 1942 I came first to Hungerford. It is then, in most years on or about the 5th of the month, that the mayfly delirium comes to the Kennet at Hungerford - though at Kintbury a few miles downstream, it comes a week earlier. For me it was the beginning of the Hungerford era; it lasted for the remaining years of the heaven that the Hungerford fishing was.

Hungerford enraptured me. Then a smiling tranquillity lay upon the place; the sense of the water, of its fishing, pervaded there, seemed almost to soak its very walls. But this was 1942, a war year: ubiquitously, amiably idling about the town, in the High Street, in Bridge Street, were the first newly arrived American soldiers. In that placid place they were very martial in steel helmets; but below the helmets the faces were ones of deep innocence.

"Gee," they said to me when learning that I had been in London throughout the Blitz, "you must be brave." So much they were to learn.

From Mr Betts at his pharmacy in Bridge Street I bought my fishing ticket. For two weeks I had such fishing as I had not had before. I had not before fished a chalkstream. How ultimately lovely all seemed to me. Hereabouts, I told myself, someday I shall live. And after long waiting so I did.

In another war year, in another mayfly season, I was at Cricklade. Cricklade is in Wiltshire but not of Wiltshire's chalk; its walls are softly grey, of a mellowness of limestone, quietly on the banks of infant Thames. The stripling river runs there a meadowy course, under its ancient willows, not dreaming of its famous future.

So it was then, so long since. Is it too much to hope that still so it is? Can degenerative time have touched its peace? I hope not; I must hope that the manic over-populating of our species has not sucked away the little stream. Then in its minor way it had profundities. Its meanders had made mysteries of deep eddies under its banks; glides rumpled into chattering shallows, making a miniature of greater streams. Even, in mayfly time, I had been told, great old trout came from their holts under the willows to suck in the mayfly. At my time of coming the mayfly's fever had passed.

In the winter of 1943 I came again to Hay. I came this time, as it seemed to me, as by a summons; that this time it was appointed that I should catch a truly epic pike. Already my mind's eye - as I supposed prophetically - saw it, hugely long, most elegantly formed, the baleful amber glare of its eyes under those frowning brows.

"Down there on the Moor water," Dansy said, "that's where those big old pike are. Monsters down there under the roots."

Thus I went, downstream, contrary to authority but by local usage, walking the track of the little branch line, till there was the Moor water, here narrow under its banks so caverned and gnarled by root and limb, that it beckoned with prickling sense of monster pike.

A willow bough prostrate in the surface, all about was thicketted and meshed by bough and twig; it promised that surely here must lie a great pike. So there one did. I brought the bait closely against the bough, limping, as though sickly vulnerable. With no fuss, quietly, it was taken. When I struck then was such a sight as almost to stop my heart. An enormity of pike rolled from under the bough, showing its mighty length in that small space of water, closely girt. It ran towards the open river so that for a terrified second I thought I might take it. It turned, came back, ran under the bough. The parting of the line was like a shot. That, so long gone, has left me still not really daring to guess the weight of that biggest pike I ever saw.

The war's later years had much of tedium, the tedium of waiting for what of certainty was to come but desperately frustratingly was long in coming. On that, from day to day, hung life's expectancy. But a quickening came. At about that time Tony Baerlein came into the office to let us see the glory of his newly won wings. He was rather shyly proud of them, liking the way they looked on his uniform. Then, so newly fledged as a bomber pilot, he went on his first operational flight over Germany. We were not to see him again. He did not return.

By then Jack Hargreaves too had gone, leaving a tangible absence. I, at first revealment, had found him rather startlingly odd. He had not much chin and it passed easily into his slope of throat. His teeth were dubious. His eyes - those eccentric spheres, had a thyroid bulge which made of their rotation a spectacle. Jack told stories; he told them often and in a manner curiously inimical. His way was not declamatory, not epic, but flat, quite flat. Aided by the roll of his pawky eye, listening was compulsive. And so much was gained by his freedom from mere truth, his disintegrating humour; all that augmented by the pregnant rolling of his outrageous eyes.

In spite of so much, or because of it, he attracted many women. All that, conscripted into the army, soon converted him into an officer in tanks and thereafter into army broadcasting.

At the late culminant time of the war I lived in Sussex by a lake: when by the lake was a millhouse pub-converted. Then, when self-conscious ruralness was still not in full possession of the home-counties and though so close to London, it could still show a fairly convincing resemblance to countryside. Birdsong was more to be heard than internal combustion, there being a wartime denial of petrol.

But over that peace there fell an apocalyptic blanket. It was the time of the thousand-bomber raids on Germany. Evening by evening the whole gentle vista of summer sky to the eyes' limit was canopied by the host of Lancaster bombers. No birdsong now was to be heard under the thundering sky. Each evening we watched in silence, thinking of what was in each one of those aerial bellies.

At last on a morning blissful and still with summer, about 11 o'clock, there was a radio announcement. This was D-Day. Allied forces were in full assault on German-occupied France.

Now optimism could spread its petals; now soon it would be over. And, fairly soon so it was; but after so hard to endure an interim. Stoicism, encouraged into softening by D-Day, must be buttoned down again.

That first night was to be sickly immortal for all who lived through it. The approaching aircraft had a sound that was not familiar. We knew the sound of German bombers; their sound was like the smell of death.

This was a sound of most bowel-turning menace, very darkly heavy. At first pulsing distantly, it growing to an engulfing saturation. Then, terribly, silence; nerve-shattering silence for stretched seconds. Then close and huge, the explosion. Thus began the 'Doodlebugs'. Thus all that first night; thus all next day; thus all succeeding nights and days.

Their purpose was dual: of course to kill, multiply, but more to terrify. At first and for a time it did, sickeningly. They had, curiously, a power for terror denied to the worst of the bombing by manned aircraft. These things were inhuman, unmanned and by that frightful by being monstrous. Their close succession made of them nightmare. Morning came and still they came, no respite, no pause, no ease for the quailing nerve, though in the light and stir of day something of the nightmare was lost.

But as always it is with that most elastic of organisms, the human soul, it adjusts. The greater part of the doodlebug's efficacy lay in first shock. Every day and night endured lessened its strength. By degrees we adjusted, at last to that self-fortifying state of being able to joke about it.

Then intensity slackened. Allied advances were overrunning launching sites. First torrent of terror became intermittent. But still for a while they came. One night brother Bert was on the usual citizens fire guard duty. A doodlebug arrived; it did not pass on, it did not cut out. Overhead it went into a rotation, a persistent circle just overhead. "It's rather trying," said Bert.

After doodlebugs came rockets, things of devilish silence in approach, instant death from nowhere. But of those I had no experience.

But VE-Day did come: the day when it was over, the day when we knew there was to be no more bombing, no more fear, no more death.

CHAPTER XIII

Mr Crabtree Finds Birth

A NEWSPAPER has no possession more precious than space. Its hunger aches incessantly. How then did we get through the war, and that still undernourished time immediately following its end?

In the salad days of peace when paper is plentiful, when news demand has taken its share of space, competition for features space is fierce. So then in starveling times of war, how was the paper to reflect life's day to day events and to cover the greatest war that history had seen? To do that we had but four pages, one folded sheet.

After the first few months of peace the bonds were eased a little; we were allowed six pages. This was not a wide freedom, not a spacious one to cover a nation's aspirations of escape into peace and all the pangs of war debilitation. But, nevertheless it stimulated pent urges of creativity to stir.

For me a first gift of space was coincidental with Harry Chapman Pincher's joining the *Express* - he so tentatively out of the army that still he was in uniform. He was Science Correspondent; in collaboration we produced a strip cartoon called 'Science Strip'; in well digested form it covered various fragments from the edges of science. One particularly I remember for its sharp relevance then. A fishing boat is burning in mid-Atlantic; that, declared the strip, could change the weather of Europe. I recalled that when we were told that atom and nuclear bomb tests would not have a distortional effect on climate.

Now, occasionally, I wrote fishing pieces, illustrating them with drawings. And there was Iris. Iris? Iris almost could be said to have been historical. Iris was the Weather Girl. Each day I drew her for her small corner where she gave the day's weather forecast. I gave her such winning ways as I could. Nevertheless to the people of today the being of Iris must seem entirely unremarkable. But only quite lately we had emerged from a long war; for its duration there had been a total blackout on weather news - another of war's depressions. Now here was Iris, prettily each day giving the weather. She was very popular though so inconspicuously in her corner.

But, pre-eminently, now was the birth of Knife Malloy. How unhappily, frustratingly, so promising a life was to be so short, unfulfilled. The pity of Knife Malloy. By the editor, Great Christiansen, it was ordained that I should create a strip cartoon about crime, about an engaging sleuth. I asked for and was granted a script writer: he was Jack Hargreaves. Our scripting sessions were memorable, made so by the quirk and oddity and askance frisking of Jack's humour. So much a pity it was that entertaining as was working with Jack, his small regard for deadlines was damaging to the nervous system.

Knife Malloy, our sleuth was called and of course he was Irish. He was leanly tall, rangy, quizzical of eye, a little uncertainly on the fence between reputable and disreputable. And of course when he acquires a girl assistant she is from most dubious circumstances, drily saucy, quick and wise, earthy, utterly of London.

I needed a setting which could be made to suggest the necessary shadow of threat. I prowled the East End of London, seeking to haunt myself with a sense of lurking felony. This was in those probably forgotten days when Wapping could still suggest such things. There at Wapping was that pub, delightful, law-abiding. It had a Dickensian air; at its rear it overhung Thames's turgid tides. How darkly sinister, I thought, that could be made to seem, how darkling an atmosphere. We called the pub 'The Virgin of Kent'.

Far from sinister was its atmosphere a night that I was there. A landing party of sailors from a ship of Her Majesty's Navy anchored in the Pool of London had boarded and were happy. They had invested the place, filled it fully with their presence. They were there for fun, they were there to 'dance and skylark'; dance they did, in a circle, arms round each others' shoulders. Meanwhile glumly round the walls were the girls, fully dressed out to charm: never was allure less rewarded. The buoyant happiness, light-footed, of the sailors clearly was a severe aggravation of the girls' neglect.

Here, as it should have been, would have been enacted, much of the living and doing of Knife Malloy. Alas, alas, those doings were never to be seen. The grant of six pages was withdrawn. Knife Malloy lost his space before he could have the freedom of it. He could have been held over until added pages were more secure. But it was otherwise.

By virtue of the strip the Editor had raised my salary to a level that then in Fleet Street was thought to be high. I had no reason to doubt that the Editor would have let me coast on thus until the lost paper should be restored - meanwhile I was amply needed otherwise. But just at that time he was absent for a period. Assistant and Features Editor Harold Keeble, for the time being in charge, declared the need for me had ended: he put me under three months' notice. Subsequently, rightly or wrongly, it was my impression that he told me I could forget the notice: immediately that I did. Three months passed peacefully. Then one day I supposed to be normal Harold Keeble said to me, "Your three months is up. You've finished here."

I was out of a job; I had done nothing about finding another. As so it happened nor did I need to. From the *Daily Mirror* there came an invitation to join them; and I did. But it was reluctantly that I left the *Express*; Arthur Christiansen's *Express* had been wonderfully stimulating. A few months later, by chance I met Christiansen in the Press Club. "See what happens when my back's turned," he said.

It was in 1946 I became a 'Mirror man'. 'Once a Mirror man, always a Mirror man' it used to be said. Only in recent years has the truth of that lessened. Newspapers have changed.

The transition from *Express* to *Mirror* was startling. I was startled that the inner being of two great national newspapers could feel so apart, so without common texture. Both, as is commonly the way of newspapers, had had their vulgarities; but, so indicatively differently. The *Express* was somewhat smugly righteous because it did not believe in anything beyond producing a very successful newspaper. The *Mirror* was rough-grained, looked with a plebeian eye: its beliefs were strong, forthright. The *Mirror* of my time often was not decorous; but it was honest, had social purpose. In one way I had enjoyed my nine years on the *Express*: quite differently I was to enjoy my seven years on the *Mirror*.

I became a part of something that was tacit on the *Mirror,* was not talked about, probably was not at conscious level: it was an unspoken acceptance that in its rather vulgar way it was there to be on the side of what was good for all the men, women and children that, day to day, amounted to what was called the Public. The *Mirror* had to keep an eye on things. When something was observed to be scandalous the *Mirror* would shout very loudly about it in a thoroughly vulgar way. It would publish a Shock Issue - and it usually was quite effectively shocking.

Many citizens who had a care for their show of respectability would look at the paper, if at all, only discreetly askance; it did seem rather common, and, hm, it was a bit salacious wasn't it? That referred to the careless cavorting every day in her underwear of Jane in her strip cartoon. How utter the innocence of Jane compared with what fills the media now.

My first assignment was with the dreams of readers. They were invited to send their dreams: I thereupon would select from them, do drawings of them in strip cartoon form, and an enlisted psychiatrist would interpret them. The response of dreamers was enormous.

Their letters filled boxes, then shelves, quite soon accumulated in a room. Through it all I must cull for those most interesting. Many dreams suggested that their owners were as unadventurous in sleep as in waking. But, culling through the mass, there was queer reading, oblique and strange, sometimes heartily uninhibited, sometimes shadowy. Many were stimulating for drawing, sometimes tempting along the edges of consciousness. Predictably the dream strip was popular. I never knew why it was stopped.

Perhaps because a need was felt for a gardening strip, perhaps it was felt that the dreams were digging a little deeply. Anyway to me was passed a gardening strip. One thing may lead to another, as retrospect so often shows; but indeed that gardening strip gave little promise of leading down any path of interest. Destiny nevertheless was in it.

All my adult life I had had a strong taste for gardens and gardening, but mine was mainly of plants and trees and landscaped sweeps. I knew enough of gardening to know I knew too little of that gardening which was of allotment and back garden vegetable plots. I needed a script writer. Jack Hargreaves became he. Jack had flair for scripts; his had movement and were lively. Soon it was evident that his grasp of the garden plot was less secure. But he remained long enough to give a name to our gardener. He called him Mr Crabtree.

So soon after his birth, the life of Mr Crabtree passed into the hands of another writer for the script, one who, undoubtedly, was amply learned in gardening. But the script was lame, slow, limping in its heavy garden boots. It struggled on until after the turn of Christmas.

"Well, what's Mr Crabtree to do now? Nothing happening in the garden," said Phil Zec to me.

I, not knowing the hand of fate, suggested that he could go fishing. He did, that January of 1947. His garden saw him no more. It may be seen now that Mr Crabtree was really somebody not of my

Jack Hargreaves with Bernard Venables.

devising, consciously made to capture a known audience. He was involuntary; he emerged unbidden from me, was essentially of me, was self-creating. He had innocence; the innocence was mine. His innocence touched the minds of a multitude of boys eager for discovery of angling's vernal delights. A great many of them, magically absorbed, identified with Peter Crabtree.

Bobby Cooper and I meanwhile, continued to play musical chairs. In advance of my going to the *Mirror* Bobby had made that crossing. Soon after my arrival he made the return journey. Quite mistakenly he thought himself to be in danger - he had 'seen the red light' he said; he said there could not be room for both of us on the same paper. The Editor declared himself happy to have both of us. But Bobby, unconvinced, departed. He returned to the *Express*.

A little later there came from him a note. 'Bernard,' it said, 'what have you been doing?' He enclosed a letter from a wronged and angry young lady. Her deceiver had told her that he it was who drew Iris, the weather girl.

Quite soon I was summoned to the editorial presence.

"You are now Angling Correspondent of the *Daily Mirror*," the Editor, Bish Bolum, said. "I don't want to see you in the office - I don't want your copy to smell of the desk. Just come in one day a week to pick up your letters." That was easy to bear: now, wholly I could give myself to the country - it was by edict. Also by Editor's edict not a word of my copy was to be changed; I was to be free from the pains of sub-editing.

It was a happy lot. Each week I must do Mr Crabtree; I must write a column; I must keep a perceptive eye on the angling scene, reflecting it in any odd pieces that suggested themselves. Also I must devise and run the *Daily Mirror* angling competitions.

The national press, till then, had had no consistent coverage of angling. Such coverage as there had been was casual. Some papers had offered weekly or monthly prize rods for best catches, but there was little more. Angling journalism had not been invented. I must begin at the beginning.

For the competition I established two main sections. That for angling clubs was for their aggregate catch for the whole season. The other part, for individuals, was divided into senior and junior. For the club section winners received money which could be used for any benefit to the club that was appropriate. For the individual winners rods and reels were given.

Experience of the first season showed clearly that such simplicity fell short of justice. With almost devastating certainty the prizes went to those already blessed with the fortune of living in the areas of the finest fishing. This must have been bitterly plain to those whose fishing had no better chance than mediocre canals; how were they to share fortune with those already more blessed?

I divided the country into three areas of comparable opportunity. In the least favoured a roach of, say, $^3/_4$lb, might balance one of 2lb in the most favoured areas. That I applied both to clubs and individuals. It did work reasonably well, though of course I could not expect to achieve entirely unblemished justice.

I hoped that just the winning of our awards would give considerable pleasure; but I wished to crown it. We devised the annual Angling Awards Luncheon at the Savoy Hotel in London. This was in the 1940s. The war was still recent: the blackouts had only recently come down, still there were restrictions and shortages; life was still lean. The times were apt for conjuring a sense of luxury.

To all winners went an invitation. It requested the pleasure of the company of each winner to a luncheon at the Savoy Hotel for the presentation of awards. For juvenile guests the invitation included an adult companion, the rail fairs of both being paid by the *Mirror*. Always the day was a Saturday; always, unless memory puts its deceits upon me, the weather was lovely. We spared nothing that could make the day forever memorable. It did appear that our guests enjoyed it enormously.

It was partner to that first of our angling lunches that first I went on radio and television. Saturday night then was the night of 'In Town Tonight'. "We stop the mighty roar of London's traffic," said the announcer, "to bring you interesting people who are 'In Town Tonight'," or something very like that. In the evening of the lunch I went on the programme.

My fellow guests were contrasted; of them two were so dazzling as to obscure the rest of us. He was the current Hollywood Tarzan, not so much tall as high, golden and god-like. The spread of his shoulders, the column of his neck, his splendour of poise were those of Greek sculpture. She, who was his wife, was Arleen Dahl, herself a Hollywood star of great lustre. She was no less glorious an object than he, bespoke made to match him, ecstatically tall, goldenly beautiful. They were remote.

It was when the eyes were turned, readjusted from the brilliance, that there was to be observed a quiet man who sat inconspicuously. He was Tennessee Williams.

Now also was my baptism of television, so long ago that it was at Alexandra Palace - Ally Pally - and, as programmes were then, live. With me I took two of our winners, and they, under the assault of lights and cameras were in danger of seizing up. From that common danger of first television exposure I had to help them. On this

Jack Hargreaves and Bernard Venables with Phil Zec (speaking) at the Savoy.

A Daily Mirror *prize for Ian Matthews.*

John Eastwood of ACA fame.

programme too was a film star, Geraldine Fitzgerald, as exceedingly small as the other two had been exceedingly large. She, not at all Olympian, was very friendly.

It was about this time there came a letter for me, a letter from an angler. A great many letters came from anglers; this one was unlike the rest. It was long, closely written on foolscap sheets in a small neat hand. The letter, first of many of its kind, was impressive, and largely discursive about carp. About carp it was illuminating. Hitherto there had hung over carp an aura, one of awed mysticism; it had seemed to be of a presence beyond the merely visible, and of a sagacity not quite explicable. It was to be seen, undoubtedly solidly material: but there was the queerness of it. It hung hugely just below the surface, amber, blue-backed, almost, it could be thought, touchable by a reaching hand. So it was to be seen in many still pools rather secretly embowered under trees; often such places had a witchy air. It enhanced the sense that carp were not quite of common things, that not diminished by its being apparently proof against all human wiles. Now almost in a moment through the eye of this correspondent they were to be seen as one more fish - still queerly formidable but nevertheless susceptible to guile.

The name of this writer of illuminating letters was Richard Walker. I had not heard of him before. I arranged that we should meet. Meeting did not lessen the impression made by his letters, but did qualify it, confuse it. He, a Cambridge trained engineer, came to fishing as to an engineering problem, combatively logical rather than passionate, technically brilliant rather than inspired. Previously he had been much involved with the eugenic problems of breeding rabbits. To fishing he applied the same mode of thought. I found in him an oddity I could not for a time identify. He had a gift for perceiving the essential material fact from which all else stemmed: he had great perspicacity in a technical sense. He was not intelligent, but was almost boundlessly innovative. He was, as someone said of him a brilliant fifth-former. He was and remained immature. I also detected a coldness of spirit which lay behind the various aspects he displayed.

About the man I had such reservations but believed that his talent should have the fullest scope. To him I vowed to do all to further his progress in such ways as I could. Having persuaded him to write a book about stillwater angling, I found him a publisher and helped the book on its way to publication. The book was very successful; it is unfortunate that its long-term effect has not been for the good of angling.

The technical means and tactics the book taught were faultlessly practical; they did greatly increase the reader's ability to catch fish, but imbued an alien spirit. In an obvious and entirely misleading way it may be said that the object of angling is to catch fish. If too persistent, failure to catch fish is dispiriting: the catching of a fish very large for its species, at last so gloriously, most beautifully on the bank, is an occasion intensely poignant to one of the true philosophy, cancelling all previous frustration. The inner nature of angling is a recognition of the sublime gift of having life on an earth by nature made boundlessly lovely. It is in living water, in fish so subtly living their lives that most fascinatingly it is to be felt.

The book led its reader most successfully to the catching of fish: it led him away from the philosophical and spiritual delights of angling as an initiation into the rhythm of nature. The spirit of the book was of conquest, of aggressive intent upon fish. The author was prone to the quoting in support the more martial voice of Kipling. At the time the book, if a little suspect in tone, seemed not only innocuous but a boon to those younger anglers impatient for such success as their insight had not yet earned them. Here was the way: as Walker had said, see fish as the enemy to be overcome.

He had also indicated that the angler should go forth in the spirit of the Elizabethan adventurers! Also inculcated was the principle that 'serious' anglers devoted themselves wholly, as to a Holy Grail, to the pursuit of 'specimen' fish; to do less was to trivialise their commando cause. It caught the fledgling imagination of many, hitherto in their untampered innocence. 'Specimen groups' sprang up widely in deadly dedication. Thus into the quiet privacies of angling was brought an athleticism, a seeking of achievement, something for chest-beating. It was far remote from the true nature of angling. In its extremest form is the bizarre absurdities of latter day carp fishing. In justice to Richard Walker, he would probably be aghast if he could see what has followed from his teaching.

In the late Forties it was suggested that I should make of the Mr Crabtree strip a basis for a book. On nothing could I have seized more gratefully. I was, and am, in love with books - not alone for their reading. Books are objects of trust that should be, sometimes are, also beautiful artifacts. Of this one that now I must make, it was as though I must allow it to emerge unbidden. Here was an open brief. Here was a deep contentment, to make a unity, its text, its design, its illustration. All that into one living whole.

To those strips which had been in the paper I added more strips, watercolour illustration, a text. I wove in pages of colour, of waterscapes, of fish, of flies. I let my loving pleasure run as it would.

Then it was done. When I had received an advance copy Jack Hargreaves happened to call upon me.

"This," he said, "will sell a million copies."

So it did, and more than another million. Now, more than fifty years later, I find myself - to my surprise - part of a family of millions. It is sad that from that huge sale no profit came to me.

When I was cogitating the production of another book, it became necessary that I should make an exploratory tour. It was January, of that mild and dreaming-skied kind that January may sometimes be. My tranquil way took me through the whispering levels of the Great Ouse, through Suffolk, into Kent and Sussex, then westward till I came to Devon. There at last I came to Slapton Ley, so strange a freshwater mere suspended between the hills and the sea's close intimacy. Then it was as it had been, justly famed, a fishery for pike and rudd and perch.

Overnight I was in an hotel above the Ley. As resort hotels in winter may be, it was bleakly empty but for one other guest. He, lately an officer of the Royal Navy, was on a mission - he was proselytising some sort of Christian message, travelling the country so to do.

"But, well, really you know," he told me, "it does get me away from my wife."

Bernard Venables and son Julian presenting a copy of Mr Crabtree Goes Fishing.

Returning, stopping one night in Mere in Wiltshire, I rose in the morning feeling unwell, soon unmistakably in emergency. I drove to reach home while still within the margin of capability. It was of course a haemorrhage. For some time it hovered in doubt as whether or not to be terminal. Slowly, clutching at life I gained purchase: once more I survived. During the first period of doubt, the Editor, as I was to hear, declared, "Bernard must not die." It must have been a difficult directive.

Having lived as directed, I took a blissful week painting at Dedham in Constable's Stour valley. But, the Editor told me, I must take a month, for that month idling somewhere in a place of my choice. I went to Co. Clare in Ireland's Celtic twilight west. I had been there before; I had a love for it before ever I saw it.

Before the war, seeking a place for fishing, far removed, a place of imagining, I heard of Corofin. The distant music of the name enraptured me. How could a place so named be anything but enchanting? I did not get there then, and the war intervened. In 1947, still instinctively drawn to Ireland, I went, wandering widely, constantly drawn westward. Still in my mind there lay that name, Corofin. I was drawn as if inevitably. In Co. Clare I found Corofin. As I had expected so it was, a place pale grey, tawny pink and moss green, a place of limestone crag and water. Everywhere lakes, quiet, inviolate, gently reflecting the sky. On everything an elusive reticence not of secrecy but inward shyness. I remembered a house there where I could stay, up from the River Fergus at Kilnaboy, crouched above Fogarty's Crag.

Kilnaboy is about three miles up the road from Corofin, a road white with limestone dust, humped with limestone. For those who went decently in ass carts it was a road good and adequate. If insistently you should go upon it with a car it was salutary in imposing low speeds.

At Kilnaboy began the Burren, a heaven-touched wilderness, stretching almost to the Atlantic coast. A barren waste of limestone terraces so it appears, able only to give comfort to the fairies. But in every crevice, under every stony shelf there is a surpassing richness of flora: where the Burren drops away to the sea at Black Head there are alpine meadows where orchids of every species thrive as closely as buttercups in a meadow.

So I, with a month for dalliance, could think only of Corofin and Kilnaboy and the Burren. There I went, but not to idle. I painted; I fished; I sent back copy abundantly.

I fished freely, having to have regard for no privacies, going as I liked. So I was, on the river at Elm Vale, when I met a man who was gently courteous. He was concerned that I should have such sport as the water could give, showing me places best known to him for giving good fish. Subsequently I enquired as to who was this kindly man. He was the owner of the valley there; the water was his. He was, they told me, quite recently out of prison. Why, I asked, should this obviously most decent man have been in prison?

"Ah sure he hit a garda." A garda is a policeman.

One day, driving into Corofin, I was stopped by a garda. He must see my papers. He was severe in his manner, firmly official. But he saw my rods in the back of the car.

"Ah, so 'tis fishing y'are," he said as absently he handed back my papers. "Sure if you go up there at Kilnaboy, sure the fishing's fine there."

Though it appeared not to be considered in Corofin and thereabouts that there is such a thing as time, that there are beginnings and ends, my month ran its course; the outer world reclaimed me. One of its first demands was that I should see the doctor, and he was admonitory. Once again, he told me, I had been lucky. Luck, he said sternly, has limits. Another haemorrhage might be the last. I must have an operation.

"They do a lovely one now you know. Not like that beastly thing you had before - that was a long time ago, things have moved on."

So again in January, but now in 1951 not 1935, into hospital I went, into Nuffield House, Guys Hospital. There Sir Heneage Ogilvy performed on me the lovely operation. And when convalescence was over, a lovely operation it proved to be, approximating to re-birth. Now I could eat what I liked. With negligent pleasure now I could enter a pub as before, with envy, I had seen others do. I was well; I was fit; I could give way to my ardent urge to live. The curtain of emergency no longer dropped. Life could sing. Out of 1951 into 1952 I went on wings of optimism.

I had, in 1950, been elected a member of the Savile Club: it was in the bar there in 1951 that Howard Marshall told me of his idea. He then was a very famous broadcaster - again a reminder of how fugitive is media fame. Who today unless elderly and with a good memory knows of Howard Marshall?

Now in the Savile bar he said to me, could there not be a fishing weekly newspaper? A tabloid newspaper, rather in the style of the *London Evening Standard*?

Would I, he asked, consider joining him in such a thing? It would be necessary to find a third party who could provide backing and production means. This being achieved, would I consider becoming of it to run the editorial?

The idea was stimulating; it stirred creative excitement. But on the *Mirror* I was happy, I was secure. I had a strong sense of loyalty to the *Mirror*. In the midst of dilemma, now came Howard Marshall to tell me that he had found the third party. There was nothing now he said to prevent our taking the plunge. But only for me was there a plunge; Howard in his secure job could continue till retirement and pension - which he wished this venture to augment. For me was a monopoly risk-taking.

It was coincidental that now there came to a salivating public a murder case of more than usual disgust. The *Mirror* in its coverage before the case came to trial was in breach of the law. The Editor, our own Bish Bolam, a man of considerable social conscience, was arraigned and brought to trial. He was found guilty; he was sent to prison for three months. Perhaps it was no coincidence that soon after he died.

His successor was Jack Nenagh, hitherto News Editor. My first contact with him in his new function was to give him my resignation.

"That's all I need," said Jack.

I had decided to join Howard Marshall and R.P. Winfrey in founding a fishing newspaper to which I gave the title *Angling*

Times. That decision made, I was put to sharp temptation to revoke it. I was called to a meeting; those present were Jack Nenagh, Cyril Morton who was Managing Editor, and Hugh Cudlipp, later to become Lord Cudlipp. Hugh Cudlipp suggested to me that I should reconsider, offering as inducement a higher salary. Not to accept was sharply painful. I had been happy on the *Mirror*.

During the *Mirror* years an incident seeming not of great consequence, was in effect, to reach far. Noel Carrington was producing for Penguin Books a series called Puffin Books; they were slim paperbacks for children, of great charm, probably of fascination for children. They were, largely to be seen, an evidence of one man's own quietly personal visual pleasures. He had a love of the classic 19th century natural history illustrators; that particularly in the context of their having been done by direct hand lithography. In his zeal he pursued a mission: he sought no less than to stir into being a revival among contemporary artists of the right inclination. Thus it was his purpose that each artist doing a Puffin book should draw his illustrations directly on the lithographic plates. Noel Carrington asked that I should write and illustrate a book on fish and fishing for the Puffin series.*

So to Ipswich I went, there to do to the lithographic work. I went with trepidation and lust for the experience of this, to me, new medium. At the works of W. S. Cowell there also was Peter Scott to do his Puffin about birds. In pauses in work we gossiped. I invited him to lunch at the hotel. This was in that immediate post war period when no menu could be free of suspicion: when there came the steaks we had ordered, we had deep dubiety. We said nothing, not wishing to arouse anxiety in the other. We started to eat: we did not continue. Neither of us had known whale meat before; we did not recognise it: but, surely, we should have been warned by what we saw, so darkly repellent. This noisome flesh should not be described, not it or its evil smell. Peter, unhappily, took it amiss. Our aquaintance for many years thereafter never quite came out from under that shadow.

**Fish and Fishing, 1948.* Published in Britain and in a French edition.

Sir Allen Lane was of course the creator of Penguin Books, thereby bringing revolution to the world of publishing. And, how incredible now it is, sixpence then was the price of a Penguin book. It was the suggestion made to me then by Sir Allen that has had far consequences. He, and Noel Carrington talked to me of the splendid 19th century tradition of colour-illustrated natural history books. How beautiful an idea it could be, Allen Lane said, to revive that old glory, to do a series of books covering natural history in Britain. Would I feel stimulated by the idea of doing such a thing about British freshwater fishes with most devotedly meticulous colour illustrations? I was enraptured: I would do this as never it had been done before. I would not, as before it had been done, paint fish carcasses. I would paint from living fish, flexing and quick in water.

At this time of writing that book has not been published. It is profoundly sad that Allen Lane had no option but to abandon the lovely project - its cost would have been so enormous as to threaten his company. I, unwilling that altogether it should die, have continued a book deriving from that. It is complete; perhaps it may sometime be published.

CHAPTER XIV

On the Birth of a Paper

IT IS an easy truism, partially, variably valid, that the best way to learn a job is by doing it. Briefly at the *Daily Express* as stand-in for an absent Bobby Cooper, I had been learning that job. But though for sixteen years I had been soaked in newspapers, not for one of them had I faced Editorial Direction: nor in all that time had I made up a newspaper page or learned the ways of typography. I had almost no knowledge of typography. Now, forthwith I must do these things: all else of the editorial function, daily must be my concern. Through those foregoing years, undoubtedly much of all that must have seeped into my sub-conscious and could be raised.

I drove over one afternoon to see my old *Express* colleague Maurice Wiggin. There and then he gave a quick lesson in page make-up, in typography; also he lent me books on typography; and, immediately, I found myself bewitchedly in love with it, thirsting for its further practice. That love has lasted. The lesson was succinct, about forty minutes: I was ready to start.

In the most relevant respects I had not been unready apart from those specifics. For those sixteen years of total immersion in two newspapers I had worked every day but Saturday, and sometimes on Saturday too for the *Sunday Express*.

Newspaper life no doubt has changed since its dispersal south of the river. Fleet Street, not merely a street, was a separateness, a seclusion - rather to be compared to those sailors whom I saw so exclusively dancing in the Thameside pub. I recall how once I being with Bernard Wicksteed in a rural pub he said, "Do you know, I find it hard to get on with people who aren't Fleet Street." Fleet Street was inclined to see itself as the epicentre of the beat of life. Fleet Street to inmates was 'The Street'. It was quite apart from all outer places from which came copy.

But now, far was I from Fleet Street, far from its sense, smell, touch. Nor now was I in a metropolis. The company that backed us was EMAP - East Midland Allied Press - based in Peterborough, and was a publisher of a series of local evening papers. Necessarily it was provincial in feeling. What must be produced was to be about fishing which, not having the clang of national news, still must have a national feel. That Peterborough had on its doorstep much angling scope for editorial staff was valuable: what at once clearly was imperative was that I, while keeping close understanding with Peterborough's provincial sense, must not become of it. In the whole country there are many other provincialisms, other localisms. The paper must retain the sense of all.

In Peterborough paternalism was a problem; Pat Winfrey was he who wore it. To him had come inheritance of EMAP from his father. It was cardinal to him that the world radiated from Peterborough, or anyway the better parts of it. He was very urgent that I should settle in the vicinity of Peterborough, so the better to be absorbed into the paternal shade. As urgently I was determined so not to do. Apart from the paper's best interests it was not tolerable that the rest of life's creative spirit should there fall into dessication.

We had less than six months before first publication in which to formulate the shape and nature of what was to be. This 'we' - the editorial staff, also contained Tiny Bennet. He had come with me

The launch of Angling Times.

With Alf Waterhouse of the NFA.

Angling Times *sells 100,000 copies. Bernard Venables and Howard Marshall celebrate.*

from the *Mirror*, having been there a staff photographer, and as that so now he came to us - doing that by his own special plea because his passion was for fishing. He was 6 foot 8 inches: he was bearded, had a loud bass and fruity voice. So conspicuous as was he, he was to be an asset in the building of an awareness of the paper - by his nature's compulsion he was a performer, an innocently amiable show-off. To that he gave himself with happiness. He was warm, loyal, and a child: such a pity it was that also he was somewhat irresponsible.

In the Strand in London we began with one upper room. Its only practical working surface was its floor boards. But soon we were promoted: in Breams Buildings, a stone's throw from what then was the *Mirror*'s building, we were awarded two rooms and tables too. Our creature soon to be had begun to quicken. Editorial and production staff were established at Peterborough. I retained an office in Breams Buildings, going to Peterborough one day a week.

All of us in our ways, as now I see, had an optimism so quietly warm as not to question itself. But beyond that relative modesty was no smallest gleam of foresight of the giant which finally was to evolve from our projection. Probably Pat Winfrey had some small light of hope that this minor rocket might lift him out of the confines of his few evening papers. Not he nor any of us foresaw the giant that was to grow from the modest birth of *Angling Times*.

We approached our D-Day not unobserved. Observers observed variously and not all optimistically. Alf Waterhouse, who was then President of the National Federation of Anglers, was firm that we should be lucky to sell 3,000 of the first issue. We sold 30,000. Contrary to the usual pattern for new publications, there was no circulation drop-back after the first issue. First publication came on 10th July, 1953.

From birth its health was rampant: hope and zeal were ratified. We could draw easy breath.

As Editorial Director to me fell the shaping of broad editorial policy - to create the taste and feel of the paper, its atmosphere. Our readership was of the widest kind, at its extremities of tastes almost irreconcilable. At one outermost wing were the hardcore match anglers. They, in tolerance or in contempt, called those of the opposite end 'Pleasure Anglers', so making the stringent charge that they were mere dalliers, butterflies. I resolved that by confining match fishing (since have it I must) to the back pages. In the rest of the paper I pursued the assumption that anglers are by nature naturalists, a little of philosophers.

In charge of week to week production was Colin Willock as Editor. He came to us from being Assistant Editor of *Lilliput* magazine: he was an experienced journalist of a kind apt for such as *Lilliput*. I think he found *Angling Times* not entirely to his natural style - nor could he find any comfort in getting on with Pat Winfrey, something not fairly to be held against him. This difficulty, becoming acute, led to his departure after six months.

During the run-up to first publication, to Richard Walker I offered a regular weekly column. His response was less an acceptance than pounce.

"That," he said, "is what I've always wanted."

'Dick Walker's Pitch' appeared in the first issue. It ran for most of the years until his death. Often it was controversial, destructive of sacred cows. For many it was compulsive reading, by some it was fervently detested. Walker's fixed purpose, he told Tiny Bennet, was to push me from my eminence, there to put himself.

When after its first six months *Angling Times* must take to itself a new editor, Pat Winfrey produced for my approval (which meant acceptance) two candidates. Both, he insisted, should be mine. As Features Editor there was to be Jack Thorndike: but, parallel, free-floating, as News Editor was Peter Tombleson. They were to be 'co-equals'.

This was a queer ship to take to sea: how fair a course could it steer with two rudders, two skippers? After two jerky years of inconsequence Jack Thorndike became full Editor - to me a gift of much contentment. Through the years that followed we, Jack and I, had the happiest of working relationships.

But that, in the paper's first year of being, was still to be. Through 1953 circulation rose steadily, which fact was observed in Ireland. Ireland then still a poor country, needed tourism; so in

Jack Thorndyke (far left), Bernard (centre), Peter Tombleson (standing second from right) with Howard Marshall and R. P. Winfrey both seated.

need she lay in the midst of an enormous and unexploited potential. She had so great a bliss of waters as hardly to be rivalled, a country so veined with lakes and rivers as to shimmer. And, then, all in a countryside so quiet, still so unstirred in forgetful ruralness as half to be a dream.

Fogra Failte, which was the Irish Tourist Board, approached *Angling Times*. They asked that I should make a tour of Irish waters, assess their potential for attracting anglers from England. They wished that I should go to Ireland, they said, as the 'first ambassador of angling'.

At that time still I felt in Ireland's more western distances as I had on first impression, a sense of its being not wholly of what was visible, of being as much of what was sensed. The very air was fey. Here, in such an air, was fishing more of dreams than of hope of anglers of England's industrial confinements. And, in this bliss of chance unlimited not once did I come upon one who fished.

To Cavan I went because there I must meet Barney O'Reilly. Barney was one of those few who did fish and knew the fishing. When I came to Barney's door he was not at home: but as I stood there came bearing down upon me most purposefully, a garda. But no stern official garda was this.

"Bernard Venables is it? I'm Garda Fox. Ah yes sure, we knew you were coming. Barney'll soon be here." And soon he was.

They took me, Garda Fox and Barney, through labyrinths of lake and river that could have given fishing for a multitude and they without sight of one another.

As at Cavan so were all places in an enchanted vagrancy that weakened my sense of worlds more mundane, floating inconsequentially, never without the glimmer of water. At Athlone the Shannon, broad between its banks, flowed as though no wind or flood or any sharp mood could ever touch it. Then there was Cong, resting incomparably on its narrow waist of land between two great loughs, Corrib and Mask. Beyond, out from the flat lands, close to the myth-misted mountains of Connemara, where the air whispered of things unseen, I heard fine old stories of great fish caught in Corrib.

Pat Donaghue ghillied for me and, as we fished through the day, told me stories of pike of fearsome size that had come from Corrib. Of one he told me - and he swore to its truth - which had been caught far up the remote last westerly arm of Lough Corrib.

"'Twas a great fish entirely," said Pat.

"What was its weight?"

"Sixty pounds was the weight of that fish. Ah sure 'twas a monster."

From village to village in the echoing lostness of that last arm I threaded, that I might find that one to which belonged this epic. In one village enquiring my way I entered a shop: being there I thought to buy a bottle of whiskey. Never before had I come upon the shop; never had its owner seen me. But when I, ashamed, discovered I had come out without money the shopkeeper was placid.

"Ah 'tis nothing to be worrying about. Sure it's yourself will be bringing in the money the next time you pass - and you having the pleasure of the bottle the meantime."

He was entirely unsurprised when next day I took the money in.

I came at last to the village where lived the man who had caught the great pike. He was lean, a little elderly; he spoke quietly, as though he heard other voices than mine. On a three-inch copper spoon of his own making he had caught the fish, trolling the spoon behind his boat on a handline of heavy cord.

"How did you know it weighed sixty pounds? You weighed it?"

"Ah no - I guessed that weight. 'Twas a big fish."

"How big was it?"

"When I held it up like this with my arm straight over my head its tail was on the ground."

He was a man of middle height or a little less: the fish could not have been less than 6 feet long. On Lough Mask (I cannot remember with certainty that Mask it was) in the early 1950s a pike was brought up caught in a net. Clearly it was seen by all present before it ripped out of the net: it was 6 feet long. They agreed that its weight was about 100lb.

What happened to the Corrib pike?

"We ate it. Every one in the village had some of it."

When I left Ireland's curlew-haunted lonelinesses of bogs and mountains, I wrote a report for Bord Failte: on it was founded policy for attracting to Ireland's manifold bliss of waters England's anglers. In *Angling Times* I wrote a series of pieces in praise of that near paradise that in Ireland beckoned the angler. I, in Ireland again a few years later, was told a result had been a benign revolution in Ireland's rural economy. Perhaps - and poignantly I hope - it has not diminished the gentle loneliness of those fey places. Anglers from England did migrate massively to what at the time was called the 'Promised Land'.

Had I not, a few years later fallen under the queer bewitchment of Lough Nafooey, that strangely improbable meeting with Mr Alston would not have been. I have written of that elsewhere, but it is worth repetition.

Its name had ensnared me; it induced a brooding sense of something beyond the edge of tangible. Sight and sense of it when I came to it confirmed and deepened my distant response to its name. Its approach was through the wild bogland, wide-skyed, saffron and pink. Then, abruptly, it constricted; on either side mountains rose darkly. There, narrowly within, lay Nafooey, a little ominous. But its people on the road were softly spoken and were courteous. The children from school, talking in Irish, dropped politely into English to bid me 'Good Day.'

There had been stories of great pike taken from Nafooey's darkling water, and for a week I fished there: but I was too late in the year. November's bitter winds drove in from the open eastern end to send pike deep and comatose.

One evening coldly bitter, the boat grated on the stones and I, chilled and stiff as they, got ashore. From the road high above, a man was descending. As he, treading carefully down the stones, came nearer, I saw his clothes were black; he wore the collar of a clergyman. Martin Coyne who was ghillie for me, had told me of a clergyman who came day by day over the mountains to fish, even if only for half an hour. This, said Martin, was he.

He was tall; his eyes were those of one long in lonely places. His voice was that of parsons of the old style, rather with the pulpit's intonation.

"Mr Venables I presume," he said, "My name is Alston."

I think that should have gained my attention. Gained it was but not by the name; here, in this far haunted corner of Ireland, was this clergyman so undeniably English and Anglican, who came over the mountains daily to fish - and clothed as though immediately out of the vicarage door. We talked, climbing up to the road, and in a casual context he mentioned rudd. Rudd! Alston! But could it be, in this place so removed from probability? He confessed that truly he was that Rev. E.C. Alston whose name had been on the record fish lists so long as almost to be legend. Who of us did not know his name as we knew of Marco Polo? Every one of us knew that in one day in some misty past he had caught two rudd - one which was the record weighed 4lb 8oz, the other

4lb 4oz; and in that same time he had caught two tench which weighed 7lb each and were for so many years the record. And this was the Rev. E.C. Alston, here.

I had supposed him still unobtrusively in his Norfolk parish, not known beyond. And here, by the sullen water, where the speech was Irish, here was he. He lived, he told me, in Connemara twenty miles on over the mountains. Would I care to go with him to his home? As I followed his tail lights, November's early darkness fell. When we came to his house it lay over a black void.

"The sea lies there," said Mr Alston.

In that space-besieged place he lived alone but for his ancient housekeeper. Paraffin lamps were lit to throw their uncertain light into reluctant shadows.

"In all my life," he told me, "for only three years have I had the blessing of electricity, so much have I lived in secluded places."

The light revealed walls hung with cased fish, and of those that legendary brace of rudd. Mr Alston released his pipe from his mouth that it might be his pointer; there was that other brace, two tench, each of 7lb. The evening had become not quite of reality, as it remained on the journey back, over the mountains, through the dark defile of Nafooey.

In those same years of the Fifties I met Charles Ritz, but in no wild Celtic twilight. Most properly I met him in the Ritz Hotel in London. Charles was son of Cesar, that Cesar who invented the metropolitan luxury hotel, by that making of his name a definition. To the Ritz I was taken to meet Charles. There was nothing accidental about the meeting. Charles was a fisherman deeply addicted, most thoughtfully erudite in its devices. He was also very shrewd.

He designed a range of rods that collectively were called Parabolic: they were excellent rods. For their making he had formed an alliance with Pezon and Michel of Amboise. It was needful that the world should know of the excellence of the rods. In the world of fishermen I had editorial influence. Potentially then it was good for Ritz rods that we should meet.

We met in his room. He was a small man, neat and quick, very

Bernard with Charles Ritz and Bertin, the angling barman.

European. His hair was stiff, erect as if mown; he had a small close-clipped moustache; his brown eyes sharp with perception. I was aware of a quickly scanned assessment of myself. He was easy, friendly, but not attempting to hide his sales talk, going straight into it as though sure I would share his conviction. He had good reason so to suppose. I, flexing them, had a mishap which might have killed the newly opening bud of friendship.

Bedrooms in the Ritz Hotel are luxurious in the Edwardian manner, much given to gilt and mirror glass. I had not noted behind me a glass and gilt screen. I hit it; memory is sharp still of the sound of rending cane. But Charles was mellow, magnanimous, tactful to ease my embarrassment - "We will make a new top joint. It will be easy."

Our association prospered. I saw much of Charles, staying at the Paris Ritz as his guest, being, so to speak, introduced to his particular pride. The Espadon restaurant was not of that gold opulence that otherwise was the Paris Ritz. All that was utterly of Cesar, gold and gorgeous. The Espadon was Charles's. The Espadon it was called because '*espadon*' means swordfish, and there hanging was a stuffed swordfish. Charles could not keep his obsession out of this which was his dear creation. And indeed, in the Espadon bar just across the foyer, the barman was Bertin, an angler too. Lovingly he told of his carp fishing in the Dordogne.

But fishing intruded no further in the Espadon restaurant; its dedication was to other things.

"I designed it very carefully. I designed the lighting. You see the lighting? It is tender and lovely - in my lighting all women are beautiful. Even Americans."

With Charles I went to Amboise - a journey needing no other purpose than its pleasure. Amboise is gracious in the French provincial fashion, crouched under the splendour of its chateaux. But in Amboise they make fishing tackle: there is the works of Pezon and Michel. For lunch I was entertained at the house of M. Pezon, and for tea by the ladies of M. Michel. They were shy and charming.

To Normandy too I went with Charles to fish the Risle and, in the morning, we met outside the hotel in the Place Vendôme where Charles's car was waiting. Happy in ignorance, I had put on my fishing clothes. Charles, a man I had thought well proofed against social shock, was shocked.

"The clothes. No not like that; put on proper clothes. Take fishing clothes with you. There will be luncheon." Charles was destabilised.

The full experience of Charles's driving was not revealed to me on the outward journey; he wished me to see the country and drove meditatively, drifting through the villages. It was a day of a referendum, *oui* or *non* on some matter of national importance which I have forgotten.

"You see," said Charles, "this is the day they decide their destiny, ruin or salvation of the country. You see how much it excites them?"

Over all were layers of rural peace, a communal dosing.

"You see? It is a day off, a holiday."

A friend of Charles, a rich banker, owned the water and to his house we went first, to the fishing room, there to change into fishing clothes. We could have done much more than that in the fishing room: it was more ample than any I have seen before or since. Then into the car again and to the river. It was time to fish.

There was the Risle, a chalkstream no less exalted in France than is the Test in England. There was the same almost divine clarity. But the weed; where were the viridian tresses of ranunculus? Why were they not swaying gently in that crystalline current?

The gravel was bare; there was no luxuriance of weed to give habitation to all those creatures that are food for trout. Nor was there weed to give concealment for fish or fisherman. It was by putting the fly tightly under the far bank that, at last, I did hook and land a trout. For its length it should have been svelte and lovely and over 2lb; it was about a pound. Charles, it was to be seen, concentrated almost entirely, and deftly, on casting into small openings in overhangs of willow.

Our hostess, much admired as a fly fisher, had recently taken a trout of 2lb. This I was told to impress me.

Lunchtime came. Into the car and to the house again, into the fishing room; out of fishing clothes, into presentable clothes. I could well see that the butler would have viewed my fishing clothes without approval. I think our hostess would not have thought well of them. There were about twelve of us to luncheon. One was a large young American who lit cigarettes between courses.

"Could he not understand," our hostess said afterwards, "that he insulted the food I offered him?"

We did not dally on the return to Paris.

"Forgive me that I don't converse - I like to concentrate on driving."

I too found that I must concentrate on his driving. It was notorious rather than well-known, and, as I was to learn, those who knew did not volunteer as passengers with Charles. To my relief and against my expectation we did attain Paris.

At an intersection near the Etoile a large elegance of Rolls Royce crossed our path.

"There goes another Swiss millionaire," said Charles. Charles was Swiss. On one occasion, in a connection I have forgotten, I remarked that very rich people were often mean. Charles said nothing but looked at me oddly. Charles was very rich. I seldom remembered that.

The International Fario Club could probably have emanated from nobody but Charles. He invented it; he ran it; he subsidised it. He was its benevolent dictator. The IFC declared he, was an association of the world's top fly fishers, and indeed it did include some who could be so described. But Charles, ever pragmatic, could sometimes see other factors. The Prince and Princess Lichtenstein may well have been very talented fly fishers - as I have seen, they cast well; but anyway their membership did add a degree of lustre. They were very pleasant people. Charles invited me to membership: I had editorial influence.

The duties of membership were simple and delightful. Each year in November we must attend a banquet in the Paris Ritz Hotel for which we paid only a nominal sum because Charles subsidised it. As could be expected, a meal devised by one of the world's greatest cooks matched the desire of a gastronome. The first year I arrived before lunch; it was a mistake. Lunch was vast. In the evening, still under the load of lunch, I was appalled. How was I to face the banquet? I failed to stay its course. In subsequent years I arrived after lunch.

It was the custom that on the morning following we all must go to a lake in the Bois de Boulogne there to cast with Ritz rods so completing our whole duty as members of the IFC. It was extremely pleasant.

In its early years so it was; it was small then, so small that all of us could be seated at one very large round table. And, though not all of us had language in common, it was intimate. Charles, presiding, made a speech in French; only a very poor job I made of following it. Then came one who was, as I could see, a much admired writer on fishing - though I cannot recall his name. He was so small, so delicately fragile that I would have been nervous of nudging him. Little as I could follow him, his eloquence was obvious, gracing out his words with small gestures, faint nods.

In that mixed small company some were French, some Belgian; there was a Swede, and a Swiss, and a modestly charming

American, settled in the Pyrenees. From England there were two of us; Frank Sawyer was the other. There were the Lichtensteins, and happily the good Pierre Creusevaut.

But year by year it grew. The round table became a long table, then a top table with leg tables. Its intimacy was gone. Particularly of the Americans there were some of a spirit less acceptable.

An end came. Charles, past eighty, died. When he died so died the International Fario Club. It had lived the best of what was its virtue. The early years were ones I am grateful to have known.

The International Fario Club.

Chapter XV

A Rural Sanctity Saved

Charles Ritz and Sandy Mac Mahon could have served as foils each for the other. Both were exceptional men, both of a brilliance peculiar to themselves. That of Charles was apparent; Sandy's could be fully found only by long intimacy. By modesty he was self obscuring.

Early in the life of *Angling Times* I perceived its need for a biological correspondent. One whom for a time I considered was Fisheries Officer to a River Board. On a morning appointed for our meeting he arrived in the Breams Buildings' office before my own arrival. On that same morning the post had delivered a fish: it, a fairly average chub, had come because its sender believed it to be a record roach (a not unusual occurrence). I, on passing, asked why someone had sent us a chub. When my visitor had gone I learned that he had for half an hour been crouched over the fish counting scales and fin rays. He sought to identify it.

My need for a biological correspondent continued. About that time I had come upon a Penguin book which engaged me curiously. *Fishlore* was its title; its flavour was suggestive of more beyond the relatively superficial coverage of its subject - as though it were a simple enticement offered by its author out of his large erudition. Its sense was of gentleness and intelligence. Its author was A.F. Magri Mac Mahon: thus to Breams Buildings came Sandy Mac Mahon. Gentle and intelligent so he was, shabby, modest, his spectacles thick-lensed. His voice was deep, rich as old mahogany, Italianate in style and accent because Sandy was half Italian, half Irish. His hair was greying, as was his scrubby moustache; his eyes behind their lenses were weak but wise, quick with humour. Thus was Professor A.F. Magri Mac Mahon. I had found my biological correspondent.

Only by years of Sandy's acquaintance could be revealed all that was Sandy, so much was his modesty a concealment. His modesty was of that kind induced in those intelligent enough for awareness of how much could lie beyond their own attainment, to know enough to know how much is still to be known. His gentle slightly wry sense of humour touched all he saw. In that best of ways he was a fisherman, as an inseparable part of his being a naturalist - ichthyologist, botanist, entomologist. He was a considerable linguist and, being so, was a regular contributor to the BBC World Service.

Beyond that he was very poor and would never be otherwise: his self-effacing modesty would allow no remedy. For a few years more Sandy lived in London. But the stridencies of metropolitan life had outpaced his tolerance. He must migrate; in Ireland he would find a haven.

He bought a bicycle. On it he wandered randomly through Ireland, so going till he should see and know that in this place he was to live. So it was he came to Kinsale.

In utmost snugness Kinsale is in the Co. Cork; no place could be more comely, of gentler serenity. It lies by the inner harbour secure from turbulences. Eighteenth century houses of most elegantly quiet good manners group down to the water and all is wrapt in peacefulness. So it was as I saw it when there I went long since. That change has touched it I know and have seen. Deeply I hope no drastic broom has swept too roughly. It was at Summercove, a small hamlet overlooking the outer habour's sweeping prospect that Sandy settled.

Also to settle at Kinsale came Elizabeth Friedlander. She was a distinguished typographer who had designed the typography of a number of Allen Lane's Penguin books. She was Jewish; her misfortune was that she was also German. The coming to power of the Nazis in 1933 forced her to flee.

In Italy, alone and in distress, she was found by Sandy: as was his way he befriended her. When, later, Sandy came to London, she followed him, there to become associated with Penguin Books. On Sandy's migration to Ireland there too she followed, settling in a cottage just up the lane from him in Summercove. Though without firm evidence, I am fairly sure that between them there was no sexual relationship: he was large of heart; she was grateful. In him she sought and found security. Probably fondly, she tyrannised his gentleness. Because Sandy fished, so must she. In a boat doing so she was alarming. Her way with a spinning rod and a lure well armed with hooks made cowards of all also in that thus perilous boat. There was a day when she, wildly active, nevertheless caught no fish when all but she did.

"The fish," said Sandy, "are anti-semitic."

In Kinsale there was also Tom White, and he too no native. He was English, and indeed of London as such of his remnant of speech declared. In the First World War Tom had been bayoneted in the face; he was apallingly scarred, his speech distorted. For him also Kinsale was final haven.

Tom White was a fisherman; more precisely he was a bass fisherman. For bass fishing Tom lived. Nowhere but at Kinsale could his passion have been more wholly fulfilled.

Now all that is utterly past. Tom, poor Tom, has gone: perhaps it is well he did not live on to see how later times have diminished that for which he lived. Sandy too has gone. All that era that was Kinsale is over, history already misting over. Kinsale remains lovely as last I saw it. But is it that place which drew to it Sandy and Tom?

In those quite early years of *Angling Times* there raged a battle now so soothed by time that probably few remember it. Very loudly it raged for several years. Its cause was for the saving of the canals, threatened with abandonment: canals, being not natural waterways, if abandoned first become choked then entirely dry and cease to be. So great a loss was not to be suffered; for so many in whom was the urge and the need to fish, the canals were their only means. Hardly less they were essential to boaters, naturalists, and others for whom they were places for walking.

Angling Times led the fight, it and I were deeply involved. We enlisted Members of Parliament, carrying the fight into the House of Commons, where, eventually, there came success. The canals passed into the care of the new Inland Waterways Board.

Uproar hardly less led me to the founding of a system for the recognition of record fish caught on rod and line. There was a day when Dr Cameron, an earnest and innocent angler, was fishing for salmon on the River Annan in Dumfriesshire. He hooked and landed a fish that for him, salmon angler as he was, was irrelevant. It was a chub. That it was such a chub as none had seen before entirely escaped worthy Dr Cameron, though it did seem to him rather large. Large it was; it was vast. It weighed 10lb 8oz. It was the biggest chub ever caught.

Little of consequence as that was, north of the border, south of it immediately there arose great passion. The catching of a chub of so dreamlike a size was anyway of so historic an importance among the coarse fishermen of the south that no other element for drama was needed. But had there been respect enough? Had this noble fish been honourably preserved in a glass case for the wonder of generations to come, or, alternatively, returned with honour to the river? There were uneasy, even ugly rumours.

This fish, so dreadful rumour claimed, had been taken home and fed to the cat. Such outrage looked as though it might brew up another Cullodden Field. But rumour in its treacherous way was false. Salmon fishers the Scots were, but not barbarians. The good Dr Cameron did perceive that his chub was not as commonly chub are. He took it home that others might see it, putting it with care and respect in, as it appeared, a place of safety. But - here began the rumour - the cat, enterprising as cats are, found the fish.

So many, and so engaging were the facets of this event that for *Angling Times* it was a great story, and, it appeared to me, one for the archives of angling. To Dumfriesshire I went to investigate. Verification had no difficulty; a number of unquestionably reliable people had seen the fish, and as certainly it was a chub and no other species. *Angling Times* declared it to have established a new record

That more or less settled the immediate matter, but equally it showed the need for a routine means for verification of record claims. There must be a record fish committee. To all interested bodies I wrote asking their co-operation. I wrote to the National Federation of Anglers, to *The Field* magazine, to Dr Jack Jones of Liverpool University, and others. A committee was formed sponsored by *Angling Times*, chaired by Howard Marshall, and including Sandy Mac Mahon, and representatives of those I had invited. So was founded the British Record Fish (rod-caught) Committee. It functions still.

From the birth of *Angling Times* has come most of what now is the world of angling - at least that of coarse fishing - and that for better or worse. Often a melancholy falls upon me when I see such absurdities as now are acceptancies. Angling, true to itself, is a retreat from stridences that predominantly are the stuff of modern life. Angling was and still should be a philosophy of quietness and acceptance that our most vital birthright is that we are of earth, and that we forget it to our great loss. Increasingly it is to our peril that we forget it.

But to angling now has come an athleticism, a vieing, a competitive urge. Even there is talk of the importance of angling. Exquisitely angling is not important: its importance is its unimportance.

One result of the advent of *Angling Times* was sad: those two aromatic old journals, the *Angler's News* and the *Fishing Gazette*, both intimate, a little quaint, well loved, could not survive. In fondest fashion they were amateur. The *Fishing Gazette* was a family property, that of the Marston family: I think they found it hard to forgive me. I cannot blame them.

From quite early in the life of *Angling Times* it had at its heart a maggot. For me it was to prevent its best fruition. Co-founder R.P. Winfrey and I were intrinsically unblendable. Before the birth of *Angling Times* the East Midlands Allied Press had no national papers. Its entire scope lay in a few local papers. It was provincial. My entire journalistic experience had been with national papers: the difference is fundamental. Nevertheless there need have been no difficulty.

But, there was Pat Winfrey. Unshakably he believed all from the metropolis suspect, lacking in worthiness: equally he was sure that truest worth was settled firmly at Peterborough. Hence whatever was of my devising must, alertly, be guarded against. He was adamant that only in Peterborough could there be final trust.

He had no sense of the pride of craftsmanship and its essential importance in journalism as in all else. His most deadly shaft against me, often used, was that I was 'a perfectionist'. I put that in quotes to convey its special and very critical sense as he used it - as of a social defect.

Pat Winfrey was urgent that I should transfer myself to live in the Peterborough area, thus assimilating into the EMAP family - as I think he not so much thought it as felt it. He was, quite sincerely, paternalistic. But his fathering was to an extent tyrannical, often choleric. His falling out of temper was spectacular, and by that much used as a tool. He would seem to swell, his head bulging down into his shoulders and his face suffusing, an alarming sight, and an effective deterrent. I found it peculiarly an irritant. Pat, rather smugly, as it seemed to me, called it having 'a paddy'. The pattern was that if Pat had a paddy it was a determiner of all. I, not a natural combatant, was always by that very coldly roused to opposition.

I did consider whether or not I should emigrate, thus to be absorbed. But, so I found, I could not. I feared it could blunt my professionalism; I knew also I would find it claustrophobic. I had tact enough not to say so. Pat Winfrey I fear was much frustrated.

At that time I lived in Sussex, and from there every Thursday made the journey to Peterborough there to spend a day in the office. Beyond that I kept in daily contact with Editor Jack Thorndike by telephone. So effective and intimate was our rapport that, working thus at home I could more sensitively direct editorial policy, write my weekly column, and do all the sub-editing of the features material. When later I moved to live in Wiltshire I drove every Thursday to Peterborough - a rather tiresome round trip, summer and winter, all weathers. But I was free of that sense of encompassing that Peterborough put upon me.

Incompatibility tended to stressful board meetings; often I think, to Pat Winfrey I appeared to be maddeningly stubborn.

"Just get it out," he would say, "just get it out."

Then would come that most damaging charge, that I was a perfectionist. Constantly it was apparent that we had no common ground. When crisis came it was with no pre-meditation.

In addition to my work on the paper, also there were books. Would it not, it was suggested, be good that I should do a book, a book so beautiful that, being under the *Angling Times* banner it would be an enhancement of the paper's aura.

No suggestion could have been more hungrily attractive to me than was that; I was afire to do it. The book was *The Angler's Companion.* I wrote the text, did the illustrations, designed the typography, designed the jacket and the binding. Its period of my producing it was stormy - necessarily it was slow, it being concurrent with my work on the paper. Pat, in a constant fume of impatience, harried me.

"Oh just get it out - all this bloody perfectionism - get it out." I, following my vision of a most beautiful book, plodded on. At last, at last, it was done: it was printed. My hoped-for happiness in the result was somewhat blunted by the quality of the colour printing (it was printed within the group). But it was very well received; it won most excellent reviews. Pat Winfrey made no comment to me, good or bad.

I think that in this, and in all his dealings with me, he was, perhaps not admittingly so, influenced by his absolute conviction that all that was Peterborough was unquestionably better than all that was London. I had come up from London, full of national press show. The more my work was successful the more distasteful that success may have been.

But *The Angler's Companion* was successful; its success prompted more books. In the paper I had been running my cartoon strip, Mr Cherry and Jim; I made it the basis of a series of paperbacks. To the strips I added a running text and additional drawings, designed the pages and the covers. I had done *Fishing for Roach with Mr Cherry and Jim*, *Fishing for Pike with Mr Cherry and Jim*, *Fishing for Perch with Mr Cherry and Jim*, and *Fishing for Trout with Mr Cherry and Jim*. Now I was working on *Fishing for Grayling with Mr Cherry and Jim*. As was my normal way I was seeking that all about it and the others should be comely and good. Pat Winfrey was growing daily more restive, prodding and urging that I should cease such time consuming fussiness. He served upon me a series of letters not so much persuasive as hammering. I replied as equably as I found it in me to be, and worked on. It was the cover design that brought the crack. For the previous book I had used a strapline title. Just, roared Pat from the letter page, drop the word 'grayling' into the strapline of one of the previous cover lay-outs. I pointed out that 'grayling' could not be dropped into a space that had accommodated 'perch' or 'pike.' Now, I suppose, we had both become tinder-dry touchy; it was a small thing. It was enough.

To all members of the board I sent copies of the entire correspondence. In my final reply to Winfrey I wrote - 'It is apparent that our difficulties of association are at crisis point.' Thus ended my nine years as Editorial Director of *Angling Times*. Under my contract I had full protection. But, I was advised, the manner of my going would be interpreted as my having ended my job myself. I received no compensation.

Old history all that is now. From the burgeoning of that first modest plant has grown a huge international magazine publishing company, EMAP. A few years ago I received from its Chief Executive an invitation to their AGM and luncheon. In his speech the Chief Executive declared that all the fortune that had come to the company, "had sprung from that editorial genius Bernard Venables." A huge photograph of me was thrown on a screen. He did not introduce me to the Chairman. I thought wistfully of all the treasure that was said to have derived from my 'editorial genius'.

CHAPTER XVI

A Change of Life

THAT this record shall be faithful demands here a gathering of strands. Life had not been exclusively of *Angling Times*: of it, I need say no more here than that what it has become since I left has no resemblance to that which I fathered. Though for painting time had been so restricted than was acceptable, it had continued. But there had been movement; rather a vagrancy.

While still I was on the *Daily Mirror* for a period I had lived at Mill Pond Farm. How pleasant a rural sound that has; and superficially that had some supporting factors, raised as it was above a lake and its millhouse converted to be a pub. But at the heart of that undeniably pretty apple there were maggots.

From the house a track dropped down beside a hedge in which nested hawfinches. The track at its bottom crossed a bridge which was my entrance and spanned a brook of great delight - if circumstances had allowed delight. This at-a-glance rural seclusion, just in Sussex out of Surrey, had a spirit suburban, only scantily wearing thin rusticity.

But there did appear means that should have been of happiness. In those first earliest ecstatic hours of summer morning and in the mystic twilights of their evenings there were fatly amber tench to be caught in the lake, and in winter pike. In the brook I did find a bliss of forgetfulness from what otherwise could have been unendurable. It was an outfall from the lake: for half a mile it ran through land I occupied, secretly under the fields' level. In its shadowed course of meanders under its alders it had a privacy so reclusively removed as to give relief. In spring when minnows became gallant in pride of spawning dress, there too in the clear rumple of the shallows, were the brook lampreys, *Lampetra planeri*, also at their spawning, but so much without spirit compared with sprightly pleasure of the minnows. They, the males, so gay with red and sparkle of gold and the females, more modest, but prettily pricked out with emerald gleams. But the lampreys - idly each one by its suctorial disk anchored inactive to a stone - for them little apparent mad joy of spring's renewal. I, wading in the whisper of current, in the tremble of light through leaf and bough, merged not only with minnows and lampreys; there were the bullheads, still even in this new dance of life a little glum as is their way, and the stone loach. They, skulkers as they are, did seem to show some lift of spirit. But a gay sense of new life did sing through the brook in spring. In summer's heat I could swim most privately in the deeper pools.

The semi idyll did not last. Mill Pond Farm was sold; I, its tenant, must leave. Very longingly I thought of further places, westerly, where good rivers ran, where country truly was country. So, passionately, my inclination was. But it was in the hands of circumstance; and what could be the wisdom of bearing with me to a better place the burden of a bitter marriage? To Hove in Sussex it took me, Hove and its sister Brighton, pleasant places, with their urban sea and 'Prinnie's lovely legacy of terraces and crescents and a fancy so elegant as is the Brighton Pavilion. During those years of Brighton and Hove, with fair consistency I exhibited at the Royal Academy: mostly my pictures were sold. Of those only one trips memory now - 'The White Bull Of Bramber' was its name;

it was bought by Mrs Elsie B. Beever. So pleasant a place as it was, for a time was stimulating. But a town, whatever its fancifulness, is a town. As certainly I am a countryman. For five years I compromised.

How odd it was that, returning then to what was to serve as country, by circumstance again I was carried; to Crawley, Crawley just into Sussex, just out of Surrey, a great pink-blanched waste of raw new urbanism dumped there to be a new town, as it was to become. Already then the gorging up of the countryside was creeping outwards, but the house I took still then was out of sight of what so dreadfully was advancing.

The house was 19th century and rather fine: a little grandiose and self-conscious in the manner of its time, but undoubtedly very pleasing, very rich in atmosphere. It stood upon a brow, its lawns dropping away in a series of terraces to fields that fell to a small brook. In its seven acres, mostly woodland, it was isolated, approached only by a long drive through great iron gates. It was also painfully expensive to run, a great deal more so than I could afford. My wife, of then, fell very easily into an exhilarating sense of costly grandeur. I too enjoyed the hard tennis court which had relapsed into wildness, a wild abandonment of rock roses (*Helianthemum*) in a lust of colour. I liked the fox that lived in the wood and came at breakfast time to sit on the terrace. The rhododendrons were flamboyant, a little declamatory; the bench seat set in a recess in the great yew hedge was a little suggestive of a patricianism. It gave my wife abundant patrician ideas too grand for my sustaining.

Not far off, darkly hidden, there was a pool. It lay, hardly approachable, deeply under a clustering of lofty trees, in a Sleeping Beauty entanglement of nettle and bramble. The pool was not large, perhaps a hundred yards long, in broad daylight dark within the loom of trees. Its owner was an elderly woman whom no one saw. So greatly she loved cats that in tiers against a wall she had thirty or more cats shut in little hutches. I, in the way of anglers, sensed that water was in that wilderness. Darkly snooping, following my nose, I penetrated, found the pool. There it lay, seeming that never had a ruffle of air stirred it. Just sub-surface, silkenly slowly, idling, cruising, were great fish, their backs blue, of a solidity a little queer in the slight unreality that there was on the air. It made of the fish a sort of immensity. They were carp.

I found the bailiff. "The missus doesn't like anglers. Thinks they're cruel - never gives permission for fishing - see the cats? But if you were to come after dark, leave before it gets light, it'd be all right."

On a night blackly dark I came, bearing rod, tackle bag, a sack, ground-bait and hook-bait, and the big landing net. All swung perilously as I climbed the rails of the iron fence. In the menacing dark, rustling, murmuring furtively, the nettles received me, forested above my head. After some penetration the crunch underfoot of shingle of glass told me I was passing a derelict greenhouse. Then, blindly stumbling, down a sharp fall of ground suddenly there was water.

Most of that first black night was unshared but for the rats: they scurrously pressing, ravenous, scuttered over my feet for the groundbait. But of such things there was culmination. When for two hours motionless I had sat in the pitchy tangle, for all that time holding the line in light touch of finger and thumb, that line, hardly bearably shrilling in the nerves, began to slide. It was slipping away - in that black water there was a life; it was taking the line. It was nothing of ghostly nature that responded to my strike. The heavy plunge, the searing run, were massively of substance - somewhere, somewhere, in the black insubstance of the night. It became dreamlike, strange in the clinging dark.

Many nights thereafter I climbed the fence. In others of them in the queerness and the silence I found the carp. Each time in the black anonymity the power astounded me, but still for that was more of dream than substance.

That haunted place they tell me, now is a public park. I suppose the light has been let in, the pitchy jungle gone. How inconceivable: I do not want to conceive it. I must never see that place again. I suppose I never shall; so much has moved on.

Just one other association there is of Crawley and that fine house.

It was there, finally, that I succumbed to Howard Marshall's persuasion. I agreed to throw in my job on the *Mirror* to join him in the *Angling Times* venture. Jack Hargreaves was urgent that I should not do it.

"You've too much to lose. Howard just wants this to take care of his old age."

I said that I had a good solid contract to look after me. Well, for Howard so thus it did work out that way. For the rest of his life he had an income from the paper. He had a pleasant house in the Lambourn valley and a delectable stretch of the river. At the time of my break with *Angling Times* he did not support me.

Then ugly destiny was approaching Woldhurstlea, that fine house. It was time to leave. A blanket of small houses was soon to smother all I knew. It was time: the cost was ruinous, too much even for my wife's aspirations.

I went to Ardingly. I found an ancient house. It was of the 14th century, dense with time. Time respired from its walls, soaked its air, smelt of its generations. Some of the generations would not vacate: the house was riddled with ghosts.

We came to know them all, with no sense of chill, no discomfort; we shared the house. There was that young lady who in one room was persistent; always she must draw back the curtains which had been drawn. I would not have known she was a lady young or old, but once in a train I fell into conversation with a man who revealed himself as having lived in that house for eighteen years before my coming. He had seen her, in a nightie.

We heard him who tramped the upstairs corridor in heavy boots. Julian, demonstrative with the bravery of teenage, declared that he and I should each take one of the two staircases at either end of the house. We did, and so met, finding nobody. Just another ghost. We came to know him well.

Constantly by night in a spare bedroom, endlessly talking, were an old woman and a small boy. Of course the room when entered was empty, but then the talking stopped. One had intruded.

My wife once was in that upstairs corridor sorting linen. When someone pushed heavily by her she was annoyed. On coming downstairs she said to her mother in the way she had, "Why the hell did you push past me like that upstairs?"

"I don't know what you mean. I've never stirred from here," her mother said.

It was an exceedingly attractive house, with high potential for happy living. It lay in pleasant neighbourliness with a farm still jogging its aromatic old way, not yet neutered into ugly 'efficiency'. It and we were poised on an abrupt plunge to a valley: in the valley ran a brook. That brook, so modest under its tunnelling of branch and bough, was more populace with fish than optimism could have suggested.

On a fine day of winter once I caught a beautiful sea trout. It was out of season. I never caught another.

Then in the midst of one summer's opulence, with no premonitory shadow, foot and mouth disease was identified on the farm. The squad moved in: slaughter swept through. The animals lay everywhere as execution had come to them, cattle and pigs, on their backs, stiff legs vertical like posts.

Of the corpses was made an enormous funeral pyre. The smell of its burning was fatty, oily-heavy; for days the pall hung.

Otherwise there was much that could have made happiness. On first coming to the house I was enchanted; I planted trees, worked the garden. In spring and early summer death-watch beetles emerging from the beams dropped on my desk as I worked. By that I suppose I should have been disturbed: but they did me no ill. They were as inevitably of the place as the bats that hung so bountifully in the great attic. They, sometimes, would intrude into the rooms: then I with a landing net must catch them for ejection.

How could I, it might be thought, so give myself to the house and garden when in it I must live out the unhappiness of a wrong marriage? But so for many years I had been living, with a sense of looking over a wall at the world beyond that had no part for me.

Already I knew when Julian was born. There were better times and worse times, but never were better times better enough. But Julian was born; a human life with life to live, to have childhood. I must stay. I would stay until he should be twenty-one.

So it had gone, year by year. Now Julian was twenty and perhaps that nudged me. Perhaps so it was; but the pressure was becoming less tolerable, biting more deeply each day, till each loomed so darkly as hardly to be born. Then it was not to be born. On Boxing Day 1958 I crammed into the car all that I could of working materials, fishing gear, and books. I drove away. I never returned. Julian became twenty-one in the March following. I left behind me nearly all I possessed. There were many beautiful things: I have not seen them again. Subsequently I did recover most of my books and a very few other things. But life began again.

Julian had a girlfriend, thirteen years older than he, and quite soon they were married. They lived on in the house, in uneasy sharing with my wife. From there each morning on a moped he rode to Haywards Heath to get a train to London. One morning a coal lorry knocked him down. For five months he lived in a coma. Then he died.

Bernard and Julian fishing the Hampshire Avon.

Chapter XVII

Event and Joy of '59

1959 was a year impossible of forgetfulness. I was free. No more of that long unhappiness. It was a year, as though symbolically, made glorious by its weather. I who have lived in most of the summers of the 20th century, remember none that fully matched that of 1959. A perfection, a kind of floating bliss, lay over all till well into late October, when in my mother's garden still there bloomed a riotous glut of summer flowers. A year of happiness sweeter for its long delay. It was as though by an ordination all might reflect that year's central fact: that in the loveliness of 1959 I laid the foundations of a marriage which, as I write, is over forty years old. In that time it has augmented by three children and three grandchildren.

I left Sussex; I left its unloved memory. For six months of vagrancy I searched, westwards, where, so long, desire had been directed. So, in July, we came to Ham. Ham was compact, neatly, prettily, peacefully set about its green. East Court stood back a little, verging upon the village but at the end of its drive, overlooking its paddock and the village beyond. In East Court we settled.

East Court had been a farmhouse and so had been from the 18th century: it sat in its landscape in modesty, unobtrusively, just touched with elegance as was the way of its time, its brick patinated by the soft kiss of time into mottlings of pink, russet, lichened yellows. In the garden the lawn sloped up on the right to a slight eminence: there stood a horse chestnut tree of the pink blossomed kind which, at the time of its blossoming came into opulent glory, tier upon tier of blossom to the summit. In the manner of its species at all seasons it had majesty - in winter a supple-limbed massiveness of form. Beyond its sentinel station there was the orchard. It is the nature of orchards that hardly may they be anything but pleasant plots, but widely differing in kind. That of East Court was of that sort: least in usefulness but great in character. In yield it had to be admitted spent but richly ripe in the gathered grace of age. Not entirely had it fallen into sterility; still a treasured ancient inhabitant there was a Blenheim Orange, which, surely beyond dispute, is one of the most loveable of apples. This tree, bent with its burden of years, gnarled and fissured, each year bore its crop of huge fruits, sumptuously orange, richly sweet in a way peculiar to its kind. That tree, alone but for one other, then, upheld bygone virtues. Still there was a plantation of filbert nuts: but the rest was colonised by huge clumping hollies, hollow, within all sorts of scrambling things. In a corner against the garden an elm towered; at the orchard's end, above the road, a columnar clustering of ashes had a perennial rookery, which every spring filled all the hours of day with its warmth of sound.

Ham, still at that time, was unspoilt. It was cosy about its green. It had its lovely manor house at the lane's end against the church; the little pub faced the green and all was as comely as it is one's right to expect a small village to be. It lay at a meeting of little roads too obscure for any notice of the world at large. Four miles away was Hungerford, shopping town for Ham. And, by Hungerford, ran the Kennet, so long of my desiring.

Shark fishing from Falmouth, Cornwall.

But when January of the year 1959 came in, all that was still to come. In that January was a train of events to match something of my childhood's fantasy. Fantasy's adult renewal fell upon shark; an obsession with shark, almost unimaginably monstrous, shadowed my mind. Surely, it grew upon me, in some dark depth of ocean there must be a shark of enormity to chill the mind.

My obsession had its origin in Cornwall. In Cornwall's offshore waters about this time there had begun angling for shark. To Cornwall I went, and soon had caught numerous shark. The first thrilling excitements of so doing by then were passed; of those caught quite a few exceeded 100lb; the majority were less. Even it became a little repetitive. But through this scale so much of reduction, I had seen much of the essential being of shark. Of those that so swarmed beyond the holiday beaches most were blue shark, creatures of a beauty coldly distilled, as though all not relevant to their menace had been reduced from them. Their backs were blue, a clear blue intensified by the milky white, suede-textured, of their bellies. Their motion, silkenly sinuous, so liquid as if not of physical intention, increased the sense of their menace. When drawn to the boat their pale eyes empty of all, flickered with opening and closing of their nictitatic membranes, making a peculiar intensity of emotionless malignancy, half uncanny. So seeing these creatures, so queerly detached in a disinterestedness of ferocity, seeing them day by day, they set upon me a deepening fascination while the catching of them began to pall.

Out of fascination grew gradually a compulsion to come upon them in their fearfulest size, to engage them by angling with rod and line. For the scanning of my mind's eye I called up the world's oceans, seeking to know where in them all I might most certainly find what I sought. That so I could in Australian waters I knew I could; I had no means of getting there. I must find some place less far. But surely it would be possible by a biologically perceptive scanning at least to achieve a high probability. So it was that I came to a scrutiny of the Caribbean's tropical waters. There it was to be seen, rose the Gulf Stream, that great oceanic river, broad, deep blue, independently flowing, going its destined way.

From its ocean birth the Gulf Stream flows north-easterly into the Atlantic, carries the warm water of that nativity. It comes to Bermuda, to the Sargasso Sea, vastly deep, inexhaustible in its richness of planktonic fertility, carrying with its warm water that gathered fertility. Still north-easterly it traverses the perimeter of the abyss which is the central Atlantic, coming to the Azores. Now, as the North Atlantic Drift, it comes at last to the mass of Europe, there to give its gift of warmth.

That is not its end: it bifurcates. One arm turns northward with its warmth; the other southward, past the Iberian Peninsular, past Gibraltar, past North Africa, coming then to Madeira.

There, biologically, dramatically, it meets the deep cold Canary Current. The meeting of warm and cold currents causes eruptive upsurge of plankton: it is from plankton there comes all else. Thus, the Gulf Stream, a river that rises in the sea, flows all its course in the sea, at Madeira an island off the coast of Africa, thousands of miles from its source in the Caribbean, at last there makes a biological phenomenon. Could it be otherwise than that Madeira was the place I sought? Whatever might be elsewhere, at Madeira, a shark of enormity must await its finding.

Where plankton proliferates vastly so all thrives greatly above in the pyramid: at its apex must be great shark.

In January 1959, by courtesy of the Bergen Line, I sailed from Southampton aboard their ship the *Venus*, still at that time, before its being fitted with stabilisers, more often called the 'vomiting *Venus*', and on this black and blowing evening of January the sea of our embarking was disturbed enough to upset quite stable stomachs. Coming out of Southampton Water the sea took us, shook us, continuing so to do with gale force 8 all the way to Funchal on Madeira.

Nevertheless at dinner that first night out there was quite a brave showing of diners. Even, faithful to our hosts' wishes, we, Ted Scott and I, had put on dinner jackets (Ted had come to take photographs). That first show alas had no continuity: the sea's incessant spite took its toll, night by night deleting diners, leaving soon but few survivors. I, perhaps a little on my mettle, continued each night to make staggering way to a bathroom, contriving unstably to achieve a bath in the absurdities of the bath, thereafter into a dinner jacket.

One lurching morning, when all heaved in one grey tossing merging of sea and sky, out of its sightless wilderness came a vessel of the Royal Navy into hailing distance. As later we learnt from our Norwegian captain, the RN commander asked had we need of help. Very proudly, our captain answered that all was entirely well with us. A majority of his passengers surely could have qualified that. But I was wildly happy. In this was a stripping away of life's day to day irrelevancies, a raw encompassing.

One morning, we dropped anchor in a soft delight of sun in Funchal harbour. The netherworld through which we had come made it celestial.

Immediate impression was of an eruption, a pile of lambent colour from the Atlantic's blue plane. That, to more settling sight, became an extravagance of blossom draped upon the island's aspiring flanks, level upon level. All had a sense of floating in evasively scented air. In the languid warmth, grew oranges, grapes, clinging small orchards of bananas, proliferations of every sort of fruit and flower and bowering tree that in sub-tropics may flourish.

For much of its circumference it fell precipitously to the sea in sheers of awful threat, evidences of what had made Madeira. Nebulously lost in earth's primordial forming, a volcano was thrown up from far black ocean depths: its merest tip above the surface sea was to be the island of Madeira. The aeons between have besieged it. Uncounted centuries of the sea's assault gnawing into its adamantine flanks. So now are left those precipices that by their fearful verticals frighten the senses. Under them, are the inshore shallows. They, to match so mighty a context, are 600 metres deep. But no more than a few hundred metres from the sun-kissed beaches there is an edge which is a frontier: it has a name which, translated from the Portuguese, is 'The Noisy Sea'. It is there that all that is of the land is lost. There is a vast plunge to a thousand fathoms and more to the ever-lightless deeps.

Imagination, pressed by awe almost could swoon for conjecture of what appalling shark there might lurk. How was I, in the light, feeling the sun's caress, to consider the awesome immensity in which somewhere, must be the great shark of my seeking. To find it, perhaps to catch it, I had ten days; of those bad weather was to rob me of five. Then the *Venus* would return and I must board her.

In a riddle so hugely amorphous the odds had an insuperable look: was I, almost, though not quite bereft of knowledge of this unaccustomed marine environment, to find a point of starting, and from it a practicable course? But not entirely was I without feel, sense, orientation: life in water, fresh or salt, large or small is directed by basic principles. All creatures in water, however modified appropriately for their niches, must eat, satisfy their chemical needs. Shark must eat, constantly, raveningly they must eat. If a place may be located with an obvious capacity for meeting so great a need, as obviously it is a place for beginning.

At Machico then, on Madeira's easterly tip, there, as also at the Azores, primitive open-boat hand-harpoon whaling still pursued its relict way (of which I will tell later in this book). Still then to the whale factory were brought whales for the bloody business of 'cutting-in'. That done the fearsome mess of blood and guts were discharged from the flensing platform into the sea. Where more appropriately should be a great shark with its gargantuan hunger?

I being under the kindly wing of the Tourist Board had for my use its big game launch, it and its crew. Of them was its skipper Augusto, his son Fernando and the engineman Orlando; Ted and I completed the ship's company. Augusto at first was a surly fellow; life aboard his *Altair* hitherto had been one of peace little disturbed by importunate calls to action; now came I bringing mess and unease. And indeed, still in England I had had warning doubts - suppose some small but essential part were broken - suppose even that it should be the gimbal of the fighting chair? I took with me a replacement gimbal.

My doubt was not unworthy. *Altair's* gimbal was broken. How providential my replacement: without it, all would have been aborted.

But before any half-considered embarkation to anywhere I had met Dr Ribeiro who then was the only big game fisherman on Madeira; he it was who told me of The Noisy Sea. He though wishing me well, said that though well enough their waters seethed with shark of all species, they knew of none bigger than 200-300lb. My conviction was undisturbed: biologically there must be in those waters mind-assaulting monsters.

By that same biological reckoning where but there should be that which I sought? Where but there could it feed so effortlessly? On a morning high with hope we turned eastward out of Funchal, going minuscule under the frightful plunge of precipice to Machico. Under the whale factory we started, making drifts with a bait of dead fish at about twenty-five fathoms of depth. Thus through the day till evening we did, finding no least evidence of shark.

I was yet to understand the crucial factor of scale in this immensity.

I, though still convinced that at Machico if anywhere must come crowning event, listened to advice most warmly given. On Funchal was an angling club; its name was *O Estaleiro* and was of a most jolly and friendly membership. At once it saw itself as dedicated to our support in all ways. They, excellent men, held a dinner for Ted and me; at the long narrow table, at one end they put Ted, at the other me. It was a simple meal, peculiarly and fondly memorable. First came tuna, which at first unaccustomed sight was startling - so very darkly red, of such meaty solidity. After it came swordfish, it by nature so good that only bad cooking could spoil it. Apart from a rich sauce nothing else accompanied the fish but a red wine of huge depth and strength. Of the club's membership one was Avelino Camara, and of memories of this adventure none lives more sharply than he. As clips of memory come before me always there is Avelino Camara, urgent, passionately participating.

In so much amorphous scope for guessing there, I who had come to Madeira rather more as a dog follows a scent and, so drawn had come to the whale factory at Machico, nevertheless was avid for all that local experience could tell me. Particularly I listened to Avelino Camara and Dr Ribeiro. Of Ponto do Pargo I was told by Dr Ribeiro. There he said, at Madeira's point of wester extremity, where the Atlantic's swells rolled down from the north, there was a lighthouse; beneath it was a place of particular gathering of shark. A bait drift started from immediately below the lighthouse would cover them.

To those who go in minor boats Ponto do Pargo is a place of frowning threat: the enormity of precipice is vertical to the remote perch above of the lighthouse. When we, venturing, came round the point the high broken crests of the northerly swells drove down upon us that we must run for shelter under the lee of the island. For the rest of that day, thinking of The Noisy Sea, we went out bearing south. A fishing boat, coming up on us waved us on, further told us, till Machico becomes visible beyond the point.

When there we came, I, seeking to take down a bait, found that impossible for all the leads I might use. The heavy force of current swept the tackle streaming along the surface.

It was then, stalled in frustration, we, Fernando, Orlando and I, fell into conversation. They told me that though we lay in such a balm of soft sun's warmth, this in their terms was winter. Being so, life within the ocean sounded to its third dimension; it went deep.

Now there came to me understanding of the vast plunge. They told me of how the commercial fishermen with their hand lines turned to the abyss, catching their fish at 1000 fathoms or more, bring up swordfish and others that in summer would be of the upper waters. They told me too of fish forever native of the black deep, never seeing light. Of these was a fish so adapted to its environment as to look hardly a fit sight for bland light of day; its body long, eel-like, its head huge, its mouth cavernous, its teeth a palisade of great fangs, its colour black or white. But not for its look was it so sought; its excellence on the table was enough.

I had come to Madeira with an outlook borne of Cornish shallow seas within Europe's continental shelf. That by comparison with Madeira's vertical deeps was almost two-dimensional. That did not lessen my belief that I must be led back to the whale factory: only by going too closely into shallow water had I been mistaken. A scent trail will draw shark from distances of miles.

Avelino Camara told me now of the Desertas, that tiny island projection 20 miles offshore from Funchal: there he said was one of *O Estaleiro's* best fishing grounds. Many shark were there said Avelino; strangely primordial looked this little archipelago when we came to it.

When the first fires of earth's beginning began to cool, when the molten upthrust solidified, the Desertas were left where now they stand, rock fangs as though newly set, their drip still not stable, yellow red-streaked; the sea's surge through them throwing up heavy white laces on the glistening spire. There is in the sense of this place, lonely, sea-besieged, that the aeons gone have passed unnoticed.

One shark I did catch there, a little thing, seventy-odd pounds - "It is winter you see," said Avelino.

My time was shortening. It came to Sunday, a non-fishing day: quite early in the day there came Avelino. At Machico he said a great fish had been caught on a hand line. To Machico we must go at once. On the beach there it was, a shark, perhaps 400lb, a species I had not seen before. Its eyes were large as is the way of fish of deep water, its teeth of nightmare ferocity. Those of the lower jaw

3 inches or more long, serrate, sloping-edged, with those conical ones of the upper jaw making scissors of frightful threat. It had been taken just offshore from the whale factory. Its suggestion was strong that from the beginning I had been right. Now I was confident, in doubt no longer. The last link in the chain was joined. This evening I must make all ready.

With Ted I walked up to Reid's hotel: there, I had been told was a Welshman on his honeymoon with his bride. I knew further that she, so staying had had pneumonia and that he was a salmon fisherman. I told him of what was toward; would he feel ready and competent to gaff a giant shark? Undoubtedly, enthusiastically so would he be.

But I said, what of his wife? Could he leave her still so convalescent? Uh yes, yes he could - "This," he said, "is important." The rest of that evening, now perceived to be historical, I devoted to the preparing of tackle fitting for my large intention. My line was of 130lb breaking strain; of it I had on the reel 600 yards.

At its end would be the trace, one able to receive much stress; it was 24 feet of powerful metal braided cable of 560lb breaking strain in four 6-feet lengths joined by swivels. But such apparent massive strength was not all. Had I not seen how powerful the strength of current, how all the lead I could use would not sink the bait? And was it not essential that immediately the bait should sink to the bottom?

Equally it was seen to be preferable that the bait should be a little clear of the bottom: my sinker must be a lump of rock, at once to be jettisoned on the hooking of the fish. To the last swivel then, 6 feet from the hook, I would tie fairly low breaking strain nylon. Upon hooking, the nylon would break.

All was ready: the next day which was to be my last must see culmination. I think I slept well that night.

Under the precipices in the morning we sailed to Machico; with us too were Avelino and the young Welshman David Bassett.

The day, my last and destined day, started fine but with early signs of threat of that torrential rain which is characteristically of Madeira's winter. On the quay there were those who had caught the shark, a man and two boys, one about thirteen, the other about seventeen. They, now of our company, put us first on a mark too far out, then moved us in, a mile off Machico. A bigger sea had begun to run; the sky darkened: the drama had begun. The hook was baited, a cluster of squid a foot long, topped off with six sardines. By its rock as weight it was lowered over the side.

But the rock, that lump of basalt, was inadequate. The current seized it, tore it away sub-surface. The seas were still augmenting. It was plain that not from the deck of *Altair* would I plumb that chasm of depth.

We put back into Machico, from there towed a small boat, perhaps 12 feet of length; in its stern was a small decking, in that a square hole. Into that now I went with my tackle - I sitting on the decking with legs in the hole. The man and the boys were to row to counter the drift, so allowing me to get the bait down. Upon the hooking of the shark we were to call up *Altair* that I might get aboard and into the fighting chair.

Now under the lowering pall of sky we were cast off on the leaden lift and fall of swell, sometimes seeing *Altair* sometimes not. Now, I could get the bait down, freed from the tyranny of current - though for that I must sacrifice 550 yards of my 600 yards on the reel, leaving only 50 yards for whatever crisis might come. But the bait was down; I felt the infinitely softly distant bump of the rock touching bottom. The rain began.

Then, so soon, after only minutes, quietly, far below, a pluck, a pluck again: then, profoundly heavy, a draw. I had struck: an answering force, vast in its distant cushioning of water; slowly as though the pull was from within the basaltine ocean floor, then wakening to a ferocity of power. *Altair* was signalled and came bucketing over the swells.

Now *Altair* had come up, yawning, bouncing in the swell. To get aboard a launch from a bouncing dinghy often is not easy: now it was not. *Altair* gave me not the stern's low freeboard but the bow, high sloped against me, railed. Many hands helped. I was aboard, soon in the fighting chair. The gimbal was of a kind, now obsolete, that for the rod's security must have a pin passed through a hole in the butt and through matching holes in the gimbal. That Avelino strove to achieve while I strove to achieve some sort of competence with the as yet unconceived enormity far below.

"Up a bit," said Avelino. I could not.

"Down a bit," said Avelino. The butt was as though welded. It was at last achieved.

For the gaining even of a yard of that reluctant line I strove, my mere human strength more desperate than hopeful. If just a little, I raised that fearful force below. The rain came now, vertically, solidly, with impact, with immediate saturation. Then strangely in that high stress of every second there was nothing but the empty heave of sea. The rod was straight; no mighty force was there. Stunned half-sick with deflation, I forlorn, wound in the limp unactivated line. There at last was the trace. Its 560lb breaking strain metal cable had been bitten through as if it were but a wisp of wool. Silently we looked; of what inconceivable mouth was that evidence?

Then renewed with trace and rock and bait, into the dinghy again. The rain passed and came again. I had out more than 550 yards of line, leaving little for what might come. Time ticked away, we rolled on the swell; an hour passed.

Then as before, from within that black pit of sea, a soft enormity of draw. I struck: again an imponderable power, too far as it seemed for connection, wrenching down my shoulders. Quite slowly, inexorably that which was there was running, taking vital yards of line; I without power to stop it. Then, a dead weight, it stopped. I gained a few yards, straining nearly horizontally backwards to steal more. *Altair* was coming up. Again the monster sheered as a movement of earth. The rod, in the hole against my leg, shifted, jammed across my shin. I struggled to free it; the rod jammed more fiercely. My leg soon must break. Then, frantically, I had freed it. I was aboard *Altair,* in the fighting chair. Below, far in the black depth, a huge guessed-at monster was fighting me for a few yards of line.

What followed has become something of no specific shape or time, an endless haze of vast and painful struggle pierced by sudden sharp illuminations of memory. *Altair* was drifting out from the land's shelter. Recurrently, violently, the rain came. Through the pain's now dream-like continuance ran a thread, blindly now, not of reason. Not one yard of my too limited line I must yield. I must gain line, stealing it by feet and inches.

My back, my arms, my shoulders, burned; thrust of feet against the gunwhale put fire in my legs but I must gain line, lift the monster. Once its sudden plunge wrenched me half out of the chair before I could slacken off the reel's clutch. Now no beginning had there been, now no forseeing of an end. Never a time when I had not been locked in this fight. The ponderous force of what was below, that and the sea's sullen heave, had thrown me so heavily and often against the arms of the fighting chair that I seemed not to have a part left unbroken.

But, not believably, there came a change; without my having sense of it. I had gained line, had lifted the shark. Change of pressure now was my ally. There came a moment as of a return to rationality, a sense that there could be an end, I could win. Then, after a time immeasurable, there came an immortal moment. Incredibly, above the surface, there was the knot of the top of the doubled line; then, most lovely sight, the top swivel of the trace. Then, 30 yards from the boat, a sight that not a lifetime has expunged, through the surface came the vast astounding head of the shark, surely too huge for belief. How was I to believe that awesome width of head though there it was? And, most strangely, its eye, which seemed pointedly to fix on mine, appeared almost unnaturally large: it was brilliant emerald-green.

There at last was my monster, so long obsessionally only of my mind, now rolling, thrashing in the surface - not in the least less a fevered dream, as much an enormity.

Later, perhaps half an hour - how am I to know? - I had brought it near the boat: it was the moment of the gaffing. For best certainty, I had told him who had the gaff, apply it in the middle of the back; he, good man was so braced for action - but not to the approval of the local men. They were insistent that in the mouth it should be, thus, as I thought, bringing into too close proximity

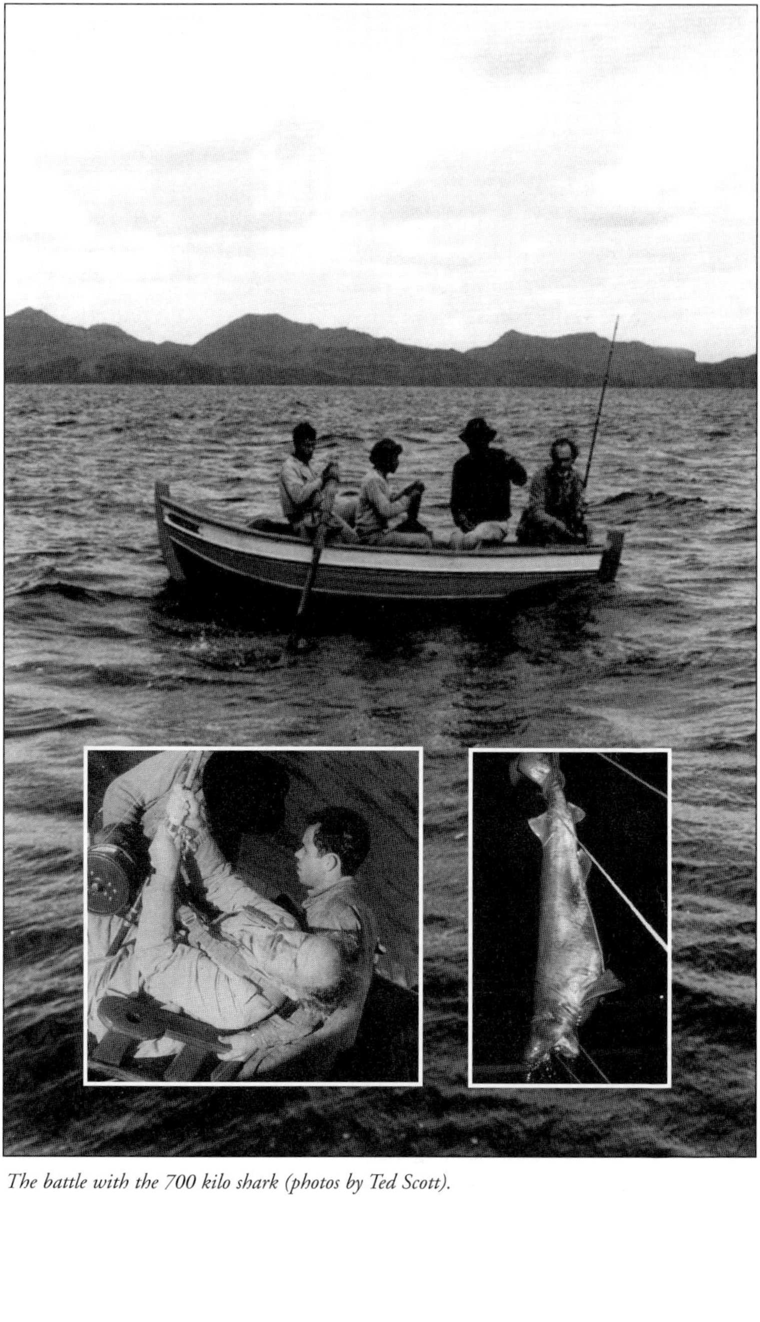

The battle with the 700 kilo shark (photos by Ted Scott).

that fantasy of frightful teeth. This led to some physical struggle in which, as I think mercifully, my Welshman won. This gaff was of the kind that has a flying head - upon the gaff's going home the head detaches, trailing a warp the end of which is made fast to a cleat, so giving a means of drawing the fish close for roping. Here again was disagreement. Rope it at the tail I had said, then by going full-ahead the shark is drowned. This engagement was won by the local men: the rope was secured round the enormous girth, raising the head from the water, where, so reachably close, it was fearfully potentially calamitous - its green-glaring eye, its multiple ranks of fangs.

Now came upon the boat a red miasma - here was the primordial monster at the cave's mouth. The men at their most dreadful peril, suddenly were armed - one with a huge screwdriver, one with a breadknife, one with my sheath knife, whatever could be seized, all frenzied at the gunwhale, plunging, stabbing. Quickly the beast was utterly subdued. Now utterly I was tired, triumphant, but passive as a noisy haze of tumult was over me.

As now I discovered, throughout all, ship-to-shore radio had been reporting. Now, putting back into Machico, what appeared to be its entire population was on the the quay - they sang, they shouted; uncounted dark hands seized mine. All the men of Machico manned the rope hauling, singing in unison so that the shark could be slid into the well of *Altair*. Now, as we steamed back to Funchal, aboard there was an air of festival. Augusto, no longer grumpy, almost jolly, produced a bottle of brandy.

At Funchal, where was gathered a great crowd, also was Dr Ribeiro, quietly supervising. From *Altair's* insufficient space a crane lifted the shark, the lorry alone was weighed: a simple sum showed the weight of the mighty shark to be 700 kilos, which, translated, was more than 1500lb. But, it was pointed out, the fish had been out of the water many hours, being by that dehydrated; it had also had great loss of blood. Final conjecture was that its most probable weight had been 1700lb. So was my obsessed vision ratified. It was a six-gilled shark (*Hexanchus griseus*).

Now all being done, Dr Ribeiro reminded me that that evening

I was engaged to dine with him and his Irish wife. I, so embattled as I had been, horrifyingly had forgotten. And several hours late in all that had been, how unacceptable a dinner guest I must be, so soaked and re-soaked, so tainted. But said Dr Ribeiro that such a day was this as to override such trifles. Characteristically his Irish wife was warmly unaffectedly friendly in her welcome.

So dramatic a beginning as was that of 1959 might have suggested a pattern for the year: it was a prelude for the better contrast with the months of tranquil happiness which followed. In July we came to East Court, there to sink into a peace not only of the present placid assuagement, but as much of all those other days lived there. The sense, almost an odour, seeped from its beams and lichened brick.

Ham lay under the domination of 'The Hill'. Almost it could be said to be dense with its sense of pre-history. In the high emptiness of its wind- and sheep-cropped grass, past and present were never quite certainly separate.

From the village the road mounted to where, abruptly, the hill's flank flung steeply up. Debouching there narrowly into the hill was 'the old road', though no road had it been. In the bottom of its deep cleft it was close, a foot-track, overhung by eroded ramparts of an ancient defence. It had guarded the ditch below, itself defensive against those of dangerous intent. Now, but for its shades, the ditch was as lonely as a forest, drowsy with drifts of butterflies; orchids crowding in the sun with every sort of plant that loves the chalk. Into it only a few steps from the road and it and all it signified were lost. Aerially on the top, soft winds stirred scents of thyme and marjoram: sheep cropped the earthworks that had been living place.

In the village, where pre-history nudged less persistently, the pub sat benignly facing the green. It and all else showed no awareness of how soon the coarse hand of the modern world was to fall upon it. Across the road was the school, a little place, 19th century brick and flint. Against the green the Admiral, at last gone from the sea, lived and, in a friendly fashion thought about God.

"Once," he said to me, "I was shipmates with a bear."

From the kitchen window of East Court the eye could wander, settling on Ben Rolfe's cottage where often as not he pottered in the garden. In that and all else he had no deviances; all was of quiet establishment, summing up his ways proven by the wearing of his eighty-odd years. All had their seasons. Summer having come to its appropriate time, Ben, pipe burning gently, would work the length of his hawthorn hedge. No modern absurdities such as shears would Ben use: his motions with his rip-hook were economical and the hook rightly sharp. It left the hedge as neatly finished as a pillow. Every evening, pipe still burning sweetly, he took his slow way to the pub because there, every evening, he and other ancients smoked pipes and played dominoes and had their beer. They were silent games: nod and grunt sufficed.

Thus it had been for time forgotten, always in the bay of the little saloon bar. An incoming landlord, with thoughts of social uplift, shunted them; he sent them sorrowing into the public bar. It was the first deed in the spoiling of Ham.

Beyond the pub Ben did not stir much about the village: out of it he did not stir at all. Except just twice a year. Then he made the 4-mile expedition to Hungerford that he might buy new underwear.

Citizens of Ham in those still simple times were more often of local, indigenous occupation than otherwise. Otherwise there were the Admiral, he of the Manor, Lady Hudson at Dove's House, and a slight dusting of those retired. There was one other. Just up from the village, there was Geoff Webb. Inescapably Geoff was of the village; by all in the village Geoff was well loved.

To us, sitting in the saloon bar on our first evening down to the pub, there came Geoff from the public bar. His coming was in effect one of official welcome to Ham. He would have been thus kindly anyway, but particularly he came in professional brotherhood; were we not both writers by profession?

Geoff was creator and writer of *Dick Barton,* that radio thriller that, reliably as nightfall every evening was on the radio. Or so it was until time came for the birth of *The Archers*, as certain in its coming every evening. Its creation and its continuance were the work of Geoff and of Ted Mason. By turn and turn about they did it.

Geoff was tall, somewhat gangling, a friend for all. Night by night in the public bar he was the centre of its ambling clubbiness, a communal uncle. He was a consistent upholder of pubs, because in pubs farmers spent much of their ample leisure, and they, swapping drinks with Geoff, were his raw material for *The Archers*. So, largely, Geoff used his days. He worked by night.

In the large-natured way that was his, so always was his car large, adequately to contain the sense of him. Things being as they were, times there were when his driving of this so-appropriate car was erratic. Against the green the road took a turn too tight for a car so large; against the road on the further side was a ditch. It and Geoff were well acquainted. As I came by one evening there was Geoff, he in the car, he and it lurched over one side down in the ditch.

"There I go again," said Geoff, melancholy in apology. I knew what to do; I told the public bar.

Immediately it emptied, almost as though routinely car and Geoff were surrounded, hand-lifted from the ditch.

It was our way, his and mine, in the evening to drive to Hungerford to post our copy. So one evening in June I went - the Mayfly was up - I after posting was going to fish the evening rise, I was not to fish that night.

At the top of the drop-down into Hungerford the road was blocked and Geoff's car, slantwise across the road, was jammed into, half under a lorry. Inside sprawled in the driving seat was Geoff. He was dead.

So it fell to me to carry this stark news to his wife. For a moment she stared. "Has he gone?" she asked.

But this was not of 1959, it was 1962, and that I knew well because it marked two points of mortality. To poor Geoff came his termination, and the birth in September of our daughter Hannah Naomi.

But for the whole sun-mellowed passage of 1959 nothing intervened to mar its days. Briefly in the first few weeks we were whisked away to Cornwall where I must do a television programme; but that disturbance soon was sunk and lost in the

Hannah, four weeks old, 1962.

Hannah, Guy and Aaron with Eileen, 1968.

Bernard and Hannah, 1963.

deep contentment of the days. I did my work, I fished, I painted.

On the Kennet at Kintbury there is a canalised length, very sweetly arboured with willow and alders. Reed labyrinths lined it, coots and moorhens forever fussed about their privacies. There very early I found a place where a faintest whisper of current crept down to pass under a low railway bridge. It was a place of congregation; teeming there, huddled even, were roach of such size and beauty as I had not seen before.

There on many gentle days we were, I to fish, she to read under a great willow, in a companionship that had no need of words.

The happy sequence of 1959 was unbroken. It seemed the glory of the weather would never cease. When November came, we eager to try out the inglenook hearth with its first log fire, the warmth of weather forbade it. Loving memory can see now that, lovely as all was, its loveliness is better seen because it was the last of many things that change has dimmed.

Still Hungerford was unaware of the bruising urgencies of what the world had become. A slow amiability lay on everything. Shops were almost as much clubs as places of merchandising: in the gracious breadth of the High Street there were two grocers of the old kind, equally cheek by jowl. Spackmans, in its 18th century bow-fronted house appeared as much a social provision as for its groceries that, anyway, were excellent.

Hungerford then had not questioned the priority of strolling feet. Old ladies meeting in mid crossing of the High Street would stay to chat. Traffic with care and courtesy, would steer round them. When occasionally a passing-through car, crudely unaware, hooted them, it caused astonishment. The High Street's concern was with such importances as how good this year was to be the mayfly hatch. Alas for that dear Hungerford before the M4 Motorway thrust through. Not then had it become a dormitory for those of London connections.

As sadly, change came creeping to eat out the soul of Ham. Ham, so pretty, so quaintly countrified, was delightfully suitable for a weekend cottage: no less how entirely right a retirement place for the well-heeled elderly.

BV in his studio at Fosbury.

Just beyond the orchard, beyond the lane, East Court had a neighbour, an ancient cottage. Within it lived a middle-aged couple in cosy retirement. Within a short time of our coming he died which a little later caused his wife to leave.

The cottage was bought, its buyer a man amply rich. The builders moved in, piece by piece dis-articulated the cottage. In one pile were stacked bricks; in another the ancient timbers that had been its frame. Into the sumptuous house erected there were incorporated the sad relict members of the cottage. All sense of what had been was lost in the new large opulence.

Hardly had so much so expensively been done than the Manor came onto the market and at once was bought by he who had done so much for the cottage. That was sold to a rich woman who, we have been told, sometimes comes there. A high wall against the road gives some security.

It is relevant to reveal that he was not in the least the sort of person these facts might suggest. He was irreproachably a nice man, honourable. Deeply he would have been shocked by any suggestion that his presence in the village was not entirely for the good of all. But his was the main agency that forever destroyed what had been the old Ham. Not for long though did he stay: after a few years he moved elsewhere.

1959 which had begun to feel a permanence, did at last slip into 1960, thence into 1962. It came to Christmas of that year: in the evening of Boxing Day the village was quietly festive. The holly wreath hung on the door of the pub; its lights were bright; its bars busy.

"Looks like snow," some said: flurries were coming on the wind.

At closing time those who had parked cars could not find them. Snow had buried them. Roads, their banks, all marks were gone, cosy under an even swathe of snow. The narrow cleft of the road to Hungerford was not visible. The high banks, the fields, all were of one level. To the pub must turn those bereft of their cars, there to be stoical for the night.

A strange world the light of morning showed, without roads, without hedges, a blind white pall that neutered all. Ham was entirely alone within its pall of snow. But Buttermere, nakedly at the mercy of weather's worst spites on the hill's bare crest, how was it faring? It at all times was its own small lost world perched in isolation. There, there was a farm, a minute church, two or three houses and much wind-assaulted loneliness. There was another farm further back, not poised on the brink of space. Buttermere on this morning was without approach, without road or track, suspended in the white void, all wires down, without electricity, without everything.

So, for Buttermere, so for Ham the first week was. Life huddled, waited. In Ham Mr Lansley's bakery ran low in bread flour. On the day of its exhaustion came homespun rescue.

In Shalbourne village a mile distant there lived a man well known to all for his insecure regard for the familiar social acceptances. He was large loud and extrovert; he lived his life fully. I recall an evening when, entertaining a lady (she was married, that I understand being his preference) for that evening, brought her first into Ham pub. In his gallantry he wore a dinner jacket, wearing it with a broad leathern belt, brass-buckled.

To Ham in its time of need came this man; over the fields from Shalbourne he came dragging a sledge bearing a bag of bread flour. Arduous as anyway this was, not entirely was it without risk, large and strong though he was. An elderly lady of Shalbourne venturing out with her dog slipped into a ditch treacherously under the snow and there died.

For three months we lay under the constantly recurrent return of blizzards. Patiently, repeatedly the snow ploughs re-cut for us channels of linkage to the world beyond, as constantly to be erased. Patiently Buttermere was restored to power and access, then again to be deprived.

On a morning of March I trudged under a drift where once had been a bank. I saw that which made my heart leap. A patch of green, 6 inches wide; grass, grass of the bank that once was there. Elated, uplifted I hastened home bearing this dear news.

We continued in Ham till 1971, and of that time all was of decline. Its entity had forsaken the village. At our first coming it had been a living organism, one body, sharing a common pulse. Increasingly its nature was drained from it. During the week it came to feel not fully vital: at weekends there came a momentary palpitance but which was not of real life. The weekenders came, possessed and on Monday were gone.

Mr and Mrs Lansley of the Post Office and the bakery retired: it was profoundly symbolic: thus ended the Ham we had first known.

CHAPTER XVIII

Creel

THE HAM years were of much else not of the enclosing intervention of snow. Ham's pattern of life for us was erratic, sometimes exciting, quite often of distress; in the ordered sight of my brother Bert, bizarre.

Having so roughly parted from *Angling Times* my need for a source of income was acute, not the less so because we were in imminent expectation of our first child. But there was more than our need of money - though that had pressing urgency.

For some time it had been growing into consciousness that I was restless; *Angling Times* had subsided into a routine; its original founding feeling of adventure had passed. It was successful; it needed little further creativity from me. Itchingly I needed again to be creative. Leaving *Angling Times* gave the prod of release that served as stimulant. Now with sudden clarity I saw what so greatly I was urged to do. I must found a magazine. It must be a beautiful magazine. The thought of that was irradiating.

What pleasures its pages should give, what graces of typography and lay-out; so good should be its writing and fond philosophies of fishing. The first tumble of ideas began to assume a pattern. First I must find a backer.

I wanted one in possession of a web offset machine. By that process, then innovative, I wanted to do my magazine. Max Reinhardt to whom I had told my purpose, told me of Wilfred Harvey, who, being Chairman of Purnell, printers and publishers, had installed a web offset machine; it as yet, was under-employed. Wilfred Harvey, classically, was a tycoon. As a thrush picks up worms, so he, stepping the sward of printing and publishing, took over companies, almost as it seemed, routinely. Of them he built the British Printing Corporation, and a gangling collection of magazines, random, un-articulated, ranging from *Nursing World* to *Boys' Own Paper*, but the creation of a new one based on web offset was appropriate. By Max's initiative a meeting of Harvey and me was arranged. It was now that fantasy stepped in.*

At the appointed day and hour I came to the great man's Mayfair office. Quite promptly I was inducted into the presence. Before me was a great desk; behind it a little man. He sat very uprightly. His hair was white, his eyes blue with a glinting as though set with blue glass particles. He was brief, sharp.

"Mr Venables," he said, "what is your proposal?"

I began but was soon stopped; clearly he had been well briefed by Max Reinhardt.

"When shall we start?" he asked, biting off his words.

I, finding my persuasions thus short-circuited, told him I proposed sixty-four pages of high quality paper, of those sixteen to be full colour, sixteen of second colour, the rest black and white (this was before the time of full colour throughout).

"No, no, make it full colour throughout," He waved a directive hand.

I, though so greatly enticed, pointed out that so great the cost must be for that as to delay break-even indefinitely. He lifted his chin.

"I don't care what it costs. I don't care if it doesn't make a profit.

*This is a story I have told before: *The Illustrated Memoirs of a Fisherman,* 1993, Merlin Unwin Books.

I have done very well from the British public. I feel I owe them something, some social service - I will do this for the public good, yes, for the public good."

My sense of reality now was softening, conditioned for whatever might come.

"Have you a car?" He snapped off the words.

No, I told him, I had been driving a company car. He called for his secretary - "Miss Sharp!" (I cannot remember her real name.) "Cheque book." She was a mature lady, reposeful, with eyes long passed all surprise. He turned to me. "Must have a car. What do you want?"

I was wordless, stunned out of speech, before my inner eye passed a wraith parade, Mini to Rolls.

"Never mind. Give you an open cheque. Get what you want." He signed a cheque, gave it to me. "Have you any money?" I murmured that, er, no I had not. He called again, "Cheque book!" He scribbled a cheque. "Here, keep you going for a while." The cheque was for £1,500. That, in those honeyed days before real inflation, was rather a lot of money.

I left Wilfred Harvey's office, floated down the stairs, thence into the street half consciously clutching two cheques. After some emergence towards reality, though still dazed, I found that I had come down Park Lane, was now walking up Piccadilly, still as though under a bidding; I came to those imperious car sales palaces opposite the Ritz Hotel. Un-pausing I walked in. A little later, coming out, I had bought a Humber Super Snipe estate car.

Not long before this astonishing occurrence, I being without a car had been grateful for the loan of a Dormobile, a most kindly gesture. It was a vehicle in want of tolerance. Its second gear was in final failure; its exhaust was extensively fractured; its floor had a hole by the front seats giving entrance for exhaust fumes; its fuel gauge did not work, thus causing reliance on guesses, which often proved fallible. It was upon this we were dependent when Eileen, terminally pregnant, must go immediately to hospital. There, gassed and rattled, I brought her. The journey, for this natal occasion was not appropriate.

All thereafter was well. She was delivered of a daughter and, in due course, ready for homecoming. Appallingly she had been conveyed there; now elegantly, she was taken from there in a vehicle suitably sumptuous, almost as new as our daughter.

Said brother Bert, "You have an interesting life. It would kill me."

Now, domestic crisis so happily secured, there was the magazine, no longer a dream of fine intent; now something to be brought to splendid birth. The way forward was lit with a glow of the work to do. Six months, I had told the Chairman, should give me time enough to achieve first publication. In, so to speak, a feverish contentment I began work.

Good as might be the contents of this magazine, first it must be titled. Such a name it must have as to encapsulate the whole sense and atmosphere of what so suffuses the minds of anglers. Simply, instantly, that it must do. The answer, when it came, had almost an inevitability. So exactly it seemed to express the tradition to which it was heir.

"Its name," I said at last "shall be *Creel.*"

As chance fell, the path to first publication was less secure than had seemed it should be. There intervened that most drastic winter of 1962-3. It imposed a paralysis. I was confined in Ham; the works were in Midsomer Norton in Somerset. They could as well have been on the moon. Not until April was it possible to do anything positive.

The meantime nevertheless was of creative intensity; largely I had found the central strength of my contributors - though that was to be adventurously flexible. They, largely, had been previously unknown, and the fresher for that. Of them was R.V. Righyni - Reg Righyni - whose large conviction, not weakened by any self doubt, was as a bastion. Arthur Oglesby, already well known in the Yorkshire school, now found a national audience. There were others of other localised schools; Lloyd Gladstone Gough was classically of the valley of the Salisbury Avon. Arthur Smith till then concealed in the precincts of the Natural History Museum, for *Creel* painted his superb pictures of aquatic fauna.

Designs and lettering for Creel.

Bernard reading an early Creel.

Incomparably they were superior to all achieved by photography - or ever shall be. In passing let it be stated that drawn and painted natural history illustration of the highest quality never can be equalled by photography.

Nor was it possible that this magazine of so high intention should be without contributions from good Professor Sandy Mac Mahon.

In these editorial matters I knew my way. In the choosing of such small staff as was needed my judgement of candidates was poor. He whom I appointed to care for promotion and circulation was more counter-productive than contributive. The assistant editor of my appointing was eager for achievement, but lacked editorial instinct. The fault was mine. Also and importantly, I appointed a staff photographer: as a photographer excellent he was.

The London office in which *Creel* had its small presence was a hive. Many companies, many magazines, which had been sucked into the group had there their editorial being - that old epic of boyhood's past, *The Boy's Own Paper* still lived on. We were a widely mixed community. The place was bursting with editors and directors of subsidiary companies. Of them all was one who was not busy, being as I was told, not hitherto of publishing connection, and being then without editorial functioning. It was said, whether truthfully I cannot say, that he was a director of a coal merchant company taken into the group. It left him, as it were, stranded on a foreign beach, unblessed with occupation.

With a predatory eye he saw the coming of any new editor, so desired as he was of territory. He took me to lunch. Very persuasively he pressed upon me that if my magazine were to rise to high success he must join me at its helm - which did indeed seem dubious since he was innocent of knowledge of angling. He was, as a start, firm with me about the title. I must discard this silly title of *Creel.*

"Oh entirely wrong my dear chap, meaningless. You must call it *Angling.*"

That already there was in circulation a magazine so named, and it the second so named he did not know. His uninformed urge to dominate was clear. With, I hope, adequate courtesy I explained that my brief was to produce a magazine that was of my particular bent. I was, I assured him, most grateful for his proffered help, but I was bound to do what my appointment was to do. I think I had given offence.

I had no time for thought of that: I was busy. I must do all apart from shooting the photographs. With a zest so I did, losing no minute of the week's seven days. I designed the pages, the typography, drew and painted illustrations. I wrote the Leader, my own column, the Diary, all sorts of extraneous pieces, and the writing and drawing of a cartoon strip. All this, and the contributed material was what had to be put into the vessel which was the central creative objective. The individual pieces must be brought together, moulded, brought into harmony, fused until they became of one entity.

If such a process in any degree loses anything of the aromatic sense of the individual contribution, it has not been sensitively done: rather it should be otherwise, the bringing into association all the parts, their intrinsic flavours may be enhanced by subtleties of contrast. So much the more so that must be so in a fishing magazine in which most contributors will not be professional writers; often though they lack those accustomed skills of writing they have those indigenous reflections that are of the place that made them and made their native angling waters. The art of the whole is that their divergences become mutually enlightening.

Beyond that is the need that the magazine should have its own singular sense of identity, its voice, only of itself; it is that which is central, which does or does not give it validity as a creative whole.

So it was that of my multiple editorial functions none was more importantly formative than that I sub-edited every word of copy. I was insistent throughout that there should be respect for style, that there should be no sloppiness of non-working words - this far from diluting the sense of individualism, heightened it.

Sub-editing is a somewhat unregarded art, unhappily so, having become a rare one. Much of what now is called sub-editing is crude space chopping - and, often, the substitution of the cliché for the communicative word. When there does come a writer of accomplished skill in no need of sub-editing, it is a happiness. But all the centuries have shown that very simple men, often can by their simplicity, quite poignantly express what is at the heart of their love of angling.

In my conception of what *Creel* should be was that all in it, whether from simple or sophisticated minds, should honour words. Good English is sacred; there is little of it now.

First publication was in July 1963. Though Wilfred Harvey had been so spectacular in magnanimity to the public, caution advised me to retain my original restricted colour. The magazine did not suffer; it was well received.

Quite remarkably well the United States received it. Joe Godfrey wrote to me; it was an experience. Joe was an ebullient man; his letters gave a sense of impact. This was his first:

Dear Bernard Venables,
Congratulations! Your Creel *is beautiful. I think all creels are beautiful, but this one of yours, the fishing magazine, is great.*

In such terms his letter continued. He took a subscription. He wrote again.

Dear Bernard,
Now back on the job . . . been fishing. We are delighted to announce to the world of fishermen for sport your election to 'The Fishing Hall of Fame'. Your 'Dolphin Award', the highest honour in sport fishing, is being shipped to you on July 11, 1964 . . .

I have it still. It is impressive, charming, a little hyperbolic in its American fashion. I have great pride in it.

Of Joe's many subsequent letters, one announced my election as an honorary member of the Sportsmen's Club of America.

The President of a major American airline wrote to declare himself enchanted by *Creel.* He was grateful, he said, for its freedom from fishing cliché.

And so great a happiness, Arnold Gingrich wrote to me. He was a man of the heart of cultural America, a friend of Dorothy Parker,

Bernard with the Dolphin Award.

of Ernest Hemingway, Scott Fitzgerald, of all of that group. He was an author and a journalist, founder of *Esquire Magazine*, still its publisher. Also probably, he was America's greatest authority on angling literature.

I have quoted this first letter in another of my books, but its relevance is such that I think it should be quoted here.*

* *The Illustrated Memoirs of a Fisherman,* 1993, Merlin Unwin Books.

Dear Mr Venables,

For more than a decade now, I've been a great fan of yours, beginning with your book Fishing *in the series 'British Sports Past and Present', and culminating in* The Angler's Companion, *where the passage on the beat on the Torridge near Hatherleigh made me pack up and go to it. That was in the spring '59, and I hurried to get there in April, to find it as you described it. And then latterly I've been most impressed by Creel, and particularly by your own contributions to it.*

This admiration has now found expression here and there, in a book I have written, which will be published by Alfred Knopf next spring, called The Well Tempered Angler. *In one chapter, 'Salmon in Connemara and Devon', it tells how I read your account of the Torridge and Hatherleigh and it details my own experience there, concluding 'Oh excellent author, oh venerable Venables and venerated Venables, every blessed word turned out to be true, down to the last, for no fish exceeded 14lb. And the beat described was instantly recognisable, from the looming sight of Dartmoor down into the high-hedged hollows, past a village, past a pretty pub. Then falling twisting under a shade of trees and past stone cottages to a bridge where the water starts, the ancient narrow massive bridge patched with golden lichen hove into view … and it was on that beat, so well portrayed in words by Venables, that the last word of his prophesy was fulfilled, for the bailiff, the man from the River Board, duly found us there on his 'mildly admonitory round', and though he was polite and friendly, almost genial, in exchanging gossip about what fish had been taken in the previous few days, he still didn't fail to bring the conversation at last around to the point where, after a deprecatory cough and saying, "Of course you both have your licenses . . ." and upon being assured that we did, still wondered if we 'didn't mind' showing them to him. So every word that Venables wrote about Hatherleigh and the Torridge was true. How many angling books, do you suppose, would pass that test?*

Sincerely Yours,
Arnold Gingrich

A fine 1960s Hampshire Avon salmon.

So warm a reception for *Creel* from over the ocean was unexpected, greatly encouraging; I was a little incredulous - rather as though I must look over my shoulder to see of whom they were talking. On this side of the ocean reception was as good if, British-fashion, more restrained. Its production demanded of me that I work ceaselessly, but I was happy in that demand. There was ample evidence that in time's fullness the magazine would break even, then on to profit. Anyway had I not Wilfred Harvey's most positive statement of his attitude on that?

After three so happily received months of publication I was summoned to the presence of the Chairman. Perhaps, I thought, he wishes to tell me he is pleased. He fixed me with the glass-blue flicker of his eye.

"We're losing money," he snapped.

Yes, I thought, wondering why he brought that up.

"Have you no sense of profit and loss?"

Thereafter as *Creel's* acclaim grew so the more did Harvey subject me to his upbraidings about the loss he had so emphatically said he was content to carry. I had told Arnold Gingrich of this unhappy state. He wrote:

> *I'm sick to think of the possibility of* Creel's *suspension, and hope very much that your sponsor will somehow be prevailed upon to come back to his original concept of the necessary breaking in period before breaking even. It has been such a beautiful job and by all odds the best thing on fishing produced on either side of the ocean.*

Throughout this, so at odds, pressure by Harvey I could not escape a sense of another presence, of a voice in his ear. How otherwise could I account for so inexplicable a volte-face?

The crisis came; I was summoned. Astonishingly I found not Harvey alone. There was assembled an audience. My assistant was there; so was the group's accountant, and others of no apparent connection. And there was he who had wanted to join me in the production of *Creel.* He wore a slight smile; it seemed to say 'This is going to be fun.' Harvey also had a small smile of similar kind.

Would I, he asked, be prepared to continue as editor of the magazine if it were reduced to thirty-two pages, on inferior paper, with no colour? My would-be collaborator smiled happily. The trap was clear, but I said that next day I would give my choice which was no choice. So it ended. I had one more issue to produce, my eighteenth. In the leader column I bid my goodbye to the readers. The magazine was not changed. A new editor was appointed. He inherited a circulation of nearly 40,000; in six months he had reduced it to 5,000.

From readers came letters, sad and angry. Captain Edwards wrote from his ship *MV Perlis* in the South China Sea:

Dear Mr Venables,
I can scarcely bring myself to believe that you are leaving us. So sudden and no word of warning. Creel *dedicated to Sanity? Pshaw!*

It was too good to be true of course, too good to last. Please, Sir, I've known you for thirty years, ever since I began to read. I beg you to reconsider for our, the readers' sake.

If I had the authority you would be confined to the ship. I feel fed up now.

Sincerely, Captain K L Edwards.
This is a bad, bad day.

Then came a letter from Arnold Gingrich:

I'm sick to hear what's become of Creel *of course, and I can just see the grubby thing it must be, with you and your cohorts out of there. But in a perverse nasty way, because I'm on your side, I'm also glad it's so lousy, now that they're trying to carry on without you.*

They tried for six months with a circulation dropping like a brick. Soon *Creel* sank, into oblivion.

Again I was pushed into a resignation which was not a resignation. Harvey having not given a written contract I could make no claim. One director confessed to me his great personal regret about the episode, and, through his kindly intervention, I did get a small pay-off. I was, so to speak, cast away in a very small boat with no island in sight. On *Creel* I had been well paid; abruptly dire poverty seized us.

Perhaps New York might have a readiness for me; perhaps *Creel* might have prepared a way for me. Arnold Gingrich thought that a probability. And indeed when I got there, by the community of anglers I was received most hearteningly warmly.

But, beyond the writing of a few articles for *Esquire*, there came no benefit.

I remember, quite irrelevantly, that on the flight out the aircraft was contending with an 80-mph wind. There was some nervousness aboard. Across the aisle from me was an American lady who told me she was an opera singer. Next to her a small man with a face made for worry, was incessant with his worry-beads.

Said the lady to me, "This feller's worry is going to worry me to death."

Chapter XIX

A Slip out of Time

At Ham we remained until 1971; but what of those Ham years has still to be told? Of the parting from *Angling Times* in 1962 the story has been told. Of that which followed, shall be told. But in those years there were other events.

About the middle 1960s Max Reinhardt, then of the publishing house, The Bodley Head, asked if I had heard of the primitive whalers of the Azores. In those Portuguese islands, remotely in mid-Atlantic, he told me, still they were hunting the great sperm whale as had the 19th century whalers of New England - just indeed as told in the story of *Moby Dick*, going day by day most perilously in small open boats, with hand harpoons and lances. This was raw confrontation having nothing in common with the safe and horrible butchery of the whaling factory ships.

Did I, asked Max Reinhardt, know of anyone who might be so stimulated by the story as to go to the Azores, go with the whalers, then write a book about it? I confessed to being so affected myself.

"That's what we hoped you'd say," said Max.

So it was that, flying first to Lisbon, I found myself, onwards from there, fading from the world of our time, declining from it by means less and less of modernity. Modernity carried me to Santa Maria and there left me. Santa Maria, most easterly of the Azores archipelago is a mid-ocean place of departure; there ends the contemporary world. Still for a while I could fly on, but by a means already slipping out of time; by a Dakota, the veteran DC3, I was carried on. It clambered into the air, ambled on till we came to Terceira. Terceira means third; it is the third island. Also it is lovely of a loveliness peculiarly of itself, of its serenity in its loneliness. It is, as Azorean islands must be, eruptive from the sea. The whole archipelago is but the emergent tops of the mid-ocean volcanic ridge which is the uneasy meeting of two tectonic plates that, north and south, run the Atlantic's length. Terceira's centre, its capital, an enchantment, is Angra do Heroismo. The little town rises from the sea in a pretty symmetry of tilted streets all, in Portuguese fashion, with pavements patterned in black and white mosaic. The houses, white-fronted under the dappling trees, have little balconies and shuttered windows, they and all else of that arch innocence of fancifulness which is Portuguese. All has a clean and shaded clarity as if not quite of common air.

A first delighted scan of Angra suggests that it was at some time past put down in one stroke of perfection, and from then had not one spoiling touch. More closely it is to be seen that in our time there has been some additional building; but, so sensitively has it been done, so instinctively of the indigenous spirit that there is no least sense of unconformity.

Perforce in Angra I must stay for three days; I must wait till Friday when I could be borne away by the little ship which was to take me further out of time. Nothing could I do but give myself to its enchantments.

Still then Portugal was under the bond of fascism; but the native tranquillity bearing it, was not of it. In my unhampered evenings in and about the cafés, I became acquainted with a young man, possibly twenty. His father was a journalist and of no sympathy for the regime. So one evening it emerged when the young man and I sat in the soft air of evening relaxed in a harbour-side café. The young man, responsive to the tender air became unguarded; his tongue liberated by a few drinks, became passionate. Passionately he declaimed of when they should throw off the hated incubus. With morning's cooling check next day, coldly sober, he was distant, in awkward unease.

"Be early," they said to me on Thursday, when I got my ticket. "She sails at 7 o'clock sharp. You should be there at least an hour before."

On Friday morning at 5.30 I was on the quay. There was the little ship; *Espirito Santo*. She, a tubby little craft of apparently limited commission, took a surprisingly broad miscellany while we the passengers awaited our turn. A cow, most melancholy in a belly sling was swung aboard, lowered into the hold. An ancient mangle went too while its black-clad old peasant woman owner watched grimly. Timber and a pile of planks, crates and boxes, ropes and bundles and things inexplicable as it seemed without end. Then all else done we too were loaded, an improbable throng, for space still there might be in the belly of the little ship. Below decks breathing space had no more to offer; I went above to the minuscule deck, there to be cheek by jowl with the stubby funnel. Space there was short but we had the air. It was later, flung by lurching seas into intimacy with the funnel, that I learned that it became too hot for touching. After 7.30 we drew away from the quay.

Till we passed the headland our going was calm; as we turned it, met the fair sea breeze, the little vessel rose to the gentle swell. There arose sounds that air and engines could not suppress. These citizens of mid-ocean were in distress; the sound and substance of it was borne on the breeze. I found it convenient to move forward there to receive the breeze in its simplicity.

Thus began a voyage of a day, of no shape, of no time, our ship a little argosy, that wandered in a dream. So going it brought us to our first port, announcing us by a siren blast outrageous for so tubby a little ship as was ours.

A port it may be called because so it served; it was the smallest of coves oppressed by raw sheets of rock. Assaulted by surf. Notched within a cramped shelf of rock, was all that was of quay. In so much seethe and fume it appeared invulnerable to entry by us; but by an adroit flick of seamanship *Espirito Santo* was coaxed until gently she tied up in a small peacefulness of water not to be guessed from without.

Of those who went ashore, though some had suffered, all were neat-footed as islanders must be. Little old women in peasant black were as ready as any when deck and jetty reached momentary common level.

Some cargo, some passengers put ashore, more came aboard. Two cows, four calves, moaned sadly when belly-slung, they came air-borne to the hold. Into this same hold came basketed wine, timber, a brass-knobbed bed. Then the affronting blast of the siren, and port fell away under the stern, lost as a spent dream.

It had been the ultimate point of the island of Sao Jorge; it gone we fell again out of orientation, wandering in an infinity of a day. We sailed on a sea blue as pigment under a tossed and turreted coast. Volcanic peaks, fantasies of precipice sheered from the sea; how could there be access to such habitation? But, a little offshore, *Espirito Santo* stopped. Into a lowered boat went the mangle and its black-mantled owner. Two crewmen rowed for the shore where now it was to be seen a little jetty of stones ran out; distantly on its end a man waited, he in the loose pantaloons, wide-brimmed straw hat that is the peasant way. The old woman and her mangle were got ashore; our ship sailed on. I left in vain worry as to how the mangle was to be levitated to its craggy lodgement.

Then that was gone, frayed wisps of a dream lost. We seemed stationary, the slow panorama of coast passing us, seen for a while then gone.

At the rounding of a point substance returned; there over the bows was a place, an open quay, houses pastelled pink and white, a dizzy towering of crag rising from the roofs. Our monstrous siren roared, the quay grew close; we sidled to a gentle mooring. There, close to the quay, my first sighting, were two whaleboats; frail and pretty they looked for such gargantuan dangers.

Of those who went ashore was a young soldier. On leave I wondered from Portugal's still unextricated entanglement in Angola? He was tall by the standard of the small Azoreans, and carried well his shabby uniform. On the quay his family, a little waiting huddle, received him, entwining him. Small mother black-clad, crying a little, lingering hands on his arm. Young sister perhaps, about eighteen, shyly worshipful, brothers, cousins. The long welcome done, they wandered away clustered. *Espirito Santo* roared its departure. The little town pretty as china against the crags, drifted again into insubstance.

The day, nebulous of form, was slipping towards evening. Soon the towering hang of Sao Jorge fell astern. In the haze over the port bow a deeper haze took form.

"That," said a neighbour on the deck, "that is Pico."

Pico. I had heard of Pico. I knew of Pico. There and on another island most intensely was based the hunting of the great sperm whale. Fayal was that other island. To Fayal was I bound.

"Fayal is just beyond," said my neighbour, "soon we shall see it. Fayal is my home."

And here was Pico, now near, of a shape classically of that mould we expect of volcanic islands rising in an aspiring sweep to its cone. The crouching cluster of houses at the mount's foot surely must be Cais do Pico which I knew was a whaling station. And there to starboard as we edged in, there it was, there the slip, there the flensing platform, beyond it the whale factory, about it active figures.

"Been cutting-in a whale," my neighbour told me, "just finished. Cooking the blubber now. Like to walk over and see?"

But first we must go in, get our mooring; there was a difficulty, shouting, a crewman running to the stern with a long boathook. He was fending off something. In a dinghy a man grappling to a floating mass to tow it clear. All about the little ship, quaking undulant masses, bulbously afloat.

"Whale's guts," said my neighbour, "they tow it out to sea later."

Ashore, against the white wall and under the oleanders and oranges and the dark olive trees we walked to the whale factory. There for my first seeing was the flensing platform, the factory, but more for first experience was the smell. All that is of whale factories is monstrous, but the most assaultive on the sense is the smell; it is heavy, fat-laden, prostrate on the air, unforgettable. It enfolds, clings.

The whalemen trod the stone wide-legged, on massive spread of naked feet blooded to the calves. They wore loose pantaloons of bed ticking patched upon patch, rolled to the calves. Their squinting seamen's eyes looked from under wide brims of conical rush hats. They were brown, leathern.

We were recalled by *Espirito Santo's* outrageous blast. Soon Cais do Pico faded astern: we turned Pico's point. Across the five-mile straight there lay Fayal. Of Fayal I knew that it was of all the islands' whaling its capital. I knew that that strip, pale pastel in the evening light, under the heights was the town of Horta. It was out of Fayal that I was to live through such improbabilities of adventure, relict from other times. The full story I have told elsewhere; this account must summarise its essence.*

In the morning they took me to the Captain of the Port for what was essential prelude to whatever might come. I must sign that document which locally is called the Death Warrant. Its effect was that whatever fate might come upon me responsibility was no one's but mine. Open boat whaling may upon its occasions be excessively dangerous.

I was carried now in a slip of time; no longer of the 20th century, but of the 19th. The 20th was still to come. In that century which I had left, the safe abominable butchery of whaling wholly was without moral plea of necessity, doing as appallingly it would. But where now I was in this lonely group of islands, an oceanic speck, almost still it was of the primeval world of the inter-balancing of the species by the mutuality of predation. The ocean was a jungle in which one species, man, desperately poor, must try to prey upon the sperm whale which itself must try to prey upon the giant squid. It was a world, historically extinct, hung in suspension in a time gone. Since I was there the cogs of time have moved on again. Now at Fayal there is an airstrip; the world has come

Baleia! The Whalers of the Azores, 1968, Bodley Head. In USA, Knopf, 1969. Also *The One that Got Away*, 1991, Merlin Unwin Books.

rudely in. The whale boats go out no more.

All to do with Azorian whaling, as still I found it, largely was as had been the way of the New England whalers; their terminology, so charged with the sense of that time's drama, was the same, partially rendered into Portuguese. Its centre was the boat, the canoa, a totem of the often frightful falls of chance - so frail a thing for its preposterous undertaking, but by that frailty giving the swift lightness for evasive manoeuvre. Largely it was as the Yankee boats had been, but at 37 feet, 10 feet longer for beach launching rather than lowering from ships. The Yankee boats in their shape, slight, pointed fore and aft, derived from the Indian canoe. By that being named. Thus, historically, was the Azorean canoa, most stringently of its purpose; but being no less an artefact, in inimitable Portuguese fashion, has a pretty gaiety of design. Along its length below the gunwale the hull was white. Along the gunwale ran a strake which by its colour declared its island of origin; that of Pico was clear blue; the gunwale was red as was the boat's interior. Fayal's boats wore a strake of yellow and a gunwale of red; delightingly inside the boat was pink. The name of the boat at its bow was carved with a pattern of leaves in a painted panel.

So small of space was all within the canoa that all must be exactingly precise of fitting and use. A minor misfitting, a moment's clumsiness, could impose final calamity. Here then is the ordering of the boat, all its contents human and artefact.

In the stem there was a cleft, a channel, its name was the chocks; through it was the running of the whale line, by that becoming polished to satin. Immediately aft, within the swell of the bows was a decked-in sunken area; its name was the box. In the box was coiled the box warp, which was of line relatively light and attached directly to the harpoon, and by its other end fastened to the main line. At the after edge of the box, only secondly crucial in possibly vital importance, was the clumsy cleat. It, a plank crossing the boat from gunwale to gunwale, had just left of its centre a semi-circular notch. It was in that that the harpooner braced his left leg at the culminating moments of harpooning and lancing.

In the stern, decked in flush with the gunwales, was the cuddy board. On it, a little to starboard, was the loggerhead, key to all. It was a bollard, about 8 inches high, relatively narrow at its base, widening to its top. It is by this small means that the skipper, who is called the boatheader, must control all the potentially lethal course of elemental encounter. As a reel is to an angler the loggerhead was to the boatheader of the whaleboat.

At either side before the cuddy board and below it were the standing cleats: footholds for the feet of the boatheader. He, upraised, standing on the cleats, had commanding view ahead and was best poised for control of the running of the line at the loggerhead and for use of the great steering oar or of the tiller. At times less active he sat upon the cuddy board. In that crucible of chance which was a whaleboat, upon the boatheader rested the agency of destiny.

Between stem and stern were six thwarts, one each for the manning of an oar. From forward going aft they were, harpoon thwart, bow thwart, midships thwart, line thwart, tub thwart, after thwart. Against the second thwart the mast was stepped, hinged so to be raised or lowered with neat speed in fraught circumstances - with what deft certainty, steel-cool, must all be done. Often in that first moment after the harpooning, a blow of the enormity of a whale's flipper has shattered the canoa's timbers. Upon the lowering of the mast, stays and halyards loosened, sails bundled, all was lowered to lie over the after quarter, there to be clear of the running of the line up the mid-line of the boat - so to avoid that fearful possibility of its being fouled.

Amidships were two line tubs, in each 120 fathoms of line coiled down with most exacting care - but one coil need foul another in the running of a whale and the kicking line could sweep the boat. Many have there been of such catastrophes. They told me of the young Mendoza. He, young, newly made harpooner, had fastened his first whale. The line kicked wild, took his ankle. He was swept away; never was he seen again.

From the after tub the line came first, thence round the loggerhead, then up the fore and aft line of the boat between the oarsmen either side on the thwarts, then for attachment to the box warp in the bows, by that attaching to the harpoon.

Before all else in the hunting of the whale were the look-outs. They, at all times from dawn till dark, were at salient points round the island with overlapping cones of vision over the sea. There, high-elevated, they kept their vigils, scanning with powerful binoculars. They watched for the blow of a whale which might be 5 miles or 35 miles offshore. For sighting so distant, weather must be benign, calm, settled; a state so favourable is characteristically a gift of a northerly wind. That which the watchers sought to see, was that low pluming hump, oyster-coloured in the sun - a whale 'having out its blows'. Then, at the initiating burst of a rocket was begun a sequence which, each time, had no certainty of what was to be its end. At the rocket's summoning crack the whalers, whatever then were their occupations, upon the instant they ceased them, dropped them instantly, ran to the manning of the boats. "*Baleia*! *Baleia*!" they shouted as they ran: '*Baleia*' means whale.

On the island of Pico one day as I was told, there was the funeral of a whaler. Solemnly whalers bore his coffin. There came the hiss, the burst of the rocket. There in the road the whalers put down the coffin. "*Baleia*!" they shouted, running for the boats. There for all the hours of that day the coffin remained till in the evening the whalers returned.

Towed by launch the boats surge from their moorings, crews hunched in the sterns, radio-guided from the shore so they go, till about a mile from the blow they stop; the canoas cast their tows. All now is quiet; the boatheader whispers; it is primary that the sperm whale has keen hearing. Should it hear, it will sound, thus to be lost. But not alarmed it idles in the sun, having out its blows in its innocence of danger.

If there is little or no wind the going on the whale will be by the oars; at the cuddy board the boatheader on his standing cleats mans the 22-foot steering oar over the stern with inch-fine precision. The harpooner rigid at the clumsy cleat, a set spring, the canoa comes from astern onto the whale's quarter. The harpooner will make his orgasmic 'dart'; the whale will be 'fastened'.

When wind was enough the going on the whale was under sail, the steering by rudder. Below the gunwale by each thwart is stowed a paddle. The men facing forward, sat on the gunwales stroking with paddles, thus almost to make the canoa skim.

Though the approach from aft, outside the whale's cone of vision, was the common way - going on the flippers - the scarifying perilous alternative mode was to go 'head on head', a way fine of skill, more thinly fine of danger. Because the sperm whale has an enormous bluff of forehead, because its eyes are set low, close to the corners of the mouth, its forward vision is restricted to a narrow cone directly in front of the head. The approach therefore must be made, appallingly finely, within that cone. In the last part of a second the boatheader puts his weight to the steering oar, just flicks the boat round the head, into vision. In that brief passage the harpooner makes his dart; the boat sweeps astern of the whale. It, sky shadowing, flings up the 12-foot span of its flukes, sounds in a boil of sea. The canoa, having skill and good fortune survives.

But for me all this was still to come when first I came to Horta. On the morning after the evening of my coming I went for a walk that as I thought was random; no less random as I thought was my coming upon Café Sport. As I was to learn, it was not in the least random. For those who come venturing in boats upon the Atlantic Ocean to come upon Café Sport in Horta on the island of Fayal was, sooner or later, inevitable - probably still is. That assumes the other probability, that there, just above the harbour, Café Sport still is.

I, on my walk that first morning, met Henrique; he was courteous; "Come to my shop." Soon we came to it; there, inconspicuously, was Café Sport. It was in the small tree-lined street, dropping from the levels of the town; its narrow frontage, blue-painted, bleached and patched by sea-salt wind's assault, was modest. Within it was small; a few tables round the wall, a few chairs, at its end a counter bearing glass sweet jars. Through the door the everlasting panorama below: the harbour, the 5-mile sea strait across to the perfectly aspiring volcanic cone of Pico; it in finest weather wearing always at its summit a tasselled tuft of cloud.

"Here," said Henrique, "is my son, José." By the counter there he was, José Azevedo, who by all who came was called Peter. "Welcome to Café Sport," Peter said: had he not said it, its sense would have been as clear. Peter, who was probably forty, had light brown eyes that twinkled. So first I came to Café Sport; by no accident had I come. I was but one of those who, having a purpose of the ocean, came to Café Sport. It was as by foretending my base. My destined purpose, being of the ocean it took me there. The ocean's being ran through Café Sport. Not only was Peter host there; he as well was a ship's chandler.

To Fayal, to Horta, I came twice, one year and a second. The first coming was unpropitious: the weather lay on the passage of the days as though an impediment. Each morning at dawn's first reluctant hint, I scanned sea and sky, assessed the wind. As slow light began to lift, picking from the sea facets as of slashed lead, morning by morning I walked the wind-searched *avenida* to the harbour with thwarted hope. But there were days of more hopeful seeming, occasionally blue as gentians. They too empty of event.

But every morning of whatever kind, of tattered skies, or delusive shine, at the harbour I would be - how calamitous should it be if one dark morning of sulky rebuff that, nevertheless the rocket should make its knell? Every morning, hardly varying so it would be; first would come Abilio Bettencourt to check the engine of the tow launch; then José Vicrente to ensure again the finally impeccable ordering of all in its place. Then came the fishermen, landing their catches and, changelessly as was their way, gossiping, dropping into passing sudden wisps of anger. Then to me, wry-faced, kindly regretfully deploring the weather. "*Noa baleia hoje*" - No whale today. They would smile sympathetically, spread their hands.

Then would come full dawn; morning grew; first people gathered for the morning's first ferry to Madalena on Pico. Then would come Peter to open Café Sport. It was full day. So, each day. Each day I started tightly ready for the crisis that, surely, it still could not be that the rocket should not shatter this stale suspension. But the days ticked off, unchanging and I not daring to leave the harbour. In Café Sport I lingered through the wastrel hours; they in there sympathised, told me old stories of great whales, of those whalers who had not returned.

On a morning of no particular difference I was on the quay in the early light. It was not very hostile, not very windy, not even was its rumpling sky without sometimes uncertain gleams of wizened sun; it was a morning of no marked entity. But I was in a fidget of expectancy unjustified by any valid promise. Till 8 o'clock the nervous itch of hope lingered, then to die in the full wan light of another day. In Café Sport the morning idled in gossip round the tables. I as always had my bag of food ready for the call that did not come, dry biscuits, a piece of cheese, rough red wine. I remember too how, idly, Peter on the pavement had a dalliance with they in the flat above who, always, between the shutters of the window, kept a vigil of statically placid observation of the passing world. There was the mother, short, swart and stout, there was the daughter, swarthy as a brown olive, as roundly shaped. To her Peter paid his playful gallantry. His friend from England he declared, was as much a slave to her beauty as he was himself.

So the morning limped till noon, no least thread of expectation left. In the midst of that depth of deflation, shattering ennui, was exultant shouting of many voices. "*Baleia*! *Baleia*!" When, unconscious of volition I had exploded to the door, they were on the quay, shouting, waving arms, calling to me - "*Baleia*! *Baleia!*"

Here it was, the trump at last, the blood-firing, belly-chilling summons. Peter was shouting, "*Baleia*!" pushing into my hands the food bag. As I reached the quay, as the engines of the tows' launches, *Cetaceo* and *Walkeria* burst into life, there was the rocket.

It rose from the roof of the whale centre in the side street, hissing, rising, suspending all, then bursting. Then from the street's narrow throat burst, as though extruded, a dark clot of men. They became apart, separate, running, shouting, "*Baleia*! *Baleia*!" I recognised he who led, José Rufino, a boatheader. As they came close I saw in their eyes cold fever: we were one in an exultant fear.

We crowded in the wells of *Cetaceo* and *Walkeria*, jostled against fuel drums and whale lines; moorings were cast off; I saw Peter waving outside Café Sport. The engines roared throatily, threw us into way across the harbour, past the tuna boats, past the pilot boat and the American yacht, and surged under the light. Now there was relief for the stretched skin of tension.

The whale's end is near. The harpoon shaft shows behind the hump.

Canoa on tow.

The men took out cigarettes, smoked erratically. The launches, following the line of coast roared on under the high stooping threat of precipice, pressing to Saloa, past lowering headlands. The sky hung in ragged shapes; the swells breaking on our bows, towered among the rocks.

Rounding a last headland, there in tossing fume and break was Saloa's embrasure, wedged into the sheer bastion of precipice behind the lash of sea. Waiting, poised on the thrash of surf were Saloa's whaleboats waiting for our tows.

The boatheaders, high on standing cleats, braced to the great steering oars, held their craft as though hovering. The crewmen as these men do, looked wild, piratical. The tow warps were made fast - first in *Walkeria*, she the faster boat - then in *Cetaceo*. The engines roared again; the wakes streamed out; Saloa dropped astern.

Steering a little east of north, Pico came up to starboard, lowering deep blue with the pale splatter of Madalena falling to the sea. On straining warps the canoas bounced in the boil of our wake, crews clustered aft. Astern, appearing, vanishing in the roll of swell, *Cetaceo* was losing distance. The radio, amplified above the engine's roar, barked continuously, guiding, correcting. Abilio with his two-note whistle signal was checking course with shore. Pico's soaring summit now had gone, lost in the pink-shot vaporous hang of blue. Over the shoulder of Pico, a translucent smudge was Sao Jorge, long, umber-mauve, half there between sea and sky.

Crowded forward in the wheelhouse of the tow launch the crew talked quietly, mouths close for the engine's uproar, clipped words dropped under knit brows, taut eyes. Beside me a whaleman smoked continually; a smell of danger was on the boat, not now its fear, now its sharp raw-edge uplift. The time of the going was too long for the first thrilled-cold quake. The raising of the blow had been far offshore; the first hour of our going came up with Pico softening on the starboard quarter, Sao Jorge enlarging and lengthening down the far sea distance. Time grew, the second hour accumulated, Pico now astern, faint, amorphous mauve.

Walkeria forged on, riding the swell, Pico lost under the stern, Sao Jorge a low recurrent wraith between the swell's lift and fall.

Cetaceo now far astern, showing on the crest, lost in the troughs. Then there was nothing but the sea, the oceanic loneliness. I thought of the lookouts ashore, still directing us; of the fantasy that they could discern, so closely locate, the blow of a whale in that heaving immensity. But, purposefully, *Walkeria* went on, undiminished in certainty, driven by the radio's constant stutter. I remembered that a blow once raised is seldom lost.

Then, out of nothing that I knew, we had stopped. The whale was near then; within a mile's vicinity. The engine purred gruffly in neutral, the sounds of the sea flooding upon us; we rolled in the embracing quiet. Abilio at the radio was consulting. Now in the boat there was awareness of forming up; I, waiting, could see nothing but the illimitable parameter of sea. *Cetaceo* now was coming up. I had a sense of time ended, it and all gone, only now this vacuity; but with a consciousness of inexorable entanglement with events' perhaps fearful course.

A canoa hauled on its warp was brought up to *Walkeria*, bringing its bow alongside, that he from the after thwart could pick his way forward over the crane gear, so come aboard *Walkeria*, making for me a place aboard the canoa. Though the danger of the hunt so overhangs, though the part of each is so pertinent for all, in their great courtesy they had given me this place. I dropped into the canoa, teetered down the dancing craft to the after thwart there to find myself at the feet of the boatheader.

He was formidable; enlarged upon life, a little god-like high in command upon his cleats - very large in authority. In his face, brown, crinkled as old leather, his eyes under his hat, high-crowned, broad-brimmed, were blue as sea reflections. His legs, his feet, almost at my eye-level, were large, knotted below the stripped bed-ticking pantaloons patched and over-patched, rolled nearly to the knee. His feet were pedestals, large, spread, horn-thick below. He had a swingeing air.

My neighbour forward, the tub oar, was elderly, sea-seamed, brown-textured as a nut: his hands were large, leather-palmed; they hung as though heavy. His eyes half smiling under his broad brim were shy, blue, faded round the edge as though the colour had been drawn from them by much sea searching.

Now I thought must be the time for fate's determination; now must we cast our tows; the men bend to the oars: almost now we are upon the fearful encounter. But still *Walkeria* with our tow, burst again to life, we surging in her wake. The boatheader high-vantaged scanned ahead. A combustion was upon him; with wide imperious fling of arm he directed *Walkeria*, hurling imprecation, head inclining like the rolling of a planet. With immensity he ordained a bearing to starboard or to port. So, searching, the boat-header's blast bludgeoning *Walkeria*. We beat about an ocean upon which there was no least event that explained itself to me. Now had come up *Cetaceo* and her tows.

In the midst of his thunder I saw the boatheader's eye seem to contract, to fasten. In that part of a moment he dropped his eyes to mine, just perceptibly he nodded, briefly smiled, privately a signal. He had raised the whale. His voice, crescendo, ordered the casting of our tow. All fury dropped from him; relaxed, suddenly softened, he turned to me. "*Eeee - Caramba*," he said. *Walkeria* veered, dematerialising, soaked into distance.

Still I, low against the sea, saw nothing within the horizon's immensity but the green heave of sea. But I knew, all knew, that he, the up-raised boatheader, had seen the blow of the whale. No more now was fear, lost now in a high thin edge of elation. In the boat now, lying in slapping rise and fall, lulled by the sea's illimitable peace clasped to a not quite tolerable tension. The boat-header, so recently gouting fire, now whispered, gentle father to his crew; now he and all of us but one in the immediacy of future about to befall us.

The harpooner came aft to midships, a young man, lean, tightly-strung, face hard-set, bleak-eyed under frowning brows. The line of the waist tub he bent to that of the after tub, then that up the mid-line of the boat there to be fastened to the box line of the harpoon. To his right at the clumsy cleat he leaned the harpoon - the first iron - next to that another - the second iron. The harpooner will dart a second one if chance allows. All was ready; the men bent to the long oars; they were inward, absorbed, smiling. Their stroke was long, smoothly powerful. The boatheader at the great steering oar coaxed the craft as though a dinghy.

Of those at the oars, rapt, contained, one was young, brown-skinned, brown eyed, still youngly soft at line of chin and cheek. Another, probably proudly of his early twenties, was dark, darkly handsome, the eyes in his long dark face great black pools under the ebony stripes of his brows. His dark beauty innocently was piratical.

Under the oars' long sweep the boat drove purposively on a course to me outside my orientation, an anonymity of ocean. We were alone now, no boat near - rarely a glimpse of *Cetaceo*, hull-down, without sighting of a canoa riding troughs and crests.

Then turning his eyes to mine, the boatheader nodded, pointing with his head beyond our bows. He whispered to the crew; "*Forca*," he said.

The men quickened stroke, forcing, smiling. The harpooner, rigid at the clumsy cleat, had no smile, his face stone-hard.

Now in softened sound of parted water, silent of all else sealed about us, we ran on; the boatheader looming like God on his cleats. Then to starboard momentarily I saw a canoa; it was hoisting sail.

There came upon the boatheader a change that I, now with sea-sense, extra-sensory, knew the whale had rounded out, sounded. Where now in so much ocean, how could man divine its going? To the crew, to Manuel, to José, Fernando, all of them, very softly the boatheader spoke; oars were boated, steering oar taken in, rudder and tiller mounted. In the crammed craft, the mast was stepped; sails were hoist, filling to the mild wind's touch. The serenity that is of sailing laid a gentling hand. We went now dreamingly, careening to the wind's caressive thrust, silent but for the lap of our bows. Tacking, going about, we beat the bounds of the sea's area which was of the whale's sounding, in inspired conjecture of its blowing again.

But there came no stomach-shrilling cry of '*Bloz*!' Now utterly we were alone; no least glimpse hull-down of launch or canoa: we went about and went about, but no sign now of whale's proximity.

No need had we now of words; a tranquillity dropped upon us. The boatheader looked at me, gently smiled, slowly shook his head. Submissively he seemed to say, the whale was lost. It had come to evening.

We lay idling in the lift and fall in peaceful abandon. The men brought out their food: most poignantly then, overwhelmingly it came to me that not since early morning had I eaten. I took out my food bag - but so differently things may appear in shore's ease and a long day's sea abstinence. Dry biscuits I had - "You can live for a day on dry biscuits, can't you?" Peter had said; too easily I had agreed. Now, 40 miles to sea how alum-dry were those biscuits, impossible of swallowing.

My neighbour of the tub oar, in the way of whalers had bread and cheese, a slab of *massa cevada* (a sort of slightly sweet bread); obliquely his eye was on me. Then upon my knee he put his wide oar-scarred hand; shyly he smiled, depracatingly offered me a large piece of *massa cevada*. Because as I could see, he had a large slab, very gratefully I accepted the offered piece. At my having eaten it, he, now more bold, offered me another piece; that too, gratefully I took. When that too I had eaten he offered me a third piece; but I, first pang satisfied, declined. Gently solicitous he pressed it on me. The boatheader, watchful at the cuddy board, quietly was reproving. I, having declined should not be pressed. Of so sensitive a courtesy are these men who, day by day pursue into death the great sperm whale. It, as it must, pursues the giant squid.

Now sequestered by sea we waited. There was no more that we could do.

The men talked, low-voiced, attuned to that stillness which follows drama. Slowly, ruminatively, the boatheader and my neighbour conversed - I, so early then with no more than a few words of Portuguese, could not interpret; but they, by glance, inclining of head, of smile, were careful that I should feel also to be of them.

Now out of quietness there came at midships a merriment. Those two, the young brown boy, the handsome pirate - though the latter, released from the shell of danger had fallen from piracy. They were joking, those two, in a crosstalk act that, whatever its theme was excessively funny; midships and forward they were convulsed. The harpooner, now free from dire responsibility, rested easily on arms relaxed on knees. Now, such is the swing of mood in states of high stresses that we now were touching an edge of bliss.

In time immeasurable, *Walkeria* materialised out of distance, gave us the tow warp. From forward the transfigured pirate came aft, smiling half in apology, from under my thwart he dragged a great bundle of polythene which, unrolled, was a tent in the stern to cover us all from *Walkeria's* drench of spray from her wake. As she lurched into throaty way, shattering sea's silence, we huddled in rough sanctuary.

Evening's cold hand had begun to fall upon us, the sky hanging low. Soon we three against the cuddy board surrendered our edge of shelter, gave ourselves to the loneliness of sea.

Within the polythene arose laughter, a bubbling of joke; those two irrepressible, till, as though drained of fun, change came upon them. They sang now, a queer wild song, desolate, of sad longing, a song of two parts, one calling, one answering. It seemed of no beginning, no end, having no solace. On the cuddy board the boatheader sat upright, swaying with the boat's motion, sightless, arms limp between his knees.

At last to the chamber of the polythene there came silence, so for a time resting upon us as though tangible. Then again singing rose, not now as before, but now, eccentric, yelping, monkeyfied, a dialogue of funniness not quite comprehensible. Tub oar and boatheader chuckled and, chuckling looked at me, smiling, with sage wagging of elderly heads. For a long time so went the singing then flagged, sank to silence, leaving nothing but the sea's hiss and scud, monotonies of swell.

Then suddenly out of that illimitable nothingness there were porpoises, a host about us. At first, in salutary caution, they kept off a little, then in their poignant innocence drawing in to full trustful proximity, within hand's touch, to individual attachment. So one went with me, palpably friendly. I felt its sense of personal association - this wild creature of ultimate freedom. How should it be that I, of our debased species so unworthily be honoured? For mile on mile they came with us in merry company, empty of untrusting fear. Then, at first amorphous forming to shape there showed that which was Fayal. With sentient sense of leave taking our escort left us, not for them land's contamination. In the boat no word was spoken.

In the toss of water under Salao's crags they left us, those men, briefly so closely of my life. We, hunched in the wheelhouse for warmth, soon were at Horta.

"No whale then," said Peter in Café Sport. "Better hurry along to Joao's before he closes, you must be hungry."

And so I was, wildly hungry.

CHAPTER XX

Tragic Monster

ON AN evening in 1966, again the little ship rounded the light, entered the harbour of Horta. There again lay Horta under the looming mass of the hills, pastel-bright in the bland light of evening. But where was that small blue façade, sun and sea bleached that so well I remembered? Could that be Café Sport, flag-bright blue, in such a flare of new paint?

When soon we had tied up, when I had walked the quay, there it was, truly itself, changed only by new paint that had also come within. There in his corner was Henrique rolling his inevitable cigarette; by the counter Peter, light brown eyes twinkling with the same lucid good humour. Beyond the door the same blue glitter across the 5-mile strait to Pico's heaven-aspiring peak. The numerous family above Café Sport still were at their window in eternal surveillance of the passing of the world.

José Eugenio, the tiny tow-launch skipper with whom I had sailed last year had taken a shore job for his better benefit, but still, they told me, when the rocket ascended he fretted, needing to remember his benefits. On the evening after my return we, Peter and I, were taking evening's freshened air at the door when there came José Eugenio walking with others under the trees across the road. Seeing me he flung up his arms, ran across, "Senhor Bernardo," he cried. While in the middle of the road our embraced meeting lasted, the traffic waited with regard for acceptable standards of courtesy.

Only minimal change had there been in my absence; day followed day, in a placidity of peace, overlying the volatile presence, always there of volcanic threat - that and the chance as constant of ill fate by whaling, with death by whaling.

"This year," they told me in Café Sport, "it will be better for whaling. So unlucky you were last year - the weather not right. Ah, but this year it is good; you will have good whaling. Just now it is not good - the wind rough, out of the south. It will pass, a few days; it is no more than the change of the moon. When full moon is passed, there will come north or north-east wind, the sea calm. Then, then, good for whaling. Soon, in a few days perhaps."

So it was in this interval that I heard of the family Fula, men of Pico, whaling men. Under the legal system governing Azorean whaling, a Pico company had a right to maintain a whaling station at Castelo Branco on Fayal: established there were the Fula men, the father patriarch, elderly but strong yet, still skippering a whale boat. Of his seventeen sons were made the greater part of crews for the two canoas there based: one, José, skippered his boat. These were men of a kind of magnificence, simple and of a tacit bravery, never questioning. I heard of them first from Bruno Vailati.

As I had come from England drawn by the epic survival into our time of this archaic remnant so had come he from Italy. I had come to write a book: he to make a film for his series, *Encyclopaedia of the Sea*. He, his crew, I too, were based in a guesthouse, by that being convenient to work together. But that first day after my return, it was Sunday; on Sunday there is no whaling: for that respite the whalemen may forget the toils, the lethal threats of other days, put on fine clothes, with their families walk in the cavernous shade of the trees. Even in Café Sport they might allow themselves a small dalliance with wine - though it was little they could afford.

But as always it is in Fayal, of such endless tranquillity as it seemed, whaling's wild thread was always woven through. Though gently a sabbatical calm was upon the tables of Café Sport, of whaling would most talk be. Not tomorrow they said would weather be right; but, probably the wind would come from the north, the sea would be easy, it would be good for whaling.

Next day, it was thought, chance there might be. At 4am at fading edge of night I was up, by 4.30 on the coast road precipitously above the sea that sinuated to Castelo Branco, I, Bruno and his crew too. There between white walls a drop of track, steeply stony between small clings of maize field, fell to the whale station. It, as was that at Saloa, lay with a look frightful with insecurity in the merest notch, morosely fanged about with juts of rock under the sheer of rock face. Only a retarded slipping run down the plunging track could attain to the crag-hemmed boat slip.

Dawn's first penumbra was lifting from the sea's blue-black edge, soon expanding, flooding up the sky, imposing the half-reality that is of the earliest hours. In this time, as it seems stolen, between dawn and sunrise, the light has a queer lean stringency that gives a hint of eternity - being neither of day nor night, thinly brief. Then Pico's silhouette softened then melted in golden blaze: behind the shoulder of the peak the sun lifted. It was day.

Still now the wind came, still southerly over the heights, but gentler, just possibly of expectancy. The enlarging light poured, pushing aside last shreds of early witchery. Just offshore, just beyond the fanged inlet of the slip lay two tow launches at their mooring buoys. With them two canoas and their crews; but they paddled in, grounding at the foot of the slip. On block and tackle, on wooden keel shoes they were hauled up. So little was expectancy that the rocket should call.

Above the slip, at the track's end, the whalemen's families waited, wives, children, wreathing the men about - for this one day more, the men were coming unharmed from the sea.

Then it was that I first met José Fula and Antonio da Costa his brother-in-law. José was small, a tiny man, lean, sea-burnt brown behind a broad sweep upturned of moustache that gave him rather a swinging air under the wide brim and high crown of his straw hat. José was a boatheader. Antonio, he a harpooner, was broad, heavy-shouldered. These two men, tough, incomparably brave, were shy.

Among those who waited were José's two daughters, perhaps nine and eleven: either side they entwined him. Soon he, they, all the men, the clinging families, wandered off, for that day free of fear. In the silent sunny loneliness above the sea we were left, Bruno and I, in a vacuum of un-happened drama; day grew, climbed the now hot blue arch of sky, there was nothing but us, a soft sibilant singing of insects in that vast peace. We who had not eaten that early-starting day became aware of need.

To find cobs of corn I wandered off on the grassy track that, against a wall of boulders, dropped away round a flank of land. In the bliss of sun, on grass gently patterned, sun and shade, above sea infinitely of peace. How could be conceived a drama so bloody as the hunting of the sperm whale? And, in the shade of a tree there was tethered a goat; it curvetted with that prettiness that goats may have, bleating winsomely, blinking its odd squinty hircine eyes, pleading that its head should be scratched. I climbed the bank there, over the wall and under olive boughs to pluck a few cobs of corn.

We lit a little fire of wood scraps that in their burning were aromatic; on that, when it had burnt to a red glow, we cooked the cobs. Hungry no more, last harsh expectancy flagged then was stilled. There came then a tiny boy, from who knows where. He wore nothing but a short little shirt, below that his little brown bottom and legs. In some far reach of child's privacy he was remote, of us unaware. What deep summer soliloquy so held him I wondered, what foetal remnant into young consciousness?

Quite soon we went. At fall of night the wind changed: there was certainty in Café Sport. "Tomorrow it will be right for you," said Othon da Rosa Silveira, "the wind will have gone round to the north, the sea will be calm; the lookouts will be able to see the blows far off. Be early at Castelo Branco."

At 4am at the thinning of night I was on the road to Castelo

Branco, where at my coming there was a shiver of expectancy; as first light seeped from under the sea's rim the men came, José, Antonio, all of them. One, elate in eager fidget to prove his mettle, was fifteen possibly sixteen. The moments this morning were taut in sequence, hard, counting as to certainty. But the hours built slowly, so separately ticking as though to defer event.

Five o'clock, 6 o'clock, then 7 o'clock. At twenty minutes past seven the brittle quiet was shattered; from a roof up the track the rocket rose, exploded, a knell rebounding from the heights, sounding, re-sounding.

There was no cry, no exultant shout "*Baleia*!" As of one imperative we were running to the boats - the brief quiet order, the shorthand movement in a sequence so long accustomed, as by birth instructed. In the canoas now, going out through the impatient tick of seconds, past the rock's ragged threat to the tow launches waiting on throb of engines. Tow warps were taken; in four minutes from the rocket we were making way.

We ran due west under that stern precipitate coast. Under our sterns the sun's molten blaze climbing the sky, still pallid in youth of day. Astern, Pico now not of rock, was vaporous, rosy-fawn. The sea folding from our wake was ultramarine, satin lined with white. In the canoas, the crews huddled aft were silhouettes against the eastern torrent of light.

On the starboard bow Capelinhos came up at the falling of the first hour; then on the starboard bow the new volcano, stark, raw-red. Surging on, Fayal dropped astern; ahead an anonymity of sea and sky, sun-glinting emptiness; no form now within the capture of the horizon. But full-throttle the boats, unhesitant, in all that blue unshapement heading upon a blow a few feet high. Fayal's tossing heights far astern now were rosy gossamer. Another two hours yet the men said. Pico now a faint pink point, Fayal a haze. Then that, all that, gone, the third hour spent. A fourth hour poured under our keels but still the horizon, inviolate, contained us.

Then with no word spoken, suddenly in the boat there was a sense, a stirring. In one launch a man swarmed the mast to scan the sea's recessions. The launches veered apart, casting as does a dog on a scent.

Then from our canoa, S. Joao Baptista, exultantly, a shout, "*Bloz*!" The men were pointing, over the starboard bow. With a boil of wake the launches sheered off; tow warp was cast. Then, in that glinting immensity, I saw it, stubby, a vaporous mushroom, pale mushroom colour, half a mile off.

The launch had stopped; we lay in a silence made more quiet by the purring of the idling engine. In the canoas the masts were being stepped, sails hoist, then filling with audible slap.

Under bellying sails, facing forward, the men, squatted on the gunwales, paddled in rapid rhythm. The whale, innocent still of danger, idled in this benefice of ocean, blowing, - 'having its spoutings out' in its world so providentially good for whales. The climactic moments were counting down. Now for whale or men must come awful disaster.

Now in painful stretch of seconds the canoa was closing on the whale. Statue-still against the clumsy cleat there was Antonio, harpoon poised. They will go from astern I thought, to go on the flipper, so slightly to lessen the appalling risk - though thus it may happen that in the first pang of agony the whale may fling up its mighty flukes, then to smash down on the boat's frail timbers. But still in the lessening moments the whale dallied in the sun, moving slowly, blowing, blowing. Its sound was as of surf washing back from a shingle beach.

The canoa did not go on the whale from astern; it came down from ahead, within the narrow cone of no vision for the whale; it came *cabec com cabeca* - head on head - straight on the great bluff of head, that way of most hideous danger, dependent on finest judgement within the fall of a second. Again the whale blew, and in the sough of its sound Antonio, in the moment of turning past the head doubling orgasmically, 'darted' the harpoon. The whale was 'fastened'.

The canoa now had passed astern, just astern, but enormously close to this creature heaved up, wet, huge, shimmering blue-grey, shadowed by an upflung canopy of the flukes. The whale sounded, the boat going about, bows wrenched down, taking water, lurching on the white seethe. The line, kicking, bucketing, was pouring through the chocks: 100 fathoms, 200 fathoms, then levelled off, pausing; suddenly a renewed plunging of line, the canoa, in tow going headlong. This was the 'Nantucket sleigh ride'. It was a wild whale in vast frenzy many fathoms deep; it took the canoa as though powered, cutting the swell in fountaining spray, for half a mile unslackening. The line at the loggerhead smoked; he of the after thwart threw water over it that it might not ignite.

The line slackened, jerked distantly vast, then slackening, rose in white smother. The sea erupted; the whale was in the surface, thrashing, blowing, beating the sea, weaving confusedly, throwing its monstrous erratic head. The flukes threw up, for a moment painted in the dazzle of sky, then rounding out, the whale sounded; in its uncomprehending rage taking the line gouted through the chocks. But not now so long, so far, so deeply; then slackened, stopped; rose slowly. The men were up, astride the thwarts, hauling line; José in the stern coiling it down with fine care that no coil should foul another.

Briefly, in frantic resurgence, the whale ran again, staccato, in the surface, weaving, beleaguered in confusion, inexorably held by the drag of line. It became undirected, pestered. The men, hauling again, took the line into the bow cleats - thus laterally to draw in upon the whale - 'bowing on the whale'. The moment for lancing was looming.

Antonio at the clumsy cleat was a set spring, for this fearsome crisis. Hauling foot by foot the boat edged on to the whale, till, just off, crouched for pouncing, it waited upon the preposterous peril of one moment that, for one or other, was to be of fate.

As by a trap released in its moment of chance, the boat went in, at an angle behind the head, closely, into contact. In Antonio the stoppered-down lust for action burst - from feet through thighs and buttocks, he drove the lance vertical downward, entered to the shank's end.

In its gargantuan anguish the whale rolled away, flukes and flippers thrashing, throwing over the boat a swamp of spray. Antonio, doubled, with drag of knees and shoulders on the lance warp, strove till the lance sucked free of the mighty body; the men at the oars, stroking two strokes, backed water. The whale seeking to sound, threw up its flukes, failed, slapped them down with a crack as of a gun. Far stricken, it sought to plunge, beating in awful futility. It turned, under the surface, ran under the boat lifting it teetering on a 3-foot displacement.

Brokenly now the whale ran indeterminately. Still it blew; the blow was pink.

Pitiful though now it was in its enormity of distress, still the whale was of possible lethal danger - which often so it had been. Cautiously with the oars the men moved on it, tentatively waiting upon chance. Edging in, on such a brief gift of chance, from 2 fathoms off Antonio, heavy-shouldered, made a tossing dart; in such a stress of moments the lance seemed to hang, then, dropping, it entered for the shank's whole length. As the boat backed water; as Antonio threw back his weight to drag free the lance, a great slow shudder ran through the whale's length. Then it blew. The blow now was clottedly vaporous, pink. On the launch was a great shout. On the canoa a red waif was hoist; it signalled the launch to move in. Inconsequentially the whale was beating about the boat, blowing, labouring. The sea's good clarity was darkening, reddening.

Now not hesitating the boat went again; again Antonio made his lobbing throw of the lance, and again. Then, as at the bursting of a stopper, the blow gushed red, now not vaporous, low, welling bloodily; whale and boat rolled in a sea of blood. The boat came in again, lanced again. Surely now the whale must be hardly still with life; it lay in the surface, awash, the blow now intermittent.

Slowly in laboured perambulation, it circled the boat, spasmodically shaken by convulsions. This was 'the flurry' close now to the end. The men, arms hanging loosely, waited.

But, abruptly, renewed life seemed to sweep the whale. It lifted monstrously half out of the water. The mighty flukes flung up, slapped down explosively. Astoundingly it sounded.

Line gouted away, vertically down, not loosely, making a rigid rod plunging, 100 fathoms, 200 and another 30. It stopped, with no movement more, the line rigidly vertical. The whale had dived to die. It was a rare event. It is nearly inviolable that the whale will die at the surface.

This I thought for these men must be a dreadful malice of fate - they of such pitiful poverty, receiving nothing for a lost whale. And how were they, seven men, to lift to the surface that colossal corpse a quarter of a mile beneath in that black deep? But they in their wondrous stoicism sat quietly on the thwarts, smoked, were placid. What would come would come. So lying in the somnolent rocking of the swell in anti-climactic peace, we waited in S. Joao Baptista, it a little down at the bows by fixed anchorage to the sunken lifeless victim of their hunting. So must we wait till help, radio-summoned, should reach us. On the foredeck of the launch I lay half-dozing while an uncounted drift of hours passed over us.

Then, minutely distant, two bow-waves were coming from the far haze that was Fayal. The bow-waves enlarged to be a tuna boat and a launch towing a canoa and its crew. They went into S. Joao Baptista, as did two more from the tuna boat so to make sixteen men in a light craft built for seven. Then they, acceptantly without complaint, with their naked hands set themselves to the lifting of the huge inert corpse. Quietly, rhythmically they began. Antonio in the bows, quietly chanting, setting the rhythm, they hauled, foot by foot, becoming fixed in a hypnosis of movement. The foot-long draws shorted to 6 inches; some of the men took off their socks, put them on their hands which the harsh wet line was causing to bleed. Unregarded, time passed, unbroken - still in faith of an ultimate successful end, still with Antonio's soft chanting, the hauling continued, out of mind.

When five hours had passed, in the clear plunge of sea the whale became visible, an uncertain shifting shape. There was no triumph in the boat, only acceptance that thus it had come to be, and of what must be made to follow.

There now the whale was, perhaps 20 fathoms down, perhaps 30; but now, head and tail together it must be brought to the surface, so to allow for the fastening of the towing strap at the tail. In so long a history as has had whaling, this as a problem probably had been before; but, almost certainly never before had it found such a solution.

With us was Bruno Vailati. He was an aqualung diver. He put on his diving suit, his air cylinder. He took a rope; with it he dived. Time now was taut: we scanned for shark that, so often are drawn by the blood of a killed whale. So incalculably we waited till there again was Bruno, ascending. He had bent the rope to the peduncle of the tail of the whale.

Not one of us now not at the hauling, in the canoa sixteen, on the boat the rest - I wondering by what fortitude the sixteen had been supported through those five hours. For us now of doubled strength the harsh line bit, muscles cracked.

At last it was done. Hugely awash, there was the great grey undulant island of corpse, so dearly won. With a boat spade a hole was mortised through one fluke, that through it the towing strap could be fastened. The whale being now without buoyancy, worriedly I did conjecture if so the towing might be precarious. A chain was attached to the towing strap, and to that the towing warp from the two launches going in line. So at two knots began the long retracing of all those miles to the whale factory at Porto Pim on Fayal. So it would go, limping through the night.

We, now emptied, drained of all impulse, discovered that comfort is relative. Gratefully we came aboard the tuna boat; it was a craft designed for practical ends, but it was roomy. We, Bruno and I, with a rolled sweater behind the back, on the foredeck found freedom for stretching of legs, leaning against the wheelhouse, so feeling to be almost a degeneracy of lounging comfort. But a tuna boat is slow; as it often may be in returns from the sea, the land seemed to retreat before our approach elusively. When we came under Capelhinos it was dark. When we came to Horta, when we dragged ourselves on to the harsh volcanic stone of the quay, we had been five hours returning.

It was in the morning that we heard that only half a mile offshore, the tow had broken loose. The whale sank, was lost. How unspeakable a tragedy was that - the whale, free in its sunny sea lost its freedom, was pestered into awful death; the men for so many hours of fearful danger and exhaustion, now in their poverty were as much so as when in the morning the rocket had sent them to sea.

There came other days when in the early light the rocket's summons sent us summarily to sea. I some days was in the tow launch, sometimes in the canoa being of the killing of other whales.

Then it came to the festa of she who was patron saint of the whalers, *Nossa Senhora da Guia,* a day most poignantly sanctified and of a bliss touched tranquillity, for all that day people going their ways smiled and were peaceful.

From quite early in the day the lilting air of morning was filled with a pretty poppling of rockets: I, waking at leisure, was filled by a light happiness that this day was with no compulsion that at dawn's early hint I must be waiting for the command to the boats.

But first, before I could fall entirely into the blessed sense of the day, there was one last part of what had been which I must attend. A whale of yesterday's hunting in which I had been, this morning was to be 'cut in' at the whale factory at Porto Pim. I walked out of Horta, past the whaling centre, along the strand of gritty black volcanic sand. There under Monte da Guia was the whale factory.

Inside, on the flensing platform, they were finishing a whale, not ours of yesterday. They were standing inside the head, emptying it. In the centre lay the guts, a slithered pile 10 feet high, dusky red, brown, gruesome yellow. Below, out a little from the slip, moored to a buoy, was our whale waiting upon the clearing of the flensing platform. In that foetid fatty air I waited too. From time to time to escape the clutch of stench I climbed to a vantage point where I might see the clear sky-reflecting blue of the bay beyond the spread of blood, to catch the sweet drift of air from the sea.

For the clearance of the guts they took cables from the winch, down the slip to pulley blocks in the walls, from there back up the slip to find purchase on the lofty quake of guts. For handling of the massive grappling hooks came a man and a boy. The man, heavy-chested, stout-legged, braced to the hook's weight. But the boy, brown and slight and smooth, trod up the paunch slither, dragging with him the monstrous hook. They set two hooks, jabbing them into a quaky hold. The winch wheezed, clanked; the pile shuffling on the stones moved down the slip, into the bay. When it was clear, oozily afloat, a dinghy took a cable from the pulley to the whale at its mooring, there to be hooked to the towing strap. Slowly, to the wheezing of the winch, the whale was brought to the slip there to strand. It looked enormous there, hugely grey, insentiently inert, rubber-smooth, seeming to be without relevance to the living frantic creature that yesterday had dwarfed the imperilled boat. Sliding easily on the noisomely lubricated stones, the ponderous tackles were taken down the slip, there to be attached by a chain round the tail. Only by the foreman's great rage, flinging of arms, was it so done, that there should be no imbalance thus to make the mighty flukes jamb across the tunnel of ascent. That achieved, rage left the foreman as would mist before the wind.

Before the ascent had ceased they who were to work on the whale had moved upon it, the cutting spades chopping softly through the white fondant-textured blubber. I stayed no longer.

Outside in the soft spangle of air and lap of sea on the strand, the unseemlinesses of the flensing platform in moments were half remembered. This day of *Nossa Senhora da Guia* was that on which the whaleboats from all the islands came to draw up on the strand of Porto Pim that they might later in this festa day be blessed by the priest. The first, bearing a yellow strake of its island of origin, then was hauling up on its keel shoes, with slow care that on this day, its paint, freshly done, should not be hurt.

Slowly I walked back into Horta through that narrow street, white walled, that passes the whaling centre which today was shut. I went in the mood of the day, idly, and all the way people were in holiday mood taking the air, smiling as they walked or at their windows. "*Bom dia*," they said to me. Soon I came to Café Sport and there at the tables were José Fula and Antonio da Costa.

When greetings were over, intertwining of arms, embracing of shoulders and the glasses of *verdellho* had come, José with finger tip drawing on the table, explained with fervour his ways of whaling. Invariably it was his way he said, to go on the whale *cabec com cabeca*. Yes, he said, how much easier to come from aft of the

Whale on a flensing platform before being cut in.

whale, on the flank where the blind zone is wider. But always he said, always there is the danger that the upflung flukes will crash down on the canoa - think, he said, just think how many times so it had happened. But to come on the head within that very narrow blind zone, under the bluff of head - if the approach has been well done - then slipping to one side of the head, at the moment of the dart the whale will be swept past and be astern before it peaks its flukes and sounds. Then how little danger from the flukes said José, smiling, in his modesty suggesting a danger no more than crossing a road. But I had seen the exactitude of a second that was vital. A big bull whale's head may be 30 feet long: in its lower jaw it has an average of twenty-two very large teeth. Immediately behind the head is the inordinate menace of a flipper, a sweep of which will shatter the boat.

But this was the day of *Senhora da Guia:* for all the floating hours of its length there was no sea danger, no rocket's summons, nothing but the gentle gaiety, the peaceful poppling of festa rockets. We dallied away the morning, José, Antonio and I. Even for a time they forgot whales to talk of home and family.

In the afternoon I went again to Porto Pim. Now all the whaling canoas had come, were drawn up, ranked along the strand, dressed over all with flags. I went on, past the factory, silent now, sunk back into bottomless peace in the sun. In the warmth of afternoon I climbed slowly, in that loneliness lulled by a soft sibilance of grasshoppers till, suddenly at the last bend, there was no loneliness. Here was the tiny white church of Senhora da Guia, the whalemen's church, poised high above the sea. Now it was thronged about, whalemen stiffly in suits, women in festa satins, children, bandsmen splendid in gold and dark blue tunics, white trousers, waiting for what would be their part in the sanctities of the day - it was from here that all later orderings of the day were to flow.

There was a second band; I found it because the climbing of the hill had made me thirsty. Following the guidance of my thirst I was led to its slaking. Characteristically it was Azorian, ingenious in its simplicity, untainted by sophistication. Its skeleton, of no powered help, was a pedal tricycle as anywhere might be seen: being Azorian it folded out elaborately, lavish with cures for thirst. Its master, unaided by any power but his own, had induced it up all the steep stony spiral of road round the flanks of Monte da Guia. There clustered was the second band, they and many others. As soon as I had gained a large glass of Pico wine I was absorbed. The *senhor* they hoped, was enjoying the day of da Guia. But after the long climb he must be thirsty; please to finish his wine and have another. All was easy, placid, smiling, without hint that ever could life be otherwise than this bliss of tarrying. That I might survive the bandsmen's care for my thirst it was necessary that I should slip away.

Because soon, as I could see, the procession would begin, for a short way I walked down the road to await it, climbing up into the falling field above the road. Such is the fertility of Fayal's volcanic soil that a clothes peg planted almost would burgeon. I lay now in a rampant riot not only of wild flowers but as much entwined with roses and others strayed from gardens. In the sea-soft air it was a lazy delight of solitude, seeing those in ascent and descent but unseen by them.

In that fragrant suspension so it was for half an hour; then the procession was approaching. Its music floating on the now nearly-evening air had a curious touch upon the soul, half melancholy, of disembodiment. The children came first, in line either side of the road wearing white, blue and pink. The procession moved slowly, with solemnity; after the children the adults, many barefoot on the stones of the road, coming in penance, carrying candles. After them, ranked across the road in white vestments, came the men. On their shoulders they carried the carved and painted figure of the saint clustered about with cherubs. With them came the priest. Though all was done so deeply suffused in solemnity, they being so devout a people, there was no sense of doctrinaire severity but rather a quiet community of a bliss shared.

Going down before the procession I met Peter coming up. Together we went down to the strand, where now all the whaleboats were drawn up under the little flutter of their flags. We waited by a Fayal boat, one from Saloa. In it waited its boatheader, not now in the rough truth of his whaling clothes, his leather-brown leanness being now stiffly pinched in a dark suit, a collar and tie. He waited fretfully, reclusively withdrawn. When slowly the procession came to his canoa, as it seemed without sound of feet in the falling light, as the figure of the saint was set athwart before the loggerhead, the whisper died. For moments, tight-lipped, the boatheader stood; in his broad seaman's hands he took the line from the after tub, snubbed it at the loggerhead and, doubling it, put it gently about the shoulders of the saint, tied it lightly. Bending, he kissed the garment of the saint. He was speaking quietly as though his inward voice was audible.

"Our lady of da Guia go with us, lead us safely. Help us that we may find whales. Guard us through the dangers of the hunt. Let your care be over us so that we may come back to our families who wait for us."

Then he was silent. Tears rolled down his sea-seamed face. For a time all were silent. Then the children were brought, one by one to be lifted, to kiss the painted garment.

We left now, Peter and I, through the twilight to the boat slip by the old Spanish watergate, to the open space between the water and the streets where, earlier, I had seen the fishing boat receiving its decoration. Now its stern was stacked with loaves. It was customary on the festa of *Nossa Senhora da Guia* that when the whaleboats have been blessed the procession shall come there to give bread to the poor.

Late in the evening, about the time of midnight, I was drawn in the leisurely throng to the pleasure ground that, hung above the town, was embowered under acacias and bougainvillea. There at little tables was a drinking of wine, and a promenading, listening to the aching sweetness of the *fado* singer. Nearly now the day of *Nossa Senhora da Guia* was done. In the morning near sunrise the whale rocket would hiss and break.

CHAPTER XXI

From Paddington to Meet Mike

ON A night of July 1966 I was on a flight which, through the night and beyond, was to translate me from all familiarity to deepest Africa. It was my first long-haul flight, unless my transatlantic trip to New York is to be so counted - a mere 3000 miles across the sea. Now I was going 6000 miles, crossing the Equator to all things exotic and far. Though air travel has destroyed so much of the magic of travel - dissipating its sense of exoticism - some remained in the now mist-wrapped years of the Sixties. Then, still, there were landings on the way, goings ashore.

That thus I was on this aerial way was part of as unplanned a course of events, as accidental, as Darwin's Natural Selection. From first consciousness I had had an undoubting acceptance that a traveller I would be, and that I would provide any determination needed to that end. But chance forestalled.

About the time that commercial television came to be, there made himself known to me a film producer-director of whom I had known nothing. His name was Max Munden. His wish was that I should be his subject in the making of a little fishing film for television. His client I think was the Gas Council. We made the film; I never saw it. I thought no more about it.

In 1964 Max Munden returned, bearing a proposal. *Creel,* he suggested should sponsor a series of angling films to be used on television. I was to be their presenter and in some the angler. Such was his persuasion that he won agreement. We made the films; the BBC accepted them, running them twice on BBC2 then twice on BBC1. They bore the title 'Angler's Corner'. In passing I have to say that when a few years ago I saw videos of some of them, a red rash of shame swept me. I was horrified, apart from all else, to hear myself tainted by the prissy nit-picking accent which was of that time. I had never known it. It was demonstrated that filming for TV has made strides in the interim.

Still there was aroused no sense of a destined path before me. I had been invited to do a job; I had done it, it had been well received. Then came 1966 and Max Munden returning to tell me that he and I were going to Africa; for the Zambia National Tourist Bureau he was to make three films about angling in Zambia to promote Zambian tourism. I began, not very clearly, to suspect an emergent pattern; here was I, projected into the night sky, involuntarily swept to what was my life's ardent seeking.

There were landings on our way and, terrorism not having then begun to stalk, freely we could go ashore. At Cyprus, in the airport silenced by that dead of night, we drank local brandy. In the morning we floated in a white torrent of sun; below, amazing in its truth at last, lay the Sahara Desert, an apparent infinity.

After the desert another infinity, the bush, endlessly dun green below, with no feature for the untrained eye until to starboard a lake. At 600 miles an hour we were most of an hour in the passing of its length. Later experience tells me that was Lake Turkana, which then still went by its white man's name of Lake Rudolf. There was a little lake, a mere park pool as it looked; we were three minutes in the passing of it. Then we came to Entebbe in Uganda, by vast Lake Victoria, there to land again. The airport had the aspect of an enlarged cricket pavilion with a little picket fence in front and a bar within where we had a beer because with Max Munden beer was a punctuation. The African barman served us with very clear distaste; he would have preferred to throw it at us. By the runway, as we took off, there were marabou storks, huge and odd at first seeing, hunched-shouldered with beaks like logs, dishevelled. Then we were held in the sky again with the slowly passing bush below, until about late lunchtime we came to last landing, Lusaka in Zambia.

I liked immediately the man who met us as the airport. Perhaps I should have had a premonitory sense. He was Deputy Director of the Zambia National Tourist Bureau; his name was Mike Blackall. I think it relevant to sketch the path of his years which had brought him there; they were to have much bearing on the path taken by my next thirty years. He then was thirty, I nearly sixty.

In the Royal Navy Mike had done his national service and, that done, was casting a speculative eye at the world. Life was before him. The world was wide and stimulatingly profound with possible excitements. In the care of a completely open mind, he chanced to be walking down the Haymarket in London. His mind though open was not quite itself; the previous evening there had been a party of leave-taking with old comrades. Pausing for the support of a window, he observed it to be that of the Northern Rhodesia Commission. In the window was a notice inviting young men to become District Assistants in that country. Mike entered, found himself taking a cup of tea with he who was in charge. Three weeks later he was in Northern Rhodesia, and only a little later, at Mumbwa, very inconspicuously far in the bush. At Mumbwa was a District Commissioner, a District Officer and two District Assistants and of them was Mike. In their hands lay entire day to day government of a district about the size of Wales. For his movement about this territory Mike was allotted transport; it was a bicycle. The District Commissioner inspected his new assistant, declared him green. He must be toughened, immediately and without tenderness.

He was ejected into the bush, on tour. With him went the local chief, he who among his people is akin to divinity. Also attendant

With Max Munden and Mike Blackall.

Landing a small one!

Bernard with a tiger fish.

were the chief's two counsellors, a district messenger, porters, bicycles, stores and approximately the powers of God. He was to cross the Kafue River, then on to the southern edge of the Lukango Swamps. He must collect taxes, site village wells, be bush doctor and bush magistrate; he must design bridges, houses and roads, he must be comforter of the aged. For all these functions he was by nature equipped; by nature he could exert authority and by nature he could make instant decisions as by divination.

That the tour should be toughening was fully realised; it was largely by luck, not lethal. To the Kafue River in due course they came in good order. With the aid of two dugout canoes they must cross it, and, of the African dugout canoe it should be known that it is not stable. It was early in the rainy season; the river ran high and heavy. The first canoe, bearing porters, messengers and some baggage, achieved the far bank. The second, deeply laden with chief, two counsellors, Mike, bicycles, baggage, reached the middle, there to meet the flood's full force. The canoe turned over. Swimming in African rivers must be shared with crocodiles and hippos, and, as now it was to be seen, neither chief nor counsellors could swim. Mike must be their saviour. He has said that only by very hard swimming, much helped by thought of crocodile and hippo, was he able to do that. When at last they did accomplish the far bank it was 300 yards downstream that they did so. They were alive; but by the river's theft, without bicycles, food, and with only the clothes they wore. They were 150 miles from base, without communication, unable to re-cross the river. For them no choice but to go forward.

The way forward was tangled jungle, much of it reed grass. Reed grass in Africa is unfriendly; it towers above the head, it is tough, adamant. Its long leaves, so gracefully pendulant, are steel-strong, sharp as spears. As well I was to know, they are lacerating to those wearing shorts. In that boundless but spiteful wilderness they struggled with little belief in salvation.

Feeling themselves so much forsaken, they could not believe when, apparently distinctly, they heard the *put-put-put* of an engine. But truly, somewhere unseen beyond in the spinous tangle so it was. That which emerged threw them back into doubt. There came a *La Velocette*, on it one who wore a white topi and a white cassock. On the handlebars hung a bag; it contained two dead chickens. In one of two panniers was a bottle of whisky. He was real. He revealed himself to be Father Peter from Karenda Mission. He led them to the village of Headman Chinokabo.

With the passage of time Mike, fully toughened, became first a District Officer then a District Commissioner. It was that which involved him in the Alice Lenshina affair. This was at that time when Northern Rhodesia was in the process of being transmuted into the new independent nation of Zambia. About Alice Lenshina arose a disturbance in the passage of that change.

Alice Lenshina was a religious zealot. She founded a religious sect of most exemplary principles. There must be no witchcraft, no drink, no drugs, no politics. It set up its own villages, its own churches; they were kempt, orderly, the land well cultivated. The people were quiet, self contained. The sect was a social model. But Alice Lenshina, struck down by malaria, was very ill; she passed into a coma. Physically she recovered; mentally she did not. She discovered herself to be the New Messiah and so declared herself.

The transition to independence, as inevitably it must, brought some turbulences. The ascendant party, militant in the change, was the United National Independence Party, UNIP; it felt first touch of political power, a heady draught. Throughout the country it took its ardent path to raise funds and membership, not prepared to be very tolerant of resistance.

Thus they came to the Lenshina villages. They were met with quiet courtesy, but great firmness. We cannot contribute, nor can we accept membership they said. We are a religious community with our own rules of life. We will accept no politics; we will live only as is our creed. UNIP in its pride was vastly affronted. Now, constantly, it harassed the community, which of course was greatly strengthened in its resistance.

UNIP, frustrated, brought in the army, so hardening resistance to fanaticism, anyway fierce, because Alice Lenshina told her followers that bullets would not hurt them but would turn to water.

There was slaughter, indiscriminately of men, women, children.

The people of the Lenshina sect were segregated into two rehabilitation centres; they who had been peaceful, now by bloody injustice were made a ferocity of rejection. To Mike, as Rehabilitation Commissioner, was handed the problem. He must so persuade these embittered people that they, in trust, might be led back to their villages. Mike should be their shepherd.

He went with a mobile unit, unarmed. That he was coming was leaked; it was seen as sinister. At dawn, when he came, he and his party were received with a hail of stones, rocks, bludgeons; they were surrounded, without escape. Several of the policemen fell, seriously injured; Mike was hurt but so far not seriously. It seemed they must be killed. Overhead a government pilot, monitoring what passed beneath, perceived their desperation. He put his plane into a dive, swept in as though a roaring angel of wrath just over the heads of the besieging mob. Again and again so he came till, in panic fear, they fled. Mike and his party gathered up their wounded and withdrew.

Later that day Mike, with the pilot who was his saviour, flew to Kasaba Bay at the southern end of Lake Tanganyika, there to rest and restore to unity his scattered nerves. He took a decision.

To Mike had been made a proposal. The Director of Tourism for the new nation of Zambia had invited him to become Deputy Director. At Kasaba Bay he decided on acceptance. Six months later the Director retired. Mike became Director of Tourism for Zambia.

Within that interval I, with Max Munden, was met at Lusaka Airport by Mike. Could we have known it, the touch of destiny was on that meeting.

How can I now recall first impressions of that distant day? They lie beyond the accumulated friendship and shared experience of thirty years. From first moment I think we, intuitively, found an affinity. We saw life as an optimism, as an adventure that was sure to turn out well. Within a few brisk days we, Max Munden and I, were programmed and cast upon our way into the bush.

It was a quick immersion, and for the sharp reception of impressions the better for that. We were upon a reconnaissance for the making of three films, for the assessing of locations, for getting the taste and smell of Africa which should inform the films. Over the years since then I have had much immersion in Africa, but still I can recall that first impingement. I recall that, newly from the thin air of England, that African air had a substance, as though almost it was organic. It was July, in the dry season, least hot of the months; other times as I was to learn was the air more potently tangible.

We took the road to Mumbwa, that road of Mike's probationary way, but without the modesty of his going. For us a car, enormous, a black thing of the American kind with a uniformed African chauffeur. So, inappropriately matched to the dirt road, we departed into space sharing it with nothing but, very occasionally, a lorry whose wake of Titian-blonde dust hid us opaquely. We, car and passengers, that started in our native colouration, immediately were Titian-red monochrome.

There was a sense soon that we were stationary; we drove in space that was limitless within inviolate horizons, the road a straight perspectived stripe, endlessly aimed but not attaining the mockery of the horizon. Then, when we had accepted our captivity within the horizons, startlingly, a place was come to. We came to Mumbwa.

It was startling too that, after the unrelenting enclosure of the road and the baked and barren bush, here at Mumbwa was a little hotel, one nice and neat and charming. Within was a bar and it was neat and nice, its cool beer was bliss. Behind, in what I took to be a chicken run, was a cheetah. But why should there be surprise that there at Mumbwa we should find that hotel? Was not Mumbwa the operative heart of a territory the size of Wales?

Beyond Mumbwa the road took us to the river, that same Kafue River, so nearly the ending of Mike and his party, and probably at that very place. But not now was it swollen with angry flood; it flowed in shrunken dry sea peacefulness, and with a pontoon ferry to bear car and us across. It took us into tsetse fly country. Where lives the tsetse fly, man and his cattle may not live; man, perforce, must leave to the wildlife the place that nature gave them. We were entering the Kafue National Park Game Reserve.

Gone now was the prevailing sense of man. Man here was the rarest species. Gone now was the beaten road of man, here only a bush track and about it not cultivation but primary jungle. We came at evening to the camp.

The camp was tight with solitude. When the black night fell, it was beleaguered. The sighing, cry-haunted bush held it. There was the tiny rest house and, just apart, the house where, in wild privacy hardly to be guessed, lived the game warden and his wife. They were of a precious kind, these two quiet people, of a dedication that it lessened, a little, the shame of man's record with nature. In the way I suppose of those newly in Africa, I said something about snakes. Did they, I asked, come into the house? "Oh quite often," the warden said. What did they do about them? The warden smiled gently. "Oh we just put them out." I wondered how one just puts out a cobra or a puff adder.

We ate that night about the campfire, a splendid pyre of enormous logs glowing wondrously. Beyond its light the bush was close, blackly sibilant with secrecies. Over all the singing of the frogs, warbling bass and things falsetto, a million million insects shrilled; one, huge and of very menacing aspect settled on my knee. I did not disturb it.

That night, being under a mosquito net enlarged my tyro sense of far adventure; how tropical a thing that so I must sleep (later, less naïve, I would be anxious that there should be no holes). The coming of morning revealed another fact of bush life; at 5 o'clock it was light; so at 5 o'clock we were up, the camp astir, the sun in rapid ascent.

Across the clearing, elusive under the trees, I saw dogs, of no kind that I had seen before. They were big, odd of shape and piebald, awkward on long front legs, backs sloping up to the high bunch of shoulders.

"Ah yes," the game warden was placid, "I thought there was a pack about - wild dogs."

I knew about wild dogs; that in the bush there was nothing

more implacably ferocious than a pack of wild dogs.

"They'll pass through," the game warden said gently. They were people of peace, he and his wife; theirs was a wisdom unattainable to urban dwellers of the western world.

Soon after 6 we were away, following the track, drenched in space, held in invincible distance. It was open country now, savannah, patched with herds of zebra, under a sky grey with heat. When once we paused, stopping the engine, the world swayed insubstantially in its heat; the shrilling of cicadas, which is incessant, fell upon us as of a solidity. Our passing disturbed a herd of impala which, superbly, hardly believably, in their leaping denied a law of gravity.

We were going to Ngoma; there we came later in the day, at last proving that African distance is not illimitable. Ngoma now has gone, or so I believe, submerged in the making of a great lake. Then, lonely in so much primal bush, it stood on a slight rise, a camp, a little of a fortress. Beyond its high steel-mesh fence, hunter and hunted, lion and antelope, went their ways. Within the fence, upon the fall of night, alien man shut the tall gates that he may, till dawn, be safe. Of Ngoma I remember much; but of nothing is memory so insistent as of one small bird. The black collared barbet is inconspicuous but never can I forget it. I recall little of its look, so little did I see of it. But I heard it. I hear it still. Incessantly, insistently, there was its voice. "Twubble," its call was; "twubble," it cried through every daylight hour, never with merciful respite. Somewhere I read that that inescapable call was not even solo; really, I was asked to believe, it was jointly done by cock and hen. "Twu," said one, "ble," said the other. I do not vouch for that, ready as I am to acknowledge what wonders there are within the realm of nature. Curiously, only at Ngoma have I heard the black collared barbet so insistent upon declaring itself.

Ngoma was comfortably established, almost cosy in so much raw wilderness. Its sleeping chalets were sound and solid, its dining block exemplary, its walks tree-shaded. Withal it was spacious. Then, so reassuringly, commodiously, the troops of baboons were to be seen very closely the other side of the fence. The game warden resident there was Barry Shenton; also resident was the Shenton Dynasty, perched like birds in a tree. Matriarchal was Mrs Shenton senior, then there was Mrs Shenton her daughter-in-law. In the evening to attend upon the bar there was a Shenton aunt. Shentonville they called Ngoma.

The bar at Ngoma was small, compact with its light in the boundless black of bush beyond the fence. No inch of the inside of the window glass was to be seen, so thickly felted over was it by a stirring host of insects. There, minute by minute, by our elbows, relentless miniature dramas were enacting, prey and predator, fulfilling tiny destinies. There the praying mantises, queerly sinister in their frozen posture, coldly mechanically slaughtering. Still I am reminded of them when I see a JCB about its work. Sometimes the voice of a lion, majestic and strange by night would penetrate the clogging curtain that voices have in a small space. Evening by evening in the bar, the steady Max Munden, for whom the drinking of beer had a spiritual validity, embarked upon his evening's devotion seriously. When a few draughts had eased first need, his need for argument would rise.

He was the very convinced holder of his somewhat idiosyncratic form of socialism, and, when suitably primed would, so to speak, throw down the doctrinaire garment of his views and invite all comers to walk on it.

"It's all," he would declare, demanding disagreement, "a matter of economics. That's what it all comes back to. Economics."

I do not believe that anything at all is just a matter of economics. I could not live happily if it were. My saying so brought Max to the hot disputatious state which was his desire. Only a few evenings taught me to avoid the trap. So much debate always incurred the need for further beer; we would have to rouse from her sleep the Shenton lady behind the bar. At 10 o'clock came lights out for economy of fuel. So our evening must end and our barmaid could continue her slumber more comfortably elsewhere.

Each morning, on the opening of the gates, we went out seeking locations on the Kafue River, going in a Landrover. It clearly, is not human; thus we saw more of those more legitimate presences than ours. Without suspicion they went their ways. We saw the warthog families going always in line ahead at a brisk trot. Leading is the mother, the young following, the father holding the rear; they go with tails rigidly erect. Not by any standard can a warthog be called pretty; but so seen, they have great charm.

Hippo we saw and heard, and they, unpretty creatures too, have charm. On African rivers they are ubiquitous, huge, soporific in sound. Their distant effect is a little like that of cows in an English meadow. In vast placidity they loll, often submerged with only nostrils emergent; they sigh with slumberous enormity. They burst from the water with cavernous honking, then with vast wistfulness sigh, sink back to submergence. Their effect is of infinite peacefulness.

But cows in an English meadow, except when newly with calf, are as tranquil as is the sound of them. But hippo deceive. They are testy, intolerant, very touchily territorial. Hippo are exceedingly large; they are exceedingly dangerous.

We saw many elephant, which also are exceedingly large, even larger, and at least as inequable of temper. No less than hippo, they are delightful to watch, majestic, imperious. We saw them in family procession crossing the Kafue River, adults cosseting the children across.

Down the valley of the Kafue, as with other African rivers, with the passing of the rainy season the river takes back its water, in hollows, depressions, water remains, making minor lakes. I have told elsewhere a story of such a one, but it will stand re-telling. With us was one who was our guide, opening to us the ways of the bush. We, he and I, decided to fish such a pool. First scrutiny revealed that in residence was a hippo; it lay mid-pool and seemed in placid phase. It honked warningly, sighed and relaxed. At the further end we observed the twin knobs that were the eyes of a submerged crocodile. The twin hazards thus noted, we went opposite ways, fishing round the pool till we should meet. The nature of fishing being what it is, I forgot the crocodile.

At a place where my way was through grass above head-height, as I thrust through I stubbed my foot on something which lashed.

The grass exploded. Back into the water in a smother went a crocodile, *the* crocodile. It was its tail that had tipped me. When a few minutes later we met, we sat on a rock, I feeling that a pause of peace would be therapeutic.

"Look," my companion said. He pointed between my feet. There, from a hole under the rock was the cast skin of a cobra. It was then that the hippo, patience gone, came at us. We left at once.

Passing round a thorn thicket we saw before us a thorn tree. In its dapple lay a pride of lion. Seeking to be unobtrusive we slunk away. At camp that evening we learned that the lion of that pride had a broken jaw; it must be shot.

African fauna that declares itself dramatically demands and receives fascinated attention - that indeed it so much deserves. It had mine. But there was that which impressed me more deeply.

Very early in childhood there had grown upon my notice, seized my devoted attention, the multiplicity of what I saw. I saw those greater creatures, birds, foxes, rabbits; they were to be seen by the least searching vision. But beyond, only for closer curiosity, there was an astonishing complexity of life that the moving of any stone or woodland leaf carpet revealed. I found the beetles, ferocious purple ground beetles, magnificent stag beetles, the smaller and smaller creatures that made of the beetles monsters. Quite soon consciousness grew of an infinite interconnectedness. I think I began dimly to perceive that this pulsating thronging of life, down scales too minute for the sight of eye, such a knitted-up intimacy, was something inseparable from the continuance of life on earth. The growing thought was part instinctive, part a perception. Now, so many years later, there is a name for it. Biodiversity it is called now; it may well be the single most important word of our time.

Now in Africa I saw that which in England had so persuaded me, blazoned. In that tropical place life thrummed; it burned, beat as a pulse. Its insistent sound incessantly shrilling, was that of cicadas, beetle-like creatures. By day and by night they sing; a restless incandescent sound of life. Such eruptive tropical fecundity is hardly to be imagined in our cool land.

Tropical life indeed is very greatly richer than that of temperate

Bernard beneath Victoria Falls.

places. I found myself overcome by its throbbing demonstration of what had preoccupied me more subtly in England. There, at home, I had been coming to an awareness of rhythms that, as it seemed to me, ran connectively through all that I saw of nature. Now here, in Africa, what I had heard as a whisper was a huge sound. From great to minute, life so teemed in such astonishing diversity that the patterns of it were the more brilliantly to be seen.

For our reconnaissance there were other destinations. Of those the first was Livingstone. Livingstone, lying hotly in the valley of the Zambezi, Livingstone by the Victoria Falls. Just as the idea of tropical Africa is so dominated by its large animals that the vibrating wonder of its smaller life is overshadowed, so all else that is Livingstone is dwarfed by the Victoria Falls. But even their taint of tourism, even such catch-pennies that may be about them, cannot lessen their awesome aspect.

We saw the Falls at night; they were floodlit. It might be supposed that, by that, they should be lessened in honesty, dignity, by such showmanship - which is indeed most thrilling to behold. It suffers no diminution. It was there I remember, on that fearful brink, that first in the southern sky I saw the Southern Cross.

Being there by day I saw a track that dropped away to the gorges below the Falls. A track of such invitation could not but be taken. Within only a few yards, all sense of the world left was gone, no sound but the Falls' muffled thunder, the hot air softened by the Falls' eternal spray. There was no mark of man. Life seethed, sang, rustled and was ecstatic. I was enraptured until, at a few paces distance, I was confronted. A very large male baboon stood there.

I had been told about baboons; do not irritate them it had been said. I had no impulse to irritate this daunting animal. Ill-tempered, baboons are, they had said. This one looked very ill-tempered; it wore a heavy frown, its beetled black eyes caved under its brows were unfriendly. It looked embittered. For immeasurable time we stood, I careful to make no movement. Then, very slowly, he began to back away, very slowly turned. On slow motion stalking legs very slowly I walked away.

In Livingstone we stayed at the North Western Hotel. I hope no outrageous modernity, hungry for that site, has overtaken that nostalgic colonial relic. Its long frontage was of one storey only in the old fashion; a deep verandah, running its length, treasured its shade. Magnificent trees, heavy-leaved, flanged with slender buttresses shaded it. The great boles, satin textured, bore long curved spines. Not to know the trees' identity was hard to bear. In the hotel's square inner courtyard garden a great palm hung its leaves. Livingstone's wide main street had a gracious air.

From Livingstone to Kasaba Bay then we must go. Kasaba Bay lies at the southern extremity of Lake Tanganyika; it is in a game reserve, and has a lodge. It is a place of fascination. Elephant wander through the camp; crocodile lie at the lake's margins, hippo wallow and sigh. But the sense of the place is in more than all that, enthralling as that is. Lake Tanganyika is a very great lake; its exact length I cannot remember, it is close to 600 miles. But not there even, is finally the heart of what must so grasp the imagination. Lake Tanganyika is a part of the great Rift Valley.

Just so, in many places it looks as though two great cosmic hands have taken the continent on either side and riven it. I stared, stared, striving that my sense of wonder should grasp the vastness of earth's convulsion that could spring that mighty cleft.

In October of that year we returned to Zambia. In Zambia October is the hottest month of the year. 'Suicide Month' they call it; it is exceedingly hot. We were to make one film on the Kafue River, on the fishing for those fish of *Cichlid* species which there are called bream. On the Zambezi the film was to be of fishing for tigerfish.

Each day by the Kafue we suffered the sun's assault, morning and afternoon. At lunchtime we had short respite, in the broken shade of low trees on which were pendant the nests of weaver birds, and under which scorpions had their ways among the stones. In the Landrover we must traverse an area where in the rainy season hippo had, in the softened soil, impressed their weighted steps - too widely for avoidance. The dry season had made of those adamantine concrete. The Landrover's suspension is, as they say, 'firm'. It seemed that no bone we had could sustain unbroken. At every evening's return to camp, first we must go to the bar, there to drink a tumbler of lime juice heavily salted. If during the day we went long without the taking of salt tablets, a swimming of the head would fall upon us.

By the Kafue we were hot; it was relative. This we learned when, soon, we came to the Zambezi. First we went to Livingstone; so hot was it that I, curious, must consult my pocket thermometer. In the shade of Livingstone's tree-bowered main street the temperature was 115°F. In the evening, in the bar of the North Western Hotel, it was the rule that, though the air sagged with its damp weight of heat, not a drink could you get without the wearing of a tie. At the horseshoe-shaped bar I sat in suffering little lessened by that I drank. On the opposite side of the horseshoe sat one whose eyes were fixed upon me. By hand sign he suggested I could find ease by the undoing of top shirt button, loosening of the tie. Thus was gained some relief.

But it was partial. Soon, bearing my cold beer, I escaped to a table in the less burdened air of the veranda. Suddenly, quietly, I was not alone. He who in the bar had signed to me, was there. On the table he leant on his arms; his eyes fixed mine. So for a time he stayed. Then very quietly, meaningfully, he spoke. What, he asked, had brought me to that place? I told him. Slowly he nodded, giving to that deep significance. Something, it seemed, was required of me; what I asked did he do?

"I am a hunter."

"Oh yes, er - may I ask what you hunt?"

"I am a hunter of men."

"I see. Er - you hunt men - what men?"

"I hunt communists."

"Oh really, where?"

"I hunt communists in the Zambezi."

I am neither a communist nor, ordinarily, a swimmer in the Zambezi, but a slight uneasiness began to touch me, I felt a wish for the company of my colleagues. By happy chance just then they came.

Of the communist hunter I saw no more. We moved on. The

odd encounter appeared to be over. But later, much later and on quite another occasion, I, with Mike, was in Lusaka; as sometimes was our way we went out to the Blue Boar about 7 miles out in the bush. I, being in the bar with a beer, felt it. Across the bar he was there, the communist hunter. He leant on his arms, his eyes fixed on mine.

From Livingstone we went upstream, to the region of Sesheke for the shooting of tigerfish fishing. Base was the camp of Graham Bell-Cross, who was a biologist from the Game and Fisheries Department. There being no room for the addition of a film unit, upstream we must go and cross the river to Katima Malilo and the stark (barely) basic provision of the rest house and diet out of cans. One morning at first light we came on the ferry across the river to breakfast at the camp. Mrs Bell-Cross was cooking; to our eager noses came a scent of wistful delight. Mrs Bell-Cross was cooking bacon and eggs. No more in the morning did we cross the river. Stoically at the rest house we took our baked beans.

Of the ferry at Katima Malilo there is a story I have told elsewhere, but so much does it suggest of what in Africa is not easily dismissable, that I tell it again. One morning, in the first light of dawn, Graham Bell-Cross had brought the Landrover over on the pontoon ferry to collect us for the day's shooting.

"Funny thing," he said as we waited to cross back, "used to be infested with crocodile here - used to take the women when they came to do their washing. Became quite a problem. So of course they called in the witch doctor. He came, did his thing - made his medicine you know. After that not another croc was seen, for a hundred yards upstream and a hundred yards downstream. Can't explain it of course."

Upstream we went, in the launch, threading precariously among reefs and rocks to an island. It lay at the foot of a long reach of tumultuous rapids, boiling white, the river's whole mile and a half of width a thrashing torrent. In such uncontained sublimity of nature, so daunting, we, mere men, seemed of very little consequence. Crocodiles sunned on sand spits, geckos slid before us into the water; over all the wild haunting cry of the fish eagle. Africa

Filming in Africa.

needs no better symbol, a sound that could come only from a creature of such imperious beauty. Wherever rivers run in Africa, there ubiquitously is the fish eagle. Its great span of wings is black and cinnamon, cinnamon beneath. Its head, its breast fiercely poised, are purest white, its great bill as yellow as a buttercup. In the hot exuberance of life, I fell to thinking of what could be its beginning. In what jungle fastness could it rise, what could be its infancy? Imagination so stirred became obsessive. To that source, by whatever means, I must go.

In the January which followed we returned to Zambia. We came to Kasaba Bay on Lake Tanganyika, there to shoot the film about Nile perch. We came in the rainy season, that being the time of best opportunity; and, so it might be thought, a time of inconvenience for its weather. But the rainy season is not as are the monsoons in some places, of relentless spirit-crushing downpour. In the rainy season there come showers of drowning density and storms of astonishing violence; they roar, they pass; the sun returns in freshened glory in a sky washed clean.

It was so came my first experience of a tropical storm, frightening and exalting. We were gathered in the central dining and bar building. There fell a stillness, as quiet as a tomb. A blackness climbed the sky, it mounting quickly, its weight seeming to crush to flatness all beneath. Slinking stirs of wind, soft, sinister, began to touch the crouching air. First lightning flickered distantly; first thunder rumbled afar. With giant strides it rushed up the sky, towering vastly then bursting, pounding the trembling earth. Lightning now unpunctuated, a shuddering blaze, wrapped the world. As of the opening of a celestial trap, the rain dropped, a solidity of water. The building, massively of blocks of igneous rock, staggered; windows bulged inwards. I thought they must yield. Outside a flood rushed to the lake 2 or 3 feet deep.

When it seemed our structure could withstand no longer, when we must be washed, broken away, the thunder's cannonade fell silent, lightning ceased to quiver. Nature seemed to sigh. The rain stopped. The cloud's pall parted and there was the sun, glorious in a blue sky.

So spellbound had I been as to have had no thought of Max Munden. He appeared now, distressed and in high indignation. At the storm's abrupt coming he had been in his chalet; there, perforce, he was held by its coming. Exceedingly he was discomforted, alarmed. Why, he complained, had no one come to succour him?

The work went well and I having caught the quite large Nile perch needed for underwater shots, we set up the great glass tank. In the dressing of it we must have rocks for simulation. I and another went to the loose rock jetty by the lake, and there chose our rock. We lifted it. Coiled beneath was a very large water cobra. We managed without the rock.

CHAPTER XXII

Zambezi

I HAD seen the Zambezi first far down, in its greatness. Upstream of Katima Malilo I had seen its mile and a half of width come down to a magnificence of boiling cataract. At Sesheke it had flowed with sweeping vistas; I had seen the river's incomparable plunge at the Victoria Falls. Everywhere I had seen the hardly comprehensible seethe of its fauna; its hippo, elephant, its crocodile, constantly and obviously to be seen. It is beyond those that the illimitable interweaving of life smaller, but in effect not lesser, swarms beyond imagining. The little gecko, so like a pigmy crocodile, is a giant to those on which it preys, and beyond them are incalculable creatures, almost beyond sight, of such perfect ingenuity of structure within their little compass.

I, wondering at such fecundity, so extravagant of such beauty of balancing, fell to wondering what could be its beginning - what could be its far birth, in what final secrecy of wilderness. I must go there, see what could be the inception of so great a river.

So it came at last that this place was near. It was early in the day, cool before the heat, the air limpid, unstirred. The ground dropped away, out of the sun into the dark forest. Within the forest's enclosure, as though by the throated passage of a door excluding sound, it was stilly quiet, echoless, the quiet more quiet for sounds, separately clear or whispered. In the columns of the forest there was a bird, unseen; its call, a single note, was pure, clear, bell-like. There were sounds, faint, heard by second hearing, minute shufflings. In the forest it was as though hallowed, imposing quietness of speech.

From the forest's floor of leaves, leathern-brown, deeply-layered, sprung smoothly soaring boles of trees reaching to the distantly vaulted canopy. In the canopy, arrested shafts of sun hung trapped in fuzzed dazzles, tangled in the boughs. A host of yellow butterflies drifted like motes held by the sun.

This place was saturated by its sense, lostly remote, almost of a texture. In far removal in Zambia's North-Western Province, it lay against the Congo frontier, a few miles from that of Angola. About half a mile away, in the Congo, rose one of the sources of the great Congo River.

One tree stood upon aerial roots, as though a colonnaded grotto, a pedestal for the soaring of the bole to the canopy. Within the roots was a pool, dusky brown but clear. Here the water started; within that clustered root, in eager first flow, was the nativity of the Zambezi River. From this obscure birth it was to flow unfaltering across a continent, to drain into the Indian Ocean. With a sense of ceremony I crouched, drank some of that destined water. Whatever else should come to me, I had drunk of the Zambezi's first upwelling water.

There were four of us - the Canadian photographer; Kufakisa Sifuniso whom we called Kay, who was a princess of the Lozi tribe, and was a journalist; there was I and our guide. All of us, in our several ways, I think felt awe.

Already, within those first few feet of the river's running, its certainty of purpose was clear, determined of destiny. So young, so small, it was eruptive with life. Small metallic beetles skated the surface; tiny frogs fled straddled on the water, they and little lizards. And, at once, within the roots, fish a few inches long.

Demonstrated silently in this dusky clarity of Zambezi's birth was the turbulent insistence of life. In this fructifying natal place I remembered the mature river; how fittingly I found its birth to be.

We began to walk, first steps of a journey that was to take me down all that part of the river which was within Zambia. For our guide they were to end that night at his village.

First steps they were, but not of easiness. Our way was tripped, multiply snarled, entangled with curtainings of lianas, knotted trees, darkly hung with leathern leaves. Great tree boles balked us, threw us into half blinded convolutions. Sometimes the thwarting grasp of growth became absolute; we must cross the river, step over the stripling stream; it now, 50 yards from its source, was a frontier. We stepped over the Zambezi, out of Zambia, into the Congo. Then soon, trapped again, again must step over the river, again into Zambia. So soon from its small birth, already by its little urgency of purpose, the river was growing, thrusting apart its banks. Now to cross it must be by leaping, then soon by the bridging of fallen logs, vine-entangled. Now the silent forest took the voice of the water, the sound of new assumptive little cataracts, minor cascades falling into glossy-sliding pools that at their tails broke into singing rills. Then, not a mile from birth, in youth's impudence, it took its first tributary which had run its full course in 40 yards from its welling source. Augmented, though juvenile still, authentically now it was a river. So neatly now imitative of maturity, it was as though a celestial eye looked down perspectively upon a river in its maturity.

Perhaps feet before ours had trodden where now we trod; if indeed they had it must have been a long time since. No sign had they left; all was as by nature intact. Very slowly we must go, our every step twiningly contested. For two or three miles more we struggled on; then our guide stopped. He was apologetic. He knew, he said, that my wish was to go only by the water, but no more; he thought we should move up out of the forest. Teetering, clutching, we made a last crossing of the river, out of Zambia, into the Congo. He led us, away from the river, slightly rising. The high columns of the trees began to thin a little, though still their distant crowns were dense. The ground began to rise with more conviction, then suddenly was steep; the trees stood apart. Then we were out of the forest into a flat white blaze of sun.

It was mid morning; a throbbing flood of life engulfed us, torrent light poured into all, stabbing its hot blades into cowering pools of shadow, blazing into crevices. Life beat, thrummed percussively. Here starkly, bitten into relief, was life's inexorable reality, the hot, insistent, never ceasing beating of its pulse; plants and creatures procreating, living their spans, dying, passing on their spent leases of what had made them. Preying and preyed-upon, all in seemingly appointed parts in an endless dizzy interlocking of life's myriad rhythms. Shafts of green new life thrusting from red crumble of soil about naked roots of trees, dead, bone-white, pointing white limbs as it seemed in protest at mortality. It is life which is immortal, not its units.

Here now it was open bush, glade-like, forest-patched; lonely under the searching swathe of sun, undoubted jungle, its heat-swaying air incessant with shrilling of cicadas; but, with much evidence of life, a curious emptiness. There was no game - no elephant, no antelope, no family trails of warthog; this was not a game reserve. Even in this unmanned wilderness, human pressure denied tolerance to those just inheritors.

Quite late in the day we came out of the Congo, into Zambia. There at an appointed place we found George and his abominable Toyota pick-up. We had gained George at the Boma at Mwinilunga, and that, at the time, had seemed fortunate. The District Secretary had donated them that they might convey us to key points in our walking.

George at first sighting was so clearly unsullied in young innocence; in his black face his huge white ingenuous smile surely was evidence. The future had still to disclose his childlike pleasure in killing. He drove us now to Ikelengi.

By the dirt road of our way, high trees stood, often densely, clear-stemmed with heavy evergreen canopies. Under them, smaller trees drooped with blossom; often also a shrub of serpentine limbs, leafless, massively pendant with flame-coloured blossom. Pineapple plots, banana groves patched the ground between. We came at evening to Ikelengi.

Greenly, exuberantly, it lay under its trees, trees sheltering the resthouse, sheltering all else. We stopped by the resthouse; it was about 6 o'clock, the brief twilight falling. Soon upon Ikelengi fell a soft curtain of night.

Within moments of stopping we were surrounded. The men were friendly; children laughed, pressing a little with shy inquisitiveness, peering at my white face, nudging, chattering, carefully polite. When a man came with the key of the resthouse, they hustled him a little for not coming more quickly, though to us he seemed prompt. When soon we came out from inspection of the resthouse, another man stood there.

He stood; all about him were deeply obeisant, heads bent, in a reverential half circle. He, of innate dignity unconsciously carried, was neat in white shirt and dark blue trousers.

"I am Chief Ikelengi," he said. "This is my village; you are strangers - I must know who you are and why you are here. This is important you see."

As I introduced us, explained my purpose, he scrutinised us closely. Then he smiled; we were welcome to Ikelengi he said. He was easy with us now, but faintly courtly, a little reserved, with the air of one accustomed to condescend. I told him that we, this day had been at the source. Now subtly changed in manner, he began to talk of the river, as of something mystic. Had we, he asked, seen the fish in that natal pool against the tree?

"I must tell you that if you catch one of those fish you must not try to eat it; however much you cook it, it will never die."

With diffidence, I asked him how he knew that so it was. He paused, smiling inwardly.

"I had it from my forefathers who were of the Ndembu people, who were of the Lunda tribe; long ago they came from the Congo. They were of the Kingdom of Mwantiyanvwa in the Congo, which still is our tribal centre." Of this he spoke as of what had been very distantly gone, in the time of the great King Mwantiyanvwa. He who was very great ordered that his people should build a very high

With Chief Ikelengi.

On the Zambezi.

tower that should reach the moon, that thus he should command it. But when the tower became very high, it fell. The anger of Mwantiyanvwa was so great that his people, terrified, ran from there to where now they are in Zambia. As I was to learn, there had been a great migration of the Lunda tribe to what now is Zambia about three hundred years ago.

Now Chief Ikelengi, unconsciously god-like, turned to his people; that at once dropped to a crouching curtsy. With soft hands they gave a double handclap, a flat-handed touch on the thighs, then another double handclap, this done with most deep reverence. He directed them as to their care of us. Turning to us he said that tomorrow night we must have dinner with him - that, I could see, was less an invitation than a most gracious command.

Then he left us. The night enclosed us. The men, talking softly in that rise and fall which is the way of their speech, were busy that we might be fed. Against the great base of a tree they drew together a hearth of stones. In that they made of leaves and twigs a loose heap, blew it, coaxed it, till it licked to first small flame. On the soon bustling little fire was put the revolting promise of our cans of stewed steak - which, though first food since the previous night wrought no response from our recumbent taste buds. But, soothingly, on the night air lay the aromatic fragrance of the burning of the wood. We sat in the dust and, dreamingly, drank beer. The bush has no greater priority than beer.

Our food, now taken from the fire, was tipped on to two battered old enamel plates, with no dilutant addition. We did our best, but hunger which had been ravening, wilted. Now the children had gone, the men too; the village was silent of human sound. It was about half past eight. We sat on the edge of the resthouse verandah with the beer and the night's infinity. The night was enormously secret, with its crowding millions of voices. The frogs were in full voice, unseen multitudes filling the night, high wavering trebles, throaty basses.

Last light died from the fire; we went to our rooms to lie on the beds there to sink peacefully, sweating into sleep.

When at 5 o'clock next morning I awoke, early light was fanning up the sky; rangy dogs and first piccanins were exploring the dust. First women were carrying water in calabashes on their heads with superb grace of movement. Soon after 6am we left the village for the beginning of a day that was to reveal to us much that was of George. All of George and his Toyota that was reliable was its unreliability. George drove always at no speed but the highest that could be wrung from the old bones of his vehicle, about fifty-five. It was the truck's raucous clangour of approach that denied George many intended fulfilments. Also the truck was whimsical; often, without warning, it fell into catalepsy. There, suddenly, it would be, without sign of life. George, smiling, would get down from the cab carrying an enormous spanner; unseen within the bonnet, he delivered heavy blows. Again life would stir, again we would bound from hole to hole.

So on this day it was. The Toyota ceased to breathe. We were on a road anonymous, deep in dust, not acknowledged by the map. George, under the bonnet, applied his therapy; alas, death this time appeared to be in earnest. The truck remained without interest, inanimate. In the sun's white blaze, in the dust, we stood, purposeless about the dead vehicle.

Then, as I thought hallucinating, it seemed to me that I saw approaching a lady wearing a rather old-fashioned summer dress and riding an old-fashioned very upright bicycle. It was no hallucination - the others were seeing her. She stopped.

"Oh dear," she said, "trouble? There's a village a few miles up the road - you can get help there."

She remounted her bicycle, rode away; we, silent, watched her. It was decided, after recovery, that George and photographer should remain with the body; Kay and I should walk to find such help as the village, if found, could give. The road, sun blasted, was a series of undulants, each one of which produced no village, but another undulation. But wavering at the knees, we came at last to sight of a village, there coming upon a group of gossips. The village, they told us was Mwinimilambo. Kay, who had her own language, Lozi, and several others, could find no word in common (there are over ninety languages and dialects in Zambia). They took us to the chief.

Chief Mwinimilambo was with his wives, in his enclosure. He rose, with dignity greeted us, bid us welcome to his village; in good English asking how it could be his pleasure to help us. Our need before all, we said, was that we might drink, but beyond that a few miles down the road, lay our expired vehicle and those two with it. He bowed.

"Come with me to my house."

It stood a little apart in the village centre; a few steps in the colonial fashion led to a verandah, thence into a quite large room, sparsely furnished. There was a sofa that, shabby now, was English Edwardian. He bade us to be seated. He went into a further, smaller room behind.

"See," he said; he pointed to calabashes against the wall. "Honey beer. We brew it today to drink tomorrow."

From a calabash he filled a jug with the beer - yellow-grey floating with bees' wings - brought it and a tumbler into the first room, there to stand. He filled the tumbler. Then, as though ceremoniously, solemnly, he drank it. We were to see it was good. He refilled the glass, gave it to Kay; she too drank. Then to me came the glass and I drank.

So then we drank till the jug was empty. No longer did we stagger from thirst, but we staggered. Now outside we heard the clangour of the Toyota; again it had been drawn from death.

So much delayed, we were late in return to Ikelengi.

"You were late," said the Chief,"I had my dinner." Then smiled, "But I will have it again with you."

It was as of heaven, a boiled chicken with great potatoes boiled in their skins. The effete practice of peeling potatoes had not penetrated to Ikelengi.

From that recessioned forest against the Congo in which rises the first running of the Zambezi it is about only 50 miles to its flowing out of Zambia, into Angola. In final remoteness there is the Kalene Hill Mission. Intimacies of African travel do not, broadly, engender admiration for the missionary principle and practice. It is more often of the proselytising of an alien dogma than of unalloyed disinterested healing. But there is also Kalene Hill.

Its function, primarily, is that of a hospital and a haven. It may be guessed that there, somewhere, is some imposition of dogma; if so it is inconspicuous compared with all else.

All about Kalene Hill was the hot encompassing bush. Pass its gate and in just that passing there was change, almost tangible in its air, a lightening. It was spacious, had cheerfulness. This, an immediate impression, was not for that of no depth. We were conducted on a tour; our guide, so memorably, was an English woman whom I will call Miss Wentworth. She was laconic; she was entirely splendid.

After seeing the general wards we came to a gate; its frame was powerful, of steel, covered with steel-link mesh, padlocked. Miss Wentworth, unlocking it, said, "Maternity ward - have to do this you know. Don't want trouble - the young men."

We went to a building somewhat removed, under the trees.

"Leprosy department here. Come and meet our lepers."

They clustered there, about the doorway, inside, squatting outside. Some were grossly disfigured, some bereft of hands, feet; but seeming cheerful, of contentment.

"Nothing we can do about those injuries. Not the leprosy which does that damage - we've cured that. It's lack of feeling - they burn themselves, hurt themselves on things. I think they're pretty happy here." That they were very affectionate to Miss Wentworth was obvious. To us they were smilingly polite.

"Now - I'll show you our witches' village."

She led us away from the building, away from proximities, amid trees. In this seclusion, with a screen of mat fencing, there lay the village. Though smaller, it was exactly as were any of the normal villages - of sun baked bricks, the food stores aloft on legs. The women squatted on the foot-polished ground, peeling cassava root. They were apparently ancient, sagging of all their parts, repellent, undoubtedly witchlike.

"They're all witches - said to be anyway. Hard to tell. Cast out of their villages - lucky to get here. Would have been killed if they'd been caught - ritual killing you know, strangled. They'll spend the rest of their lives here. Look very old don't they,

On Mwinilunga airstrip.

ninety or more? Probably only about sixty."

"How did they come to be named as witches?"

"Oh - witch doctor I expect, points them out - might have failed a test. They appoint a chicken to a woman accused of witchcraft. They give poison to the chicken; if it dies the woman is guilty. One so found guilty fled the village to come here - never got here, caught, strangled. Now that one over there, you see? I asked her why she'd been accused. She said she'd eaten a person - that means she'd eaten the spirit of that person, which means he'd died. And over there, that one, had eaten the spirit of her pregnant daughter they said. The girl did die. 'But why should I do that to my own daughter?' she said. But on that day the girl died, her husband took their other child to his own village; almost immediately there he too died, and the child. You just can't tell."

In that area Miss Wentworth said, all moments of daily life are permeated by black terror, a constant malignant cloud of fear of witchcraft and sorcery. There could be no certainty about the guilt or innocence of any of the women. Its terror ran like a veining through life's whole fabric in the villages. It is obsessionally believed that people become possessed by malevolent spirits of ancestors. For their placating and that of other manifold evil spirits, huts of dedication to them are made, set about with an ingenuity of protective totems.

That they may bring about their evil purposes so, without question, it is believed they have familiars. These beings are of most skin-tightening dreadfulness by being visible only to their owners or a doctor, he who is as it were a witch doctor of beneficent purpose, and who may exorcise them. Some familiars, even more of dread, are able to act of their actuation - that actuation being often an extremity of jealous malice towards their owners. Witches and their familiars, it is believed will unearth bodies of their victims so to devour them.

The visible form of familiars is uneasily various - often dwarfs with backward pointing feet, other things of shrinking suggestion, queerly sinister, of ambiguous distortion.

Sorcerers have the power to produce their own familiars, making them of evil medicines, a freedom not of witches. To them their familiars come by inheritance from dead witch ancestors and are selected by the familiars - she so selected is without choice.

In the high heat of midday we had finished the round of the hospital. Miss Wentworth turned upon us a searching eye. "Would you care to come to my house for a cup of tea?" she asked. So English, so freshly pleasant was her sitting room, chintz-curtained, that we must sigh as we sank into armchairs.

Miss Wentworth who knew how easily hunger may be had in the bush, said suddenly, "Are you hungry? Hm, yes; see you are. Better be eggs. Quicker."

Never has the passing of hunger's pangs been more sweet. As, fully restored, we took most grateful leave, there walked in another woman; it was our lady of the high bicycle on the road to Mwinimilambo.

Slowly we took our way back to Ikelengi, pausing in the villages to pass the time of day; between, restraining George from his homicidal intentions. From Ikelengi we must go that night to Mwinilunga, that at the airstrip in the morning an aircraft might lift us away. Now it was early in the rainy season; the declining day had begun to put on a threatening face. At twilight in Ikelengi clouds had begun to pile.

We had wanted to go before dark. Rainy season storms fall suddenly. Their violence may quickly turn the dirt bush road to disintegration. We had fidgeted at George; he smiled his porcelain smile; again life had failed the Toyota. There was nothing for us but fatalism; we waited while George wrought with the big spanner.

A change came upon the air; a silence, a stillness, then small wisping puffs. Last threads of twilight drained into night; a shroud, purple-black, wrapped the sky. The lightning began faint, far, then augmenting, it and thunder striding the miles, shivering down the sky, thunder towering, rolling. Now the wind rose, shrilling, pressed like giant hands. Still there was no rain.

An uneasiness touched us. We remembered there were rivers to cross, which smally innocent in the dry season, by a rainy season storm are made raging torrents, their bridges simply of cross-laid planks. Under the bonnet, still George tinkered; the storm roared. Then miraculously, unreliably, again the truck burst to life. We started, crammed into the cab. The rain began, separate drowning drops like plates, then coalesced, becoming a solidity of water. The storm rose to wild enormity; lightning ripped eerie lucidities; the whole world crouched under a pale blue shiver. George, un-awed, untouched by caution, flung the truck blindly.

"George," we shouted, "George - slow down for God's sake."

He, heedless, slewed the truck in the sleazy surface. Hurtling sickly round a bend, we plunged upon the road's first flood. Behind an upflung wave of impact, the truck careened, recovered. George kept his foot down. Wonderfully, beyond deserving, we emerged from the flood with engine not flooded. No longer with faith in arrival, doggedly expecting the worst, we lurched on a crisis way, flood to flood, oftener, deeper. And we in the hands of George, who smiled, kept his foot to the floor.

Coming to one more flood, in its centre the Toyota died again. "Well that's it," I bawled to Kay. George climbed down, bearing his spanner. Most curiously, again it was therapeutic. The engine returned to life. Still we bore on, not seeking to explain what was inexplicable.

Without forewarning, the road dropped from under us. Below, steeply below, was the first river, tossing in flood. Alarm at last seized George. He snatched at the brakes. We slid over what was left of the shoulder, askew down from the ruin of the road. In the cab we were jammed, beyond scope for saving movement. As, coincidentally, we lurched at the water, a shuddering impact threw us into counter-skid up from the river, in a slither over the shoulder, thence crosswise on to and over the rail-less bridge. Halfway up the further bank's slope, still crosswise, we stopped, the Toyota again fallen into coma.

In that inconstancy which is of tropical storms, in little more than minutes, as by a switch, the tumult fell to silence, the lightning died. Upon the night there fell a vast peace, gently breathing. George now drove soberly, the Toyota freaked no more. We came to Mwinilunga.

George, in the morning, drove us out to the airstrip. We waited, watching the eagle that floated in the dazzle. Soon, out of the dazzle, the aircraft substantiated, landed, put down its steps. A white nurse came down, helping down a tremblingly aged African who carried a chief's switch.

"Come on Chiefie," the nurse said, "carefully down - won't let you fall - that's it, good for you Chiefie."

To us she said, "May I borrow your transport? Got to get Chiefie to hospital in Mwinilunga."

George lost his smile, scowled and was sulky, shook his head. To him Kay spoke succinctly. Nurse and Chiefie were taken off to Mwinilunga and hospital.

At Lingilingenda we found the river again; it was there it came out of Angola, no longer stripling, broadly flowing. We went with it down to Chavuma. There, all its wide volume is constricted through a narrow throat between outreaching arms of rock, so giving it a sound as of *shavooma.* For the next 80 miles downstream an American missionary gave us a lift in his boat, steering clear of the crocodiles. So it was we came to Balovale.

There we met Joe who was Assistant District Secretary.

Balovale, so then it was called because it was the tribal centre of the Lovale people. Now it is called Zambezi. For the new nation of Zambia, seeking to build a national consciousness of nationhood, 'Balovale', so it was feared, had too strong an emotional reminder of traditional tribal loyalties.

But Balovale is in memory unchallengedly secure, it and Joe. Joe was an officer of the state; the formalities of that he performed with all correctness, though he strained that the beam of his friendliness should not too soon be upon us. Formalities' last wisps had dissipated when at the resthouse he had arranged that we should be fed.

"Very soon I will come back," he said. "Just time for you to eat. Then we will go to the club; we will have some beer."

Very soon back he was. We went in the Landrover, under the trees in the firefly-flickering clasp of darkness. The club, African-fashion of bungalow kind, was corrugated iron, huddled by jacarandas, tumbles of bougainvillea, the air drugged with scent of frangipani. It was early, just then the lights going on - candles where they found lodgement, dimly augmented by a paraffin pressure lamp by the bar counter. A few small tables and chairs scattered the concrete floor.

To us, at our table, Joe brought beer in correct fashion - bottles with the crown caps lifted. Then, he still with some ceremony, raised his bottle, bade us welcome to the community of Balovale; we raised ours; together we put back our heads, sucked at the bottles and gurgled in proper social form. That done, all formality drained away. A sequence of bottles followed; a happiness set in; more people joined us at our table and there were many introductions. We were now very relaxed; there was much laughter. In the twilight now only one thing separated us; two of us had sweaty white faces, the others sweaty black ones.

Joe, next morning, came to find us; it was lunchtime and he sat with us in the wood-smoked kitchen.

"I will come for you after you have eaten - we will go to the river, we will swim and sit in the sand - bring your rod; perhaps we will catch tigerfish. We will be happy."

At the river, happy so we were, we and those who came too. They joined us on the way down in the Landrover, hailing us, climbing aboard till the vehicle was crammed inside, outwardly as though fly-hung with others. All that Joe had promised, so we did. At the club that night it was as before till, at about ten, it ended. But not for us was the evening done. Joe's wife was away; for that he was apologetic; but if we, nevertheless, would come with him to his home, he would be happy. The way was labyrinthine, under the trees, till there was Joe's house, neatly snugged in the nearly enveloping bougainvillaea, the air heavy with fragrance of frangipani.

Joe was shy, thus taking us into his privacies. His wife's absent presence was clear, in frilled curtains and other prettinesses; the shelves were well filled with books. And though those memories are softened by circumstance, I do remember my declaration, roundly certain, that nowhere is there more richly splendid writing than in the Old Testament and further, to perdition with all reverend tinkerers who had, by 'modernising', debilitated those lovely sonorities. What else could better, even equal, that sumptuous roll of words, 'The Song of Solomon'?

Immediately, there on my lap was Joe's great Bible, his fingers feeling through for the place. Please would I read it aloud, he asked.

I did; whether well, whether not, I cannot know. I am rather worriedly sure that I did so with ample feeling.

Of the evening's end I am not very clear; its end was prolonged, made sad by a sense of parting. How happy a place for us had been Balovale. But now we must go downstream; we must get to Lukulu.

Of Balovale, tree-shaded, fragrant, of its people I have loving memory. Of Lukulu I have memory as persistent but unloving. But Lukulu, anticipated for one thing, was fascinating; upstream there came into the Zambezi a tributary, the Kabompo River. It was relative to that that Livingstone made what may have been his only geographical mistake. The Kabompo he took to be the main river, the Zambezi its tributary. An oddity that seemed to me. I must see for myself, if not with his first-discovering eye.

Lukulu, it seemed, must be the key. Then, perhaps, I could get camping gear and porters that we might walk to the confluence. For me to have come down from Balovale could not have been, because it would have involved the crossing of the Kabompo, without which we could not have continued on to Lukulu. Thus it was by air-hop we came to Lukulu.

We landed on the airstrip, which, in the way of its kind, lay as though prostrated by weight of the blank, sun-blazed whiteness, empty beyond mere emptiness. But we had buzzed the place; pre-arrangements had been made; somebody would come. Nobody came. We climbed out. In the hot quiver of air there was nothing, no sound, no movement.

But distantly, at the strip's end there were two figures, motionless, staying so as we walked down to them. Both were white, one bearded, non-commitally smiling, the other blonde, lean, big-boned and tall. They waited, impersonally silent. I explained; the District Secretary had been informed of our coming. Did they know if someone would be coming? They shook their heads slowly. Gently, he who was bearded edged away from involvement. In a manner hinting of sanctimony he murmured that he must get back to the mission.

He who was tall had regarded us coolly, now he spoke. He was German.

"You will come to my house, ja? You will stay with me and you will have food, and you will pay me, ja?" He smiled suddenly; his teeth were very large, very white.

"My Landrover is over there. We will get your gear from the plane."

Out of the airstrip's blaze Lukulu was arcaded under its trees - jacaranda, flamboyant, acacia, its vistas swagged, clustered with bougainvillaea, ipomaea, frangipani. The buildings mostly were white, mostly of the mission, which was Catholic; Lukulu was a most priestly place. It was beautiful but its atmosphere hung vaguely with an oppression, silently. Its African people and their gardens circumscribed the hush of mission centre, whose brilliance of sun and blossomed shade had a sense of darkness concealed.

The house of our host - whom I will call Helmuth - stood a little apart from the mission's shaded sanctimony. The house, squatly ugly, was poised above a panorama. At Lukulu is the last of the high land, in dizzy fall of hanging gardens to the river. It, now great, receded distantly into the Barotse Flood Plain's level enormity.

"This is my house. You will stay here, ja? Now we will have some food."

In the kitchen we did have food, after Helmuth had crossed himself and muttered with bowed head. He was there, he said, at the mission's behest, to teach the people to abandon their tribal practices of subsistence farming, to pursue instead the good modern methods of chemical culture which, so effectively destroys the soil's humus, imbues the crop with chemical residues. For my furtherance tomorrow he would take us to the Boma.

At the Boma it was desiccated, a waste of dust and scrub, dizzy with heat, a mile from the mission. Those there, listless, profoundly without interest in us, told us that, no, the District Secretary was not there. Tomorrow he might be there, but he might not.

At the mission we found a priest, a pallid man with eyes turned upon the ground. And no, he could not help us. Perhaps the Irish fathers - they had a boat.

The bungalow of the Irish fathers was poised at the high ground's most sublime point of prospect, as though floated there. The windows were closely curtained.

At our knocking, the door opened enough to show half the face of an Irish father. We explained our two-fold need for a boat - to reach the Kabompo confluence, thereafter to go down-river to Mongu; he listened. Then he came out, pulling the door closed behind him. Suddenly he smiled, blue eyes twinkling.

"Ah sure yes now," he said, "wouldn't I be liking to help you to the Kabompo. But I'm thinking our boat's out of order. Goodbye, and good luck now." The door shut.

Lukulu's freedom from interest in us had begun to set upon us a claustrophobia. We went back to the Boma; perhaps, Helmuth said, the police there would allow us the use of their radio to talk to the DS at Mongu.

After some show of official face, an ease of helpfulness emerged from behind it. Yes, but we must wait until there should be a break in police use. In the vast ennui we waited - mosquitoes zinged, cicadas shrilled, flies pestered. We waited in a trap of nothingness while against us boiled the hot throb of millions of striving small lives. The police called us. They had Mongu Boma on the radio. To the DS, Kay explained who we were, what were our objectives; could a boat come up from Mongu that we might fulfil them? The answer, ready, helpful, was that tomorrow morning perhaps the boat could come, perhaps next day. If then the boat did not come, communicate again. On no day did a boat come. The unshaped days accumulated; our urgency for escape from Lukulu grew strong. Then to us one day Helmuth said,"Tomorrow I drive to Mongu in my Landrover, you will come with me and you will pay me, ja?"

In the Landrover next morning we were in the cab; in the back packed to last suffocating inch were women of the village. So, in common sweat for all the hours of that day, we lurched across the seeming infinitudes of the Barotse Flood Plain, already beginning to prove its name. Each of the many pitchings of the Landrover threw those in the back into sprawling heaps.

The Barotse Plain has an air of brooding; its flatness is as though levelled by its weight of sky. Rarely about its illimitable space are small islands, mounds lonely as stars, higher than highest floods, each with its few resident souls. To one we came, landing there. Immediately the children surrounded us, shyly smiling, bringing gifts of wild bananas; the adults came, friendly, almost visibly wrapped with the sense of their isolation. Then we left.

So oppressed had we been by the burden of their unremitting earthen sea, in its long season one of water that closed about them, that in the evening we were glad to come to Mongu.

A year later I came again to Lukulu. I was drawn back. I could not leave unresolved the now nagging doubt about the Kabompo confluence. I came now with Dave Nash; Dave was a pilot in an air charter company and an angler. Easily he became insistent - by insistence he proved the totality of no help at the mission; by insistence he wrung the use for a day of a boat, the boat which had in advance been promised.

So oppressed had we been by the mission's clotted burden on the spirit as to be unaware of that other part of Lukulu, the local people. They, in the sun's good light, went their own ways when unmolested by the mission. But now, of sudden refreshment to the spirit, was a throng of the people from their plots, come to give us happy ceremony of departure. There they were, lodged under the sheer drop of shore, a flare of colour, purple bloom on black skin, clustered brilliance of garments. They sang, waving us good voyaging.

We went upriver, surging confidently, as we thought, at last to the confluence. But after the passing of a few miles we went aground on slabby rocks. By wading in those suspect waters we did get free, but again to go aground. As soon we saw, so it would be. None but a dugout canoe could clear the rocks.

Said Dave, "We'll fly."

We did, over the tree tops of the Kabompo Confluence. Beyond chance of mistake, the Kabompo was the tributary, the other the main river. Still then unresolved is how so monumental a geographer as was Livingstone could misread what seems so easily read.

Upon its but low eminence Mongu sits and dreams its dreams of dignities past. Spread so nearly below is that sea of land, the Barotse Flood Plain; it was the Kingdom of Barotse, home of the Lozi people. Now it is Western Province. He who was king now is Paramount Chief. But still most proudly, he is the Litunga, who half god-like, is head of the Lozi tribe. Kay is his relative.

But not for long could I stay at Mongu; I must move downstream by the now great river, down to Senanga. I went now not with Kay and our Canadian photographer, but with John Kabemba. John Kabemba was of the Bemba tribe; with us too was a black photographer. His name was Bernard.

At Senanga we were met by the District Governor and the District Secretary. That so they should meet us was of their function, but its effect was to wipe away completely the taste of Lukulu. Of that, though, it must be said that that taste was not of the people of the village. They were warm, responsive.

At Senanga the DG was tall; there in the sun I see him still, his head a little politely inclined to one side, one eye most winningly with a cast. The DS was not tall; he was roundly small and smiling. Their welcome was courteous, gently friendly, part of an urbanity that, it seemed, was settled on Senanga. The DS conducted us, as it were conjuring us from pleasure to pleasure of discovery. How could past experience of resthouses have prepared me for that one at Senanga? It, on a modest eminence above the plain, was U-shaped so the better to hold its garden, in which grew pawpaws, flowers, fragrant shrubs on whose twists of limb were chameleons, poised in sly pretence of being plant, not animal. From the garden, from the verandah, the ground declined gently to a serenity, in the evening light of the river's broad bend, of groves, of the plain's immensity that put peace upon the spirit.

"And down there," said the DS with an air of producing a culminative rabbit from the hat, "down there we have a bar, a very nice bar. Perhaps when you have eaten?"

A little later, in the soft early scented dark, we went with him under the trees down to the bar. Voices of others, unseen, went with us; murmuring, sudden laughter, the shuffling in the dust of many feet, showed us to be not alone. We, reaching the bar, were engulfed. Its sound, its light, took us as by the breaking of a wave, sucking us. The jukebox's assault bludgeoned our ears. In the stunning blast some were dancing in a removed privacy, unpartnered; spare youths barefoot in one place, with absent eyes, lolling heads.

We passed defensively to rooms beyond where, at once, we were absorbed into easeful uproar. In its intimacy, which was immediate after the soft handclap greeting, some had English, some had not. Sometimes I was unsure; sometimes we understood each other; sometimes we did not. But very comfortably we were as one.

The girl brought the bottles on a tray, caps lifted, bearing them with fine balance through the crowding of tables, making her least movement a voluptuary, the rhythm of the jukebox shivering in shoulders and hips. Her voice was high, tinkling, as though syncopated on hollow wood.

At the Boma next morning the firm observance of all proper formalities seemed leached through by a gaiety, as though all found a happy revelation that again they had the gift of one more day on so lovely an earth. With the DS, we went to the room of the DG, and how warmly good a thing it was that we old friends should be meeting again. Outside the day was still young; trees, jacarandas mauve, flamboyant flame coloured, clustered the Boma. For our goings, our comings they found it a pleasure that they should allot us a Landrover, and for that a driver who was not as drivers of Landrovers commonly are. This one was tall, polished of manner and handsome, head to foot in immaculate white. So gallantly we went.

Downstream we went, down the Matabele Plain, then on higher ground, under shade of giant straddling trees of genus *Ficus*, they of the fig kind. We went to the Sioma Falls, which, remotely lost and tourist free, threw upon me an enchantment, so wild, primary their beauty. For a day I was with a Scotsman who, ponderously large, a rancher, had a wife who was black, very young, shy and most delicately lovely. He told me that routinely he shot lions to save his cattle. He told me too of two who, camping thereabout, in the night had been visited by a lion. Under the side of the tent it had inserted a sly though powerful paw, dragged out one of them without waking the other. The man's head was found.

To leave Senanga was difficult; but my journey was not done. It continued, downstream, past Nangweshi, through the cataracts of Katima Mulilo, past Sesheke where, turning east, the river runs on through Lake Kariba, thence on past Chirundu to the Zambezi Valley; for most of that way on the further bank in what then was Rhodesia. It was an uneasy neighbouring, only academically short of war.

There still is original wilderness, still unravished, qualified by man only to the extent of being compressed by man's erosive pressure - and by man's attempts by management to control the imbalances he has created. Fortunately his restorative good intention has the backing of an agent of nature, the inconspicuous little tsetse fly. To man's domestic cattle the tsetse is lethal. So it is that the Zambezi Valley is virtually uninhabited by man who, unchecked, would have destroyed it by his occupation. Man has tried, and is trying, to exterminate the tsetse fly. So greatly it is to be hoped that never may he succeed.

It was Smoke Tembo who took us into the Zambezi Valley, he and his Landrover; none but he could have been so fortunate for us. He was a Game Guard, seconded to me by the Game and Fisheries Department. That also he was a witch doctor, a snake doctor, I did not know till later - his being young, likeable, smart in his khaki uniform, did not suggest it.

When in the afternoon we departed, we asked Smoke Tembo how far we must go.

"A hundred miles," he said. And when should we arrive?

"About midnight." So late?

"It is rough," said Smoke Tembo. Smoke as we were to find, inclined to understatement. At first, on the plateau the road was broad, fine and modern, but we came to that place where we must leave the plateau, drop down the fearful fall of the escarpment to where, below, lay the Zambezi Valley. Off the brave modernity of the road Smoke Tembo turned the Landrover, on its nose, to feel down a track, loose, erratically twisted. Slowly, with suggestive caution, Smoke Tembo crept us down till, in thankful safety, we were upon the Valley's floor where was the last village before surrender to jungle and to night. Its store, roused from closure, gave us a last beer. Against the ancient might of a baobab tree, that there, perhaps, had stood for two thousand years, we drank. Black night had begun to settle.

Shall we, we asked, soon be there?

"It is slow, last part," said Smoke.

Slowly now we went on a track of rough uncertainty in the formless night. The world closed to within the Landrover's enclosure, all else lessened to void without time or form, all slipped away. Then, without expectancy, we had stopped, the void pushed back. We were in a small village, a huddling of a few huts uncertainly illuminated by a paraffin lamp held high. People sat at hut doors; some clustered the Landrover. Black jungle clutched us in. Children came confidingly.

There, it was to be seen, Smoke Tembo had business of the Game Department. I got down and the children, shyly pressing, came about me. They and I, soon squatting in the deep dust, found a game - I finger drawing in the dust, drew a Landrover. The children, delighted, chanted "Lahndrorver". So we went calling up what was of their world - elephant, lion, giraffe. We became warm friends.

Smoke Tembo, soon returning had collected several women and a baby; they in the back were to be fellow travellers. When later we left, night was folding back upon the village. As we passed the huts, children, ranked in rows on their sides, slept in the dust because in the huts the heat was great. Then the village was gone, lost in what was past, a dream.

Now all was gone, no habitation, no road, no perceptible track, nothing that could acknowledge any relevance there for us. Our headlights slicing blades of light in the black seclusion could win no recognitions. The way was as chance fell, a constancy strung on fortuities of feasibility, diverging for fallen trees, for rocks, for pits, for pushing through.

We came to a donga, a deep dry river bed, rock strewn. The Landrover on its nose clambered down, feeling, threading; engine racing, it strove to the ascent, half vertical, of the further side. The engine stalled; the lights went out, the black engulfing jungle dropped upon us. The pause before again the engine surged to life seemed long. Clutching, clinging between rocks, feeling for certainties of surface, almost as though sentient, the Landrover achieved the top, squirmed over, its levelling beams snatched briefly from the void a creature, belly-slung on short legs, black-backed to halfway down, white below. For a moment its eyes threw back our glare. It, so little seen, was a honey badger.

There were more dongas, each bundling into heaps those in the back; of dongas and of time I lost count. The blackness into which, interminably, we bored was punctuated by momentary flashing of anonymous eyes, half seen forms. Once, lithe, spare and speckled, there was that which leaped from our trapping lights.

"Serval cat," said Smoke. "Not much further," he added and vaguely later we stopped.

"Here Mashika Camp," said Smoke Tembo. It was an hour past midnight.

We were in a clearing. There was a scatter of white-walled chalets. Stiffly the women were climbing out. Smoke was sounding the horn; to its summons came a man distraught because we were ravenous and he, just dragged from bed, fearing we might demand the cooking of a meal. Just give us a piece of bread, I told him, just till morning. Soon, under the mosquito net, I lay thinking of food, hearing the mumblings of hippos, the scuffing of their hides on the wall that separated us.

In the morning sunrise came cheerfully, revealing that Mashika Camp was neat, soundly thatched. The dread black threat of night thrust back. In a backwater of the river against the camp the nocturnal hippos now dreamed, with sudden hollerings of watery philosophies. So odd it is that a creature of such deeply slumberous sound should be, often, of such malignant intention.

He of last night now revealed himself as William Maguwi, Camp Cook. Now, he said, it would be his happiness to cook our breakfast, were there anything to cook. To camps in uninhabited country it is necessary that they who come bring food.

"Perhaps I find an egg," said William

The day before us stretched long, long and hungry, already, though early, burdensomely hot, already under rampant rule of tsetse fly.

"We hunt," Smoke Tembo said.

Hunt we did, walking many miles, I in the wake of Smoke Tembo, he ceaselessly tracking, head down, this way, that, dog-like, a predator in a tangled complexity of predators, tiny to great.

We, humanly presumptuous, might think of the primal bush as of an emptiness because it is free of us. First impression upon total immersion is of its thronging; you walk at first with a sense of loneliness - no reassuring sight is there of another human; so it may be felt when walking alone in such measureless enclosure of bush. Now, hunting with Smoke Tembo there was a nearness of sense, of a pressure of life. In the ways between thoroughfares of passage, the ground was multiply trodden, a knitted up interweaving of tracks which Smoke hound-like, read, pursued, so that I, who would have paused in captured interest, was swept on. Particularly he followed a warthog spoor till, coming up on it, it was a female with young, inviolate.

"Whose hole is that?" I asked, seeing what seemed an enormous rabbit burrow.

"Warthog," Smoke said. "It dug by aardvark - warthog take it over. Always go in backwards because of lion or leopard."

Very well I saw the practical soundness of that; the warthog at its forward end carries two very competent tusks; but how vulnerable it is at its rear.

One thing I saw so strange that, often since, I have doubted my seeing. On a bush I saw a blossom so large, so bright it seized my eye. Its long petals, daisy-fashioned, brilliantly were red, its centre lustrous black. Upon our coming, it became a flying cluster of small beetles, red and black. A little way so it went, then settled, again a daisy, red and black.

The hunting of that day gave us no warthog; my shooting of

guinea fowl pushed back immediate hunger, but that achieved laboriously. The guinea fowl, active creatures as they must have been, were stringy, dry, resistant to eager teeth.

It had come to us that the famous white hunter Johnny Uys had camp in the locality. Johnny probably was among the greatest rarities of the bush; among humans he was greatly over life-size in metaphorical measuring. None but he among white men had such profound intimacy with the bush; in the bush he had been for most of his life. Few, possibly none, could equal his knowledge of its flora and fauna. Often, when by casual chance confronted by the most minor creature, its intimacies of living would tumble from Johnny. It was my great fortune to have much bush wandering with Johnny Uys.

Johnny was killed. He was conducting a photo safari of Americans. One, often warned by Johnny of the acute danger of elephants, unregardful, tried for a shot of a charging bull. Johnny jumped to save the man. The man was saved. Johnny was killed.

There is so much, vastly much, that could be told of bushwhacking with Johnny Uys, but if this book is not to be of biblical length it cannot here be told. And I had to move on; I must come to Feira, Zambia's last extremity on the Zambezi River. At Feira my journey was to end. And here at last was Feira, Zambia's last few feet. On its left, which was to the north, there was the flowing in of the Luangwa River. To its right, which was south, was Rhodesia - at that time a hostile frontier. Opposite, to the east, was Mozambique. The sense of outpost, of finality was strong in the air.

The Boma lay against the ancient immensity of a baobab tree, its diameter was not less than 30 feet. Its hollow interior could have held a board meeting if the directors were indifferent to the virtual certainty of a presence of snakes. The tree probably had stood there for three thousand years.

In the heat of afternoon I walked out from the resthouse, back westward, by the river, towards distant mountains the colour of bluebells. I thought of all those I had known beyond them, between them and that small brown pool in the forest.

At the resthouse that evening, when candles were lit, beer bottles opened, there was company, two old men and with them the assistant DS who, I think, had brought them for the tales they could tell - very willing to tell as they were after a few beers. With rambling mumblings of wizened jaws they told of many things, of the hunting prowess that had been theirs. Also they told us, as I believe in a spirit of helpfulness, of a medicine which we could get from the witch doctor. To your wife you must give this medicine without her knowledge; if she goes with another man he will become very sick. His head will burn fiercely, awful disorders will afflict his stomach. On stomach and legs will come great swellings. Thus for two weeks he will be. Then he will die.

But also from the witch doctor you may get an antidote. Many men with sound sense of insurance get both.

Later there came into the resthouse a man of outstanding belly who wore nothing but khaki shorts, and had slung on his shoulder a 303 rifle. He announced himself as being Head of Police, answerable only to the President. I had listened to other improbable people making such claims. Then, hearing of my afternoon walk, he announced that, had he seen me, he would have shot me first and asked questions after. That I believed. There had been incidents.

Chapter XXIII

In Africa at Large

All that of Zambia, of the Zambezi River, was of the 1960s. Of travel in the 1970s there is left some confusion; of so much, only some salient events insist on remembrance. It was in 1970 that I became Angling Consultant to BOAC, with a responsibility to examine and advise on potential, and exploiting, of angling tourism.

It was an appointment suggestive of glamorous destinations and, at once, my duty was to go to Mauritius, a tropical island in the Indian Ocean. But when I came to it, set in that cobalt ocean, turquoise within the lagoon, they there said to me that it could not compare with the Seychelles, also in the Indian Ocean. It so was that, already, dreamingly, I was aware of the Seychelles. My old friend and colleague of the *Daily Express*, James Cameron, had told me of how, when, coming in a ship from India, he found himself 'stuck' in those celestial islands because not for three months did another ship call. To the office in London he must cable to explain that for that time he must endure paradise in neglect of what else he should be doing. I, knowing that imminently was coming an airport, preached of the Seychelles, of their undoubted delights for anglers.

In 1971 the airport was open; to it, with no delay, we came, Graham Long of BOAC and I. We saw the Seychelles as, since then, others cannot see them. The tourism which since has come had not then impinged. The heavenly blessing of inaccessibility had as yet hardly been touched. It was also of this trip that we must explore what, then, was Lake Rudolph and, now, and properly, is Lake Turkana, its true name. It and the Seychelle islands could not be more starkly of contrast; fully to understand, to appreciate either both should be seen.

The Seychelles then, at instant first sight, were idyllic, perfectly a fulfilling of everyone's dream. With the exception of one, Bird Island, which is tiny, of coral, most perfectly visionary - or so was then - the other islands are granitic, a sudden soaring from a turquoise sea; from their beaches to their tops, mantled by a rampant scrambling of flowery growth. Palms droop languorously over white beaches. As extravagantly, flamboyantly, fish populate the sea among the islands, growing to sizes extravagant by standards of lesser places. On one of my fishing days, a sperm whale surfaced close to the boat. After seventeen years, again I was in the Seychelles. Still their beauty was overwhelming; but that first tender sense of Eden was gone, had come to being proved earth. Eden, once so turned, cannot reclaim its original partial paradise.

So then the Seychelles, as so they were, as so they are. From them we went back to Nairobi in Kenya, on the high plateau, there to feel cold at only 65°F. From there, with heads full still of the spilling delights of the islands, we flew to the Turkana desert, to Lake Turkana which therein lies. To the Seychelles it is a finality of contrast. On the lake's further shore, that of the east, there are mountains, mountains sullenly stark, cleft and riven, seared by sun's assault. On island upthrusts of rock, in the baking glare, lie slabby hulks of crocodiles. On the western shore is nothing, nothing but the desert, rising a little from the lake, then lying in prostration under the mercilessness of sun.

We landed on an airstrip, enormously alone in the desert but for a group of men of no apparent relevance to anything and naked.

Just one wore a blanket hanging from his shoulders. He struck a posture, flinging his blanket dramatically across his chest, so a little to emphasise his nudity. No other sign did these men show of reacting to our incursion nosily from the sky. They were tall men, more than 6 feet, lean and hard, their faces impassively set as masks, which made of them an uneasiness. They, Turkana tribesmen, were reason enough for uneasiness for neighbouring tribesmen, with whom from time to time, in traditional manner, they drop into warfare. Thus, in ancient fashion, by casualties, preventing population exceeding the desert's sparse capacity for feeding its citizens. That culling should not exceed its function, fate as yet had denied them the blessing of modern weapons. Turkana tribesmen, nevertheless are very constant in the carrying of their spears.

In oddest contrast to the men, so lankly lean, are the women, who are small, small and rounded as little fruits. Nor are they naked, indeed are a little heavily dressed, though with nothing but beads. They, these Turkanas, are nomads, as without choice they must be. Their environment, to which all their lives they must accommodate, is of stony desert in which those very stones seem to crouch in the arid burn of the sun.

This Turkana desert is not of that kind blankly of sand filling its horizons; it is sun-riven, stony, sparsely scrubby, sometimes naked wilderness. But by the water under a few palms there were springs; in that kindly association was the lodge at which unadapted interlopers such as I could stay. As a place remembered, memory mainly is of fascination, of heat almost not to be believed, of thirst. Somebody had a thermometer; at 134°F it burst. The heat was of total desiccation, of a thirst always beyond curing by drinking. I did of course become dehydrated. The reason for being in this place of such small comfort, but of strange hold upon the mind, was that in Lake Turkana are many Nile perch. Nile perch tend to great size, even 300lb. The inducement is strong. But anyway its geography has grip enough to touch imagination. This queer country of the Turkanas, out of Ethiopia, into northern Kenya, has a sense constantly of something just evading grasp. It may be, though, that here still the air itself carries a sense of those

Australopithecines, part man part ape, who remotely were here on the long climb to *Homo sapiens.*

The journey south from there by air is of such dramatic delight that none should take it but those who have still the immeasurable gift of a sense of wonder. The flight should be intimate, slowly and not too high, in a small aircraft. From Turkana it should be southerly over Kenya, over the Rift valley. So it was I went, with a view at that altitude god-like. It was as though, time suspended, I was seeing those mountains at the moment of their volcanic throwing-up, as though the lava flows had barely come to first pause.

Once, further south, I was at Kilufi Creek, at the incomparably sited lodge. It appears as though hovered above the creek's opening to the Indian Ocean. Inland, trees hung luxuriant boughs over the water, constantly flickering with flight of carmine bee-eaters, insecurely, on pendant boughs, pelicans clustered, beautifully, absurdly, with constant flapping of panic wings. It was as stilly, beatifically divine a place as could be expected under heaven. The bar, under its lofty pitch of thatch, had unimpeded scan over the sublime prospect.

I, one idyllic morning, was in the bar. So also were two other men; they, with backs to the prospect, were talking. As soon I learned, they, casually met there, were comparing importances. They were, as also I learned, from the cosier south-western suburbs of London. Wholly engaged, they compared the minutes it took them in the morning to drive to the station and how conveniently near were they to the golf clubs.

It was there, fishing offshore, that first I saw a whale shark; it is appropriate to record that here. It was astonishing, a thrilling antidote for the soul-anaesthetising whiff of the suburbs. This mobile sub-surface island, monstrous, magnificent, passed under the boat, dwarfing it. Seen thus, it was deep-bluish, patterned over all with pale saucer shapes. The whale shark, as sharks are, is predatory, but so mildly, only upon plankton. It is a peaceful creature, drifting its idling days in its sunny seas, at peace with all else but plankton.

It was, as I remember, several years later that I found myself in Tanzania, which sounds as though by nothing but chance, but really

was otherwise. Mike Blackall then was Chief Executive of an African-owned hotels and tourism group operating in Tanzania; Tanzania, reluctantly, was exploding on all sides into tourism developments. Of those one was at Tanga.

Tanga is a port of no great scale on Tanzania's northern coast on to the Indian Ocean, reason enough for Mike to be preparing to open there an hotel. Potentially importantly, Tanga is on the Pemba Channel, lying between Pemba Island and the mainland; this, in the eyes of anglers of the big game kind, is distinguished water; it has a run of blue marlin. No game fish more zealously is desired. It was my function to advise on the possible exploitation of the fishing in association with the hotel.

From Dar-es-Salaam, Mike and I flew to Tanga, there to be met by John, Mike's local manager, an adroit sophisticated African. How pleasant a place Tanga appeared to me; how broadly open to its panorama of ocean, its places and ways spacious under the trees. On a corner where a side street went off, John installed me in an African-run hotel which, though basic, bore an aromatic air. At its front under a great mango tree it was set with tables and chairs, that in the evenings people might gossip over their beer.

That evening, when Mike had flown back to Dar es Salaam, there came John with a girlfriend to take us into a pleasure ground next to the hotel. Many people were at the tables and, as now it seems to me, they were all men. And as now too I realise, none but I there or anywhere there, was white. There for a time we sat; then it came to my consciousness that the rustle of talk had fallen to silence. It was as though a weight had fallen on the air. All eyes in that place were on us.

"I think we should go," John said.

In a brittle silence we walked out. But under the great mango tree the air was lighter; people were easy at their tables. Rigidity fell from us. I noticed that, nearby, there was a gaggle of teenagers as ubiquitously there as is the nature of teenagers. But John suddenly seized my arm.

"Those teenagers - they're saying that you'll have money - they'll beat you up, get the money. You must go, quickly - lock yourself in your room."

I went. I locked myself in my room. I had begun to see Tanga with less blandly acceptant eyes.

In the fine new light of next morning nevertheless, the irksome sense of an unseen watcher did not prevent my response to a place till now unknown to me. Ocean and land were beautiful; there was much for the notice of my hungry eye. I wandered assiduously. One morning, on the further corner of the diverging street by the hotel, I became much engaged by several starkly gesturing trees against the building on that corner; vaguely conscious that, constantly, khaki-uniformed figures passed in and out. Fully preoccupied, I photographed the trees.

A youth, probably sixteen, on a bicycle had stopped by me.

"I want your shorts," he said, "you must give them to me."

Upon my declining to give him my shorts he informed me, a little menacingly, that he was a trainee policeman. "I want your shorts," he said. "You must give them to me."

A little later, making notes, I was in my room. The door burst open; a flood of khaki policemen plunged in. All that was of me was swept up, as was I. Then I and mine, tightly packed in the khaki posse, were marched across the road, quickly into the police station. I was under arrest.

Then we were in a small room, rather dark; a slow 5-foot fan above rolled and re-rolled the limply sweating air. The room was crowded; a team of interrogators that, by turns, could keep up their rotting pressure, that none might weaken by fatigue or thirst or hunger. He who led them was small, of a craven hostility and sliding eye. At once interrogation began, darkly insinuating, seeking to weaken by ceaseless beating. In turn they went for food, then to return. I thought it best, lest I should appear to weaken by frightening, to adopt an attitude of lightly careless co-operation.

As though looking for lice, they combed through what was mine; they found my Admiralty Charts of the seaways of that coast and were exultant. Slyly they looked - I having those! Did I not know that on Pemba Island were military installations? I said I had not known until they told me. And what devilry was this? They found that fly rod which had been made for me by Charles Ritz. They shone lights into the ferrules; they were looking for microfilm. Perception came to me. I was a spy.

This was at that time when in Uganda there was civil war, that Uganda might rid itself of Idi Amin. Tanzania had sent troops for the aiding of the putting aside of Amin. That, in Uganda, was quite far to the west from this Indian Ocean coast to the east. But these were zealous men.

Beyond the door now there were sounds as of scuffling; a young man, white, was bundled into the room. He was frightened, angry; seeing me he demanded of me with a German accent what was the meaning of this outrage? In mid word he was cut off, I bidden sharply to silence. He was taken away. His case when it emerged was that he, a German seaman, had in his innocence been taking photographs. The police, ravenous for spies, had grabbed him. His ship had sailed without him. Never since have I ceased to worry about that young man.

The day now was far advanced, close upon evening. I was thirsty, hungry, exhausted, weakly becoming angry with my tormentors. Then, to me as a vision, a black-faced angel, there walked in John.

He bore an order from the Commandant of Police that I, at least temporarily, should be released. In a haze of only partial belief I walked out with John.

John had had a busy day. He had telephoned Mike, he had been assiduous with the Commandant of Police, to such effect that, perhaps temporarily, I was free. But John told me, this evening I should be as inconspicuous as possible; and that night I should lock my door. In the morning I should remain so locked in until he came for me.

Inconspicuous that evening I was; one of John's staff came to keep me company and, presumably, as a guardian. "We all hate the police," he said. About midnight that night someone tried to force an entrance to my room.

In the morning, locked in, I waited. In the room's back wall was a window overlooking a long corrugated roof, terminated by the opulent overhang of a mango tree, in heavy fruiting. Monkeys swarmed in it, there and on the iron roof, playing those games that monkeys play. I watched them that I might not so rigidly count the leaden passage of fraught minutes. As so often, the pinched little faces of these monkeys had a look almost of sagacity. Let it remain just a look I thought; it is only the 'intelligent' humans who create evils. But at last John came.

He led me down that I might get breakfast. In the room was one other having breakfast; he was the Commandant of Police. To him went John, for some time closely talking. He came back.

"You are free," he said, "but you must leave here as soon as possible. Don't show yourself more than you can help. Soon I'll be back with a car and a driver."

A little later, there, coming hangdog across the road from the Police station was my chief persecutor. Too good to be true I thought - here he comes again for me. But he, so ordered, had come to apologise. Quite clearly his wish rather was to kill me. "I hope," he said, malignant-eyed, "you're not going to make a lot of trouble about this."

I stood under the great mango tree to wait for John. Immediately the youth and his bicycle were there.

"I want your shorts," he said, "you must give me your shorts." At that moment John, with car and driver, arrived. The youth vanished. A minute more and I was in the car, the wheels turning. I was on my way back to Dar es Salaam, 400 miles away. It was dark when we stopped at Mike's door.

"May a jailbird come in?" I asked.

With Mike and Vicky was Haroun Rascid. He was taking us to dinner at the Kilimanjaro Hotel. How violent changes may be; so quickly. I remembered that evening, there, on the dance floor was a most beautiful African girl, very elegantly tall, very lithe. Her evening gown, fitting as though grown on her, was emerald green satin. Superbly she and it graced each other.

Home from the hazards of Tanzania, how coolly reassuring were the placid pastures of Fosbury. How serenely lay the fall to the valley under our windows. But for so short a time for me. I must go to Djibouti.

Even distantly, as yet unseen, on Djibouti lay a fascination. It was so unsure in geographical identity, for many people hardly heard of, uncertainly of Africa or Middle East. Its seeming was of an outpost, only of itself, a place of strangeness. It is, at least in theory, a sovereign state - but so small a one, the last pigmy tip of the Horn of Africa, squeezed by two giant neighbours. Ethiopia to the one side, to the other Somalia. A place of great departures, of far distribution to all the eastern world. It is the guardian, if that word may be used, of the Gulf of Tadjoura, that small westerly sea inland into Africa from the great Gulf of Aden from which northward is the Red Sea, southward the Indian Ocean. Eastward lies all the sweep of Asia. Of Africa physically, in the sense of it at least as much Levantine. It, erstwhile a colony of France, easily so still could seem to be. There still, as before, is based France's Foreign Legion. Beyond that it is arid and searingly hot, its lakes so salty that their margins are white-encrusted.

To get to Djibouti it seemed that you must go with conviction. My point of departure was Paris, but departure was evasive. Its means was the one aircraft that was Djibouti Air, one that, once worthy, now was old, reluctant. The promise was of arrival at

Djibouti at 7.30pm; it was achieved at that time am, next day, where we, its canned, spiritually defeated passengers, were discarded.

From the airport the way was past the inevitable prelude of skulking hovels. From one, startlingly, emerged a young woman. She was tall, slender, of exceeding grace, her dress clean and nice as a petal. To suggest that such revelations were common in Djibouti would, unhappily, be misleading, but it was not uncommon; thus are many of the maidens of Djibouti's two indigenous tribes. Also there were Yemeni women; of them some too were beautiful, but smaller, more delicately moulded, suggestive of the dreaming eroticisms of the Song of Solomon. For contrast, numerously, were the squat Arab women.

It was my mission to probe the nature of Djibouti's brooding offshore waters, they of such sinister repute for the enormity of the shark that were pervasive there. Might not those waters, so awesomely fertile, be equally so for other species of angling interest?

The water of the Gulf of Tadjoura was enigmatic. So for me it must remain, as it seemed at first. This water of such pregnant promise was, so far as I at first could tell, virgin territory, unbroached. No one it seemed had made any attempt at its dark sub-surface privacies. There had been one who, being of some substance, and wishing that there should be evidence of that, equipped and put upon the water a boat for big game fishing. It was of angling incongruity that it languished permanently at its moorings.

Then through a tangled thread of chance, some of it dubious, I was led to a man of most unlikely probability. He was an Ethiopian Jew of a background so incoherent that, legitimately, he held three passports. His English was fluent, it was not to be doubted that he was not less so in a few other tongues. I am sure that he was of easy citizenship of varied worlds, probably not unprofitably. He, most excellent man, was massive, very solidly strong rather than fat.

He had been a citizen of Ethiopia, there having a business for the making of clothing that in Ethiopia's context of communism was irksomely frustrating. He migrated to Djibouti, there to set up business. Of Ethiopia he told me many interesting things; of those was that three out of four women there were prostitutes - or perhaps it was one in four - I cannot remember, but anyway impressive.

To my great regret I cannot remember the name of my too temporary friend; only one thing further I may say of him - by my previous experience he was one of the least recognisable as an angler. But that he was, passionately.

Now, in Djibouti secure, he, apparently alone, probed its local seas for what epics they might have. His boat, about 25 feet, was sea sound, fairly fast but with no fighting chair. He had for mate a youth, sleek-limbed and slender of the local tribes. I was invited aboard to fish.

Out of the harbour's shelter we turned westerly into Tadjoura's lumpy swells. On our port lay sun-wasted wilderness searly crouching, blistered rock, supine scrub. To starboard, northerly on a naked shore, rose riven mountains 20 incandescent miles or more beyond. Soon, on the southern shore, there came up the barracks of the French Foreign Legion, stark in the glare. At a mile or so offshore, we went westward, the northern bittern heights edged in upon us, investing us. As with the closing of a slow entrapment we were held, north and south coming to a fusion of savagery, a tumbling shattering of scree and tumbled rock. In it was a gap, toothed uneasily. Through that we passed.

An abrupt strangeness fell upon us, as though a smothering of the senses. In that moment the world of Tadjoura's cresting swells, scattering spray, was gone, unheard, forgotten; impalpably we were taken, of another world. We seemed now shorn of sound, of no touch. We were in a vast cup, at its bottom. Its sides at every aspect a fearful upsweep of precipice to a distance of sky. We were held in a seeming soundless immurement, perhaps 20 miles across. That which so held us was a caldera, a collapsed volcano. It was the Ghubet Kharab.

Its water lay still, as though suppressed, as though no earthly wind had ever touched it. It could not be doubted that shark, imponderably great, lurked within its shadowing depths. All lay as though embalmed.

On our left after entering, there ran out a rocky spit; at its extremity stood a Goliath heron, poised in such stillness as to appear carved. At intervals on the plummeting walls of the cup were narrow shelvings which had gathered scant growth; one had even a few palms, some shrubs. It had no visible means of access but upon it, as if stopped in a moment of action, was a camel. It stood still as though fallen into premature fossilisation. But, more queer it was, of a tawniness, of a shining brilliance, than any camel that ever I had seen. In that brief interval, soon after six, when light of day passed shortly through twilight to night, we took the boat inshore, where under an appalling sheer was a narrow sandy strand. Taking the anchor, wading ashore, we made fast for the night. The clustered night enfolded us; we ate our food with a bottle of wine; in the sand made hollows for hip, and shoulder, a pillow for head; succumbed to sleep's soft stealth.

In that hazed interval, close to my ear I heard that place's only sound of life; a rodent of some kind gnawed at a vagrant remnant of our food.

When I awoke, day's first sun was flaring from dawn's reluctant grey; the water lay still as if of a solidity, the boat welded to it. In frozen posture still there was the camel, on its shelf. Distantly, on its point of rock, stood the Goliath heron in its stillness of eternity.

For a while we fished, vainly intrusive. We came again to the place of our entering, passed through; in the moment, in the tumult of water our ears assaulted by its sound. Out now from that most queer suspension, at once I hooked a fish which I never saw. Protractedly, heavily it lunged and bored, then severed the line on an edge of rock. In the roll and toss of sea, now by contrast made a little unreal, we fished up the Gulf to Djibouti, in the going, catching as fine a kingfish as I ever saw - its weight I guessed, trying for honesty. I thought it to be about 60lb, but still all was so hung with a strangeness that stole from that its sense of occasion.

In how contrasted a context errant memory strays to Zimbabwe. No weird oddities there, but as so consistently in Africa, Africa's insistent demand for a symbol of any adequacy is hard to meet, though it seems so lavish with candidates. But all are too obvious, too limited for Africa's enormity of life. The elephant? A glorious giant, majestically arrogant. The lion? It too imperiously splendid. The giraffe? Astonishing on first beholding, of most beguiling and elegant beauty. But these creatures, so magnificent, are too self-declaring.

They are seen, acknowledged; by degrees thereafter, discovery is made of descending levels of life that, in scale, have splendour no less. Such awareness is prompted by things remembered of the hotly fecund valley of the Zambezi, as in Zimbabwe I knew it in the area about Chirundu.

Here then, in this riparian jungle are there possible symbols? There are many, from hippos to beetles of heroic sculpting, and others hardly to be seen by the unaided eye. There was one that drew me there. The tigerfish is incomparable.

Only nature, of such unlimited resource, could have designed so precise an image of ferocity; it is as though moulded of chromium, given mirror polish, then, brilliantly, tinctured with colour. For the length of its flanks it has soot-black stripes, its fins are flame coloured. Its gape of mouth is ringed with a grin of huge projecting fangs, razor-sharp. The tigerfish looks, and is, a perfected vehicle of execution. It is also an angler's quarry of immense attraction. Its maximum size is about 25lb, though in Lake Tanganyika and the Congo River is an allied species that may be close to 100lb.

At Chirundu when I was there, the tigerfish abounded, though not with the ferocious teeming they have in the uninhabited part of the valley. But teem they did at Chirundu, so still perhaps they do. Intensive poaching from Zambia on the other bank might have wrought diminution. Zambian poaching of game on the Zimbabwe bank has been so seriously damaging that game guards were empowered to shoot poachers. Many have been shot. Of such are the results of ungoverned human fructifying.

It must have been 1987 when I was in Zimbabwe, it seems so recent. I was eighty. It was at the time of England's autumn which, in the Zambezi valley is a time of greatest heat. We fished through the long forgetful hours, always as it is with fishing. The boat was one that in a moment can be put to planing which, on African rivers of heavy hippo population, is an asset. We fished by long drifts, on a river that sometimes, with its backwaters, was 3 miles wide. As properly it must be, each day before fishing, we poured into the river a bottle of beer as an offering to the river god, saying his name, *Yami yami*. The days were timeless, often of a vast peace, though great crocodiles sunned on the bank, hippos honked warnings; intermittently the flashing fury of hooked tiger splintered the bliss. So constant presences that they may be forgotten.

On one midday of crushing heat we pulled into the bank for shade and food. The promise of the river overcame caution; I stripped off, dived, deliciously swam. In mid-river awareness returned; I swam quickly for the bank.

But there were the hippos, surly beasts, so constantly apt for charging. We passed one day through a channel between outlying rocks and a lagoon against the bank; a hippo of great venom erupted from there to charge us. The boat, put to plane, evaded the charge. The hippo, turning to charge again, threw up a wave 15 feet high. The charge, repeated, passed our stern with inches to spare. Then again we were in that peace that on a river has no bottom.

CHAPTER XXIV

Kathmandu

AS IF for the greater contrast, I went before to Norway first, fishing there for a week. With only an interval of days, I went to Kathmandu. Never before had I been in Asia. I had heard of Kathmandu rather as one hears of places of an exoticism too remotely glowing to be achievable by any commonly mechanical transport. But, so commonly, I did go; first to Delhi, where at the airport I frustrated the intention of a porter to remove my baggage for his private purposes. Very early next morning a quite small aeroplane, with me and others, took off for Kathmandu, where, soon it was revealed why the plane was not big.

The ground rose before us; we climbed over a turreted landscape of mountains, then, dizzily, were over Kathmandu. It was as though a bluebottle, to reach the bottom of a tumbler, must spiral down. Within its ramparts, so Kathmandu is, deeply circumscribed among mountains. As soon I learned, there they are 'the hills'; they are, after all, a mere 10,000 feet or so. They have very lofty neighbours.

The sense of far removal from the common world was not only of my imagination. The 20th century had not yet surmounted the hills, indeed had still, in many ways, several centuries to overtake. Walking that first morning among the temples, the shrines, the sacred insignia in every street and place, what was of today, a thousand years past, a few centuries, or a few minutes, did not seem securely distinguishable. Perhaps since then all such untidiness has been sorted out; but - 'Oh God oh Montreal' - I hope not. May the mountains still guard the soul of Kathmandu.

Kathmandu is not a museum of the residues of its ancient past. That which a thousand years ago was the material, spiritual, physical, philosophical, so still is now. Now, as has been for all that time, a blend of Hinduism and Buddhism is for every day, every minute as integral as putting on clothes. Evidences are ubiquitous, constant as shops. The colour vermilion has a sacred significance; any stone of the street, that by its form suggests a symbolism, is painted vermilion. A circular shrine in the street has prayer wheels set into its circumference; those who pass will stop that they may turn a prayer wheel. Such small reverences have no severance from the normal texture of every day.

The interlacing of Hinduism and Buddhism is too anciently established for unravelment; the tendrils of Tantrism are woven through both. Common to all is the principle of attainment to the third eye which, in the middle of the forehead, symbolises a state of eternal wisdom after all the trivials of the flesh and the world are past. It is a principal of Tantrism that the purging at last from all gross falsities may be had only by extremities of sexual indulgence. Only thus, finally, the soul is drained of all that might cloud the crystalline purity of wisdom. That path to so final a distillation might be thought to be of some interest on the way. The great many lucidly explicit sculptures, everywhere to be seen, are done with great verve.

In an exuberance of sculpture at every turn, on temples at street sides, anywhere that can carry it, preoccupation with the phallus is constant. From such timeless roots, though but stone, this legacy of sculpture broods upon the senses.

The common demon of tourism is a constant threat, insidiously growing, to this as yet (when I was there) unravaged spirit of Nepal, Kathmandu its capital, and the other time-soaked towns. But they of Nepal, quiet inheritors of so ancient assumptions, will not easily bend to absorb brash alien usages. They guard the spirit by which they live. Indoctrination by alien religions is most severely prohibited and punished. There was a Roman Catholic priest who came covertly to proselytise; he had to leave very hurriedly, overnight.

They of Nepal are amiable in their religion, without zealotry. An occasional holy man is to be seen cross-legged against a temple, rather as the waist-high phallic symbol is to be seen, any day, in its constant place. Tolerance is soft upon it all, with no sharp bother as to being Hindu or Buddhist. A man, asked if he was Hindu or Buddhist, answered, "Yes."

In Kathmandu, in Patan, which lies just across the Bagmati River, in Bhaktapur, the centuries have accumulated temples which crowd and jostle, often stacked high pergoda-fashion. In Durbar Square, Kathmandu, there are more than fifty temples.

That I should see all, should absorb the sight and sense of it, was necessary. To Kathmandu where Mike Blackall had taken over as General Manager of the Sheraton Hotel, I had come to paint a mural in the main dining room. On the morning of my arrival Vicky, who is Mike's wife, took me out to lunch at the little restaurant which was at its eyrie high in the hills at Dhullikhel. Beyond, the hills ranged upwards and away, rising till they clustered to the Himalaya.

'Downtown' the main dining room was called; that, downtown Kathmandu, must be the theme of my mural - one indeed as stimulating as I could wish. Recently, sadly, I have learned how great was my fortune that I came to the work before western tourism had dragged its trail too horribly across the face of what the centuries had so aromatically matured. First cars were there, such few forerunners, a scattering of tourists, those from Germany urgent with their cameras among the sculptures, but as yet only lightly impinging. Still cows, secure in sacredness, were easy in the streets with not even slight regard for the cars. Pye-dogs wove in the traffic, but they, entirely unholy, were intermittent casualties. Porters at their pick-up stations waited for clients, then to carry their enormous burdens in suspense from a band round the forehead - with no other means of taking the weight, however outrageous. So were carried armchairs, wardrobes, sacks so hugely packed as to be bigger than he who carried them, anything else bizarrely so disproportionate. These men, some mere boys, were small, astonishingly tough; but forty was their life span - nor was the average life span any greater.

Young men, newly tinctured with alien smartness, entwined through the streets with those from the hills in dress unchanged for a thousand years. Kathmandu, and Patan, and Bhaktapur, seemed still not to have noticed that change had begun to touch. Bicycles jostled with bicycle-powered rickshaws, they with crawling cars, they with those from the sense of time's irrelevance and, even if unseen, as often they were, the dominating Himalayan immensity.

All that was my material. All that I must seek to express. The fact and the spirit for it all must be contained in a mural 6 feet by 18 feet.

It had to start from scratch; Kathmandu did not customarily cater for such activity. A roll of canvas, by Mike's conjuring, was sent from Singapore. But canvas must be mounted on a stretcher; how was Kathmandu to meet such a demand? And of that size?

"We can do that," said Mike, and he talked to the hotel's staff carpenters; he bade me explain to them what is the principle of a stretcher. He who was foreman, unlike the characteristic tough little tribesmen, was tall, very dark of skin; he was splendidly bearded, withal a fine and handsome man. If now that seems of no relevance, then it claimed the admiration of my artist's eye. The first, and tentative, structure failed; the second, if a little big-boned, a little awkward, served well. Upon it the canvas was stretched; nothing more was needed but for me to put upon it an expression of the soul of Kathmandu.

Intermediately, space for so doing was a problem, finally solved by screening off an area where incoming and outgoing baggage was handled. There, day by day, I heard departures of climbers outgoing to assaults on the great peaks, of trekkers, of Americans in haste to collect one more piece of world. Also, forever inseparable, the music. Every day it wrapped all the minutes of my work, softened by distance, reaching me through the filter of other sounds. It was not the music ordinarily of such usage; music to Mike and Vicky is important. Still, when music a little distantly comes to my ear I am again by the baggage lobby at Kathmandu - as for many, many hours I was.

At 6am each morning we went out, Mike and I, driving a few miles from town. Then, a few miles on Mike jogged; I, strenuously-paced, walked back. By 7 we both were working; at 8 we stopped for breakfast. By 8.30, or a little later, we were working again. At midday a brief lunch stopped us; at 6 my working day ended because then came end of daylight. For seven days a week, so it was for most of three months.

In my little privacy against the bustle, I worked with fair peace. Mike was stringent that I was not to be disturbed. Few were unregardful. But there came the German woman. She was in her fifties; each year had left its dire mark; on her there lay no least touch of humour, of softness. Entirely she was free of easement for the eye - gaunt, sallow, but pudgily modelled about the face, against her projective nose. For her every step she was attended by two large minders, silent, blank as paving stones. Probably for her those minders were not an extravagance.

She came that first morning, minder-flanked, stalked as by right of conquest, pushed past me, astonished in mid-brushstroke. With a bludgeoning finger she stabbed my work. Staccato she barked criticisms. Then, abruptly, she wheeled, went, minders parade-fashion wheeling with her. Next day, mission uncompleted, she returned, finished her demolition. She left, as if in jack-boots, leaving me numb with impotent astonishment. A long life has shown me few things as ugly.

In the hotel there was to be an exhibition of my watercolours, and, though I had brought with me enough pictures, I snatched several days to paint locally. As minder for me, Mike gave me a man of the hotel's security guard.

The mural at the Kathmandu Sheraton.

No such guard did my physical person need; the people of the hills abundantly, warmly, were friendly. But, and this Mike foresaw, without aid I would be hardly with a free arm for working, so closely would these good people attend upon me. No single stroke of mine would they wish to miss. He who was my guard had been a Gurkha, had served with the British army. He was formidably competent for all contingencies, also charming and, it seemed, with pleasure in his care of me.

Very smartly he took his charge; very erect, his symbolic swagger cane officially under left arm. He was delegated authority, kind but firm. The need for him was well proved.

In a close valley running into the hills, a clustering village hung above the road, a tumble of houses stacked as levels allowed. Narrow paths winding tightly between flowery hedges were stitched among houses and small bright patches of garden. There enclosed, I painted. To watch, came, I think, the village's every resident; only by my Gurkha's benign marshalling was I able to work.

When I had done, all present most kindly expressed approval of what I had done. As best of friends we parted.

Coming in the afternoon further into the hills, where a river and the road ran more deeply under the poise of the heights, from a face of rock a crystal spring dropped into a pool of white marble; in it swam fish, elegant on idling fins. Because it was a holy place, about it had been made a little temple, it of white marble too. A grove of trees, dark leaves, framed the marble's white purity. In that tranquillity, remote and blessed, I painted again. Tranquil for a time it remained, in a still spell of quietness.

But suddenly from the grove arose a man's angry shouting, the screaming of a woman. Instantly to duty, striding from my sight, went my Gurkha, into the grove. As by a switch, cessation dropped upon the noise. Back, smartly marching, came my Gurkha. From the grove came not a sound again.

Much later, when all my labour on the mural was past, I asked my Gurkha to sit for me that I might do for him a pencil portrait.

Most willingly he did; but, that stalwart man of valour, he found posing too severe a demand. Soon sleep began to creep upon him as so easily it may. The picture, nevertheless was done. A Colonel of Gurkhas whom I told of this said it would, to my Gurkha, be a pride for life. It would be hung on his veranda, where things of such honour properly have their place.

For expatriots in such places as Kathmandu, all things are good for the contriving of social occasion. Such was the Private View of my exhibition. The social life of the foreign community turns on the hub of the embassies; to open my show came the British Ambassador. The Ambassador of the Republic of West Germany, as then it was, was there; also the Japanese Ambassador, the Ambassador of South Korea, he too of Italy; and others. He of Korea bought a picture as deeply of rural England as might be, a grass-tracked lane in which rabbits grazed. A man of Sri Lanka bought a picture of my wife in the fields attendant upon our goats. An Indian bought a picture of a Hereford bull against the carcass of a dead elm. So many Asian places now thus shall be 'forever England'. I sold a number of pictures for which I was much pleased; less pleasingly they were sold at third world prices.

Before that event, at a cocktail party, I had met the British Ambassador. "Tony," said Vicky, "this is Bernard Venables." "Bernard, this is Tony Hurrell, the British Ambassador."

The Ambassador stopped, for a moment stared - "BV!" he exclaimed. The Ambassador was a man of Norfolk, and, as men of Norfolk so often are, a dedicated angler. Later, on the occasion of the Queen's visit to Kathmandu, he was to become Sir Anthony Hurrell. He now, I believe, is home again in Norfolk, there to fish, there to commune with the birds.

Week followed week; every morning faithfully at 7am I, perched on high, was at work. Most of those mornings, as faithfully, there would come Das Gupta, Works Manager of the hotel, there to stand a little while, looking.

"So big," he would say, "so big." Then slowly he would walk away, shaking his head. "So big."

He, I think, had no convinced belief that it could have an end.

But, one day about mid-morning, Mike came. I climbed down, put down my pallet.

"Mike - it's finished," I said.

It was done; its incessant demand no longer. Incessant it had been, a loved compulsion, purring on like the running of a smoothly running engine.

Now I was at leisure. Now was holiday, that made a miracle by a prolonged passion of work. One brief respite there had been; for one day I was persuaded from work that I might go into the climbing fastnesses towards the Chinese frontier. They who took me were Mike North and his wife Leonora; he, head of the Civil Service College in Kathmandu. So good a guide, so kind a host; the day of such enchantment as now to seem more legend than substance. The threading road, more ribboned track than road, sinuating into the hills, aspiring to the ultimate Himalaya, passing tiny lost villages lodged over dizzy plunges.

And now, at leisure, I could explore: not those far hills as I might have wished, but by local walking. There was much to see. Threading through the paddy fields the track took me to the old Tibetan bridge, so to cross the Bagmati River and to Patan and its temples. Above the river hung one, small, intact still, abandoned to the pye-dogs. They, unmolested, within that sanctity had all their social being. I watched them often, saw with what evolved practicality their social life ran its way.

There came upon me one morning as I walked by the riverside ghats, a funeral procession. They came slowly, bearing the body. Above their heads they bore it, prone and under no cover, on a litter. The women as they came maintained a wailing, high, thin, of no cadence, a formal desolation. They proceeded thus, as was the deceased's right, to the burning ghats.

Sometimes my way, when walking, took me by the burning ghats at the time of a cremation. The pyre, at first seeing, seemed oddly inadequate for the disposing of the corpse's entirety. It is of logs, of 6 or 7 inches diameter stacked at right-angles in alternate layers, so to allow draught. The whole standing about waist-height, its shape a rectangle. Snugly within its lower levels the body is disposed.

Such ceremony as there is at the time of committal of the deceased to the pyre, I never saw; at such times as I passed, all seemed accustomedly mundane. Attendant upon the pyre squatted he who was its keeper; he bore no sign that his mind dwelt upon matters of mortality. My sense was that he dwelt upon nothing at all as flames licked among the logs. As one day I paused in passing, an ankle and foot lolled out. The attendant, without pause from his unthought, prodded it back with a stick - which I guessed, lay there for that purpose.

Dubby, an Indian of that kind, urbane, erudite in ways both western and Asian, was right-hand man to Mike in the hotel. He took me to Bodhnath. For that he was a good guide, his mind being, like Bodhnath, suffused with oblique mysticisms, nebulous philosophies. Bodhnath, in Nepal, a few miles from Kathmandu, is Tibetan. Entirely it is of Tibet, as though lifted in that entirety from Tibet, and there put down. It is tempting to suppose that Chinese aggressions within recent time are associated with its presence; perhaps there is a refugee connection. But Bodhnath is ancient. Its roots are bedded in mists of time so time-forgetting that there is no time; past, present, future, in Bodhnath are one. It is in concretion what is Buddhism.

Dwelling enormously over all is the stupa, white, circular, towering in terraces to its great crown of gold. Huge painted eyes look from there, eternally dispassionate, eyes placid with ultimate wisdom. From the top stretched to all sides lines bearing prayer flags of many colours.

At ground level, in a wall skirting all the circumference, 147 prayer wheels are set in niches. To them at all times come the devout, turning each for the making of a prayer.

Monasteries surround the stupa, they and shops that sell the incidentals of being properly observant of sacredness. Of the many constant in passing, ubiquitously are the lamas. At one monastery they were in devotional session. Two long tables at squatting level faced each other, 2 or 3 feet apart. Along each, also facing, were lamas, shaven, saffron-robed. Between, up and down, went novices bringing to each lama a small cup of butter tea - not for his physical need but as part of a ritual sacred of intent. They chanted, rather low, of a sound a little grumbling. Behind, against the wall were two great horns, so great, so long, that their forward ends must rest distantly on the floor. At a time of deepest profundity, they emitted blasts, low in pitch but of a cavernous softness. Great as was the noise, they seemed to induce a quietness in the mind.

"Now," Dubby, told me, "you must come to the Rimpoche; but first you must get your ribbon." And in a shop we did, of crimson silk. In a monastery where dwelt the Rimpoche, we were received by a novice; he was quiet, moved silkenly. Gently smiling he directed us by minor gestures. A 'Rimpoche' it should be explained, is a lama, but one much elevated by having had previous reincarnations; he who was to receive me was credited with six. Whether my spelling is right I am unsure - it is pronounced 'reempoochay'.

He was in an inner chamber; he sat in the lotus position; whether so he sat continuously in meditation, or so had put himself for my reception, I cannot say. He too smiled, with that faint detachment suggesting that half was for me, the other half for a further dimension less solid than I. As I had been instructed, I gave him my loop of crimson silk. He put it over my head with, I think, the muttering of a few words. Then, as if now I had gained a little on the unseen, he smiled almost personally, made some movement of the hands. It appeared he was putting upon me a blessing. Leaving him, returning to the more positively material world, I felt a slightly dazed sense of a peace having fallen upon me.

It was now October: in October in Nepal there comes Dasai. Just that once a year it comes, rather as Christmas comes to us, as a time of happiness, of festival, of feasting. It brings also a multitude of ceremonial sacrificing of animals - most particularly of goats and buffalo. The sense of the time is that pervasiveness that at Christmas hangs in the air. In the hill villages, great arches are made over the roads: two quite slender trees, as tall as 50 feet, on either side, are drawn together at their tops and there bound. From that union, two ropes of plaited lianas are hung almost to the ground. There, given a seat, they become a swing for the pleasure of the children.

Outside the hotel, as everywhere, Puja was to be performed. Just by Mike's parked car, a goat was tethered, a pretty little creature, slender, white, with mazed hircine eyes. Before it, on the ground, lay a *kukri.* It, in the way of Puja, was, with a single stroke, to sever the little beast's head. Not wishing to witness this sacred act, I did not stay. Later, returning, upon the bonnet of Mike's car was a wreath of orange flowers and a smearing of goat's blood. To the honour of Mike his car had received Puja.

Before Dasai had run its course, there came for me my time for departure. It was that time, each year, when the mist of distance lifts; now with the seeming of a miracle the whole astonishment of the Himalaya is revealed. The entire northern prospect is filled with a mightiness of peaks assaulting the sky. I must suppose that familiarity, sustained for time enough, could lessen the glory of that shock: it is hard to believe.

For three or four months I had been in Nepal; I had worked very hard, had seen much that never I had seen before: I am left with a sea of memory of people whom never I shall see again. A few remain so clearly that memory shall retain them. Of those, one is indelible, another Ambassador. The Ambassador of New Zealand was Sir Edmund Hillary, first conqueror of Everest. That he and I should meet, Mike gave a dinner party.

First meeting of Ed Hillary was overwhelming. Not merely for his size which, in a confined space, must overwhelm, but also that he was so gently amiable a bear of a man. His largeness anyway was intrinsic, in essential character. That he was quiet of speech, modest of manner, enhanced his scale.

Returning from Kathmandu, I dallied briefly in India: there among other wonders I saw the crawling heaving human life. Painfully, on my rare reluctant coming to Oxford Street in London, I am reminded of Old Delhi. So it has gone, through the lived years. How steeply the perspective of them falls away.

CHAPTER XXV

'Art', Earth and Anthropomorphism

AFTER Uganda I wandered no more in far places. Now to English skies each morning I opened my eyes, familiar, tumbled, uncertain in mood. The fields of Fosbury falling to the valley were gentle to eyes that had seen the flawless early hours of African skies, that, in later hours, were brazen. On that last return it was autumn, October I think. The leaves lay wet in the woods, the scent of their decay filled the grateful mind. Nowhere, in all the far places can earth yield a smell of such poetic ecstasy.

But at Fosbury such pleasures were not much longer to be ours. For seventeen years there we had lived, loving that house that had gathered its years so aromatically, soaked with the sense of lives lived in it. He who now owned it wished to turn it into money. The agent called upon us; very winning, very sweetly persuasive. If we would vacate the house a payment would be made to us: £15,000.

"Think of that," he crooned, "you could have a holiday, or buy a car."

When too late, we had advice, it was revealed that by statutory practice, by leaving we were entitled to a sum of over £87,000. The rest is not a story worth the telling. By a final court ruling we were evicted from the cottage in the village which the estate lent to us as a condition of leaving the old house. We received no money.

He who bought the house was of such means that, as it appeared, money was of no consequence. The price was, by the standard of that time - the turn from the Eighties to the Nineties - a high one. For about two years thereafter builders were in and about the house, sometimes, if not always, seven days a week. The house, that old loved house, was ripped, gutted, spilled into skips; inevitably a conservatory gummed on to it. The oldest part, that of the 17th century, was totally ravished. It had been of two storeys, and a little third one under the tiles was revealed. All was torn out. Windows the depth of both original floors were put in, facing the garden. An original stone fireplace in the upper floor, old country fashion, was rebuilt, augmented; in the new *Homes and Gardens* style baronial hall thus made.

One of the greatest pleasures of the old house had been its windows, each period having made its contribution. All were lovely of their kind, together a harmony that only such chance can make. All were torn out. In the new splendour, all windows were of a kind, pretty, wall-to-wall so to speak. They were, as my daughter said, 'twee'. A vastly expensive vulgar vandalism had been achieved. It was entirely false.

As had been told, in our extremity, we were succoured by the local authority, finding for us a minute old folks' bungalow on a housing estate. For that we had great reason to be grateful. By nothing but chance the estate was appendaged to a most charming village in which we were received in good, friendly country fashion.

But oh, how small the little house! To the saleroom went the greater part of our furniture so long, so lovingly collected. The little dwelling did not recognise activities asking space beyond the naked essentials of sitting, eating, sleeping. We have many books, books of a lifetime, books for delight, books for reference, books that accumulate as necessities of a professional writer and artist.

Their needs threatened to exclude us from the house. Such scant space as could accept bookshelves were soon filled. The loft remained. There must go our books, stuffed into cartons. Shelves that had come with us were dismembered, laid over the nakedness of joists and plaster. There languishes our library, a jammedness of cartons. Constantly arises the need to refer to a book. But no, almost invariably, in the loft that book is immured.

And I am an artist; I am a painter; I was, till here we came, a sculptor. I have a studio; I must count my blessings - one blessing it truly has. It has a north light; that blessing never before have I had. There blessings end. This 'studio' was by intention a bedroom, one for the barest essentials of seeking rest. Into it I must put my writing desk, a word processor and printer; also must go such minimum books as daily work demands, also my drawing desk which now must serve also as an easel. Also squeezed in are drawers for storage of paper and watercolours and, stacked on them, stacked on every last ledge, canvasses. And I am a fisherman; fishing's many appurtenances are stuffed into the studio, stuffed in every last cranny throughout the house. In the studio, when working, I must restrict my movements, any movement ill considered might, often does, cause a crash. The pursuit of creative work, by its nature often impassioned, has difficulty. How odd then that out of that compressive box has come constantly a flow of pictures, oils and watercolours, several books, some journalism. But so often, with dilutants of joy.

From time to time to the unresponsive air I raise protesting hands - I can take no more. I say, can I continue thus. I must and I do. My wife spins; having room she would weave; she has fleeces to store. We are gardeners; that minuscule piece of England, that must serve for all our passion, is very shallow in its soil, inhabited by ravenous hordes of snails which compete with slugs as numerous. But gardening is an adaptive passion; from that once depressively unhopeful patch we have drawn much happiness.

But to our dreams we turn to sustain our souls. We dream of a house with a garden more fit; I dream of a house in which a spacious studio has a north light, has plenty of room for canvasses. One by one the years add. We dream on.

Life still calls eagerly for the living of it. Still I go fishing and the joy of it, quiet now, still unites me to the boy who once was put into a trance of delight because fish had hidden lives in water. That I say 'still' is not a word casually used. During the 1980s my eyes, in the way of eyes very hardly worked, had lost much competence, but latterly decline had accelerated. To a consultant I took them in the firm belief that they could be propped up for much further use.

But no, I was told; to my eyes had come a degenerative condition. They would degenerate further and seriously, but blindness would not fall upon me. Would I be able still to fish, still to paint? No, both would be denied me. How long must it be before this sentence should be enacted? About four to five years.

The passing since then of about ten years has not brought that full calamity, though so surely I think it would have done if I had submitted. Much of my sight indeed has gone; much of seeing is done now almost as much with hands as eyes. I see as much of evasive insubstance as of definition. Much embarrassment comes to me for my failure to recognise people. Then most dreadfully, there came a time when it appeared that, really, I could paint no more. Fishing was almost as nearly threatened. Was I then to fumble and stumble the rest of my life so uselessly, so drearily?

For a time I tried to persuade myself that I was willing myself to acceptance. It was useless. Of the many parts of painting, one is a sense of order, a sense of wholeness. When at the time it seemed the blow had fallen, that sense had deserted me. No longer it seemed could I keep the parts of a picture in their structural relationship. While working at one part, the rest would slip away from my control. It was not to be borne.

Just what was the nature of what I did, it is difficult to isolate. I, as it were, fastened a grip upon myself. Though, as it seemed to me, I was without power so to do, there it must have been, jelly-useless as I thought myself to be. I think that, without the knowing, I had come to a state of deeply intense willing of myself.

A few attempts at watercolour were harrowingly abortive; one lingeringly failed oil I slashed to pieces. First sign of recovery came

Studio at Upper Fosbury.

At work in Upavon.

I think when my daughter asked that she should watch me in the painting of a watercolour, thus to learn the way of it. Great as is my dislike of being watched, clearly this could not be refused. I hope my daughter's purpose was served; I think it began my salvation. Twelve watercolours followed - as if in a gasping rush for reclamation. Some I destroyed; some were successful. The doing of them induced a change of technique, imposed by limitations of sight. As with watercolour, so with oils; to paint in the mode of the past was finished.

In a way, ample with difficulty, it was a resuscitation; the old eyes had failed, the new ones were handicapped but saw with a new vision. My painting became broader, looser, is evolving continuously - and that, for an artist who has entered his nineties is something for a deeply glowing excitement. Again now, as in all those years past, it is an excitement on waking to know that, beyond the wall, in the studio, the current picture waits for that assessment which can be given by a fresh eye of a new day. Often the excitement is sharpened; how well will yesterday's work appear? Before all else I must go to the studio. If all is well, if the work seems good, a warm flood of relief sweeps up.

So always it has been, now the excitement is made poignant. For all my years of work till these last few, pre-eminently I have been a draughtsman. In early childhood I fell with passion into the delights of drawing; so for life's length it has been until the declining of sight. Particularly my draughtsmanship has been applied in line drawing - that is drawing for reproduction - often loosely, wrongly called pen-and-ink. By nearly all line draughtsmen of skill and experience it has been done with a fine sable brush. Nowadays, as is too painfully obvious, there are no line draughtsmen of skill and experience.

In line drawing I was deeply satisfied in the certain knowledge that what I did was good. I loved the fluent certainty that flowed from my hand. Alas, nothing falls so quickly victim to degenerating sight. Real line drawing - the scratchy thumbnails of today (some of which, within their limits are very well and wittily done) demands finely subtle co-ordination of mind, eye and hand. It is a devastating loss. Being so, the spiritual effect of continuance of painting is so much the greater.

Continuance of ability to paint, continuance of the urge so to do, is a gift with something of sublimity, something which is self-rewarding. In the contemporary world so it has to be. It has no other reward.

A society come to decadence has no more certain sign of its ailing than its art - or, what in its degeneration, is called art. Only our time has achieved a state beyond in which 'Art' is entirely unconnected with art - and, astonishingly, is presided over by salaried officers of the establishment. It is so far beyond rationality as to be, it could be thought, beyond credibility. Yet there it is, established, official. Some press critics, apparently mentally normal, pontificate to lengths arcanely asinine. At some point earlier in this book I commented bitterly on 'modern art'; then its practitioners still were related enough to art to use its forms and materials, if incompetently. But they did paint, did offer some small gesture to methods and materials for sculpture, but in effect deadly as disease to integrity. Art students no longer were taught as taught they should have been, that before they could, if ever they should, spread wings of inspired achievement, they first must be craftsmen, tradesmen. They must learn their plumbing. So began a rolling succession of generations denied the dignity and practicality of being skilled, professional. No casualty of this degeneration has been more tragic than the assassination of the ineffable art of drawing. Drawing, in the modern vocabulary, bears a slight smell of contempt.

In this context it is relevant to look again, with uncommitted eye, at Cezanne; there is no more established totem figure, the 'Father of Modern Art'. Some pictures of beauty, excitement, he did paint; he painted more that were ugly. He could not draw, his power of composition was limited, his handling of paint often clumsy. His series of 'Bathers' pictures, were they not so solemnly regarded, surely might cause sympathetic laughter. He had so tried. But, but, the wholly honest observer must admit, they are funny. And their compositions are obvious, repetitive.

But Cezanne was the 'Master' from whom, largely, has come all

Homo Sapiens

Summer Solstice.

the poverties of 'Modern Art'. Nevertheless, still pictures were painted; still an artist, good or bad, was a practitioner in the art of painting or sculpture. But now, now! The last pretence has gone. Not till now has it been questioned that the artist is, in his gift, one apart, that all the historic record of art has come from those so excepted from ordinary kind. And now; now it is official. Art's reality has been abolished. Now it is the time when anyone, quack, poser, exhibitionist, self-deceptive trickster can by random nonsenses be a 'Conceptual Artist'. (It has to be allowed that there are those who, quite sincerely, do believe that truly there is virtue in what they do.) Innocent or phoney, the concepts so far demonstrated by conceptual artists are to be seen as insubstance plucked from nothingness, apart from what uneasinesses are loose in the artist's head. One artist filled a shack with concrete immediately prior to its being bulldozed into infinity; another hung a dead sheep in formaldehyde; another causes an actress to lie immobile, as though in sleep in a glass tank. They won prizes. How irrelevant it appears, without remotest association with art. If a soul should be sought in Conceptual Art, it must surely be in some cranny, small, wizened, turning whimpering eyes, half knowing its imminence to death.

There was a phase in the Seventies when the unhappy student, as I am told, was restrained in white-painted cell, a visual vacuum, removed from all associations; there, free of all stimuli, he (or she) was told to be conceptual, having first been alienated, cancelled. Nothing is left but meaninglesses, rubbish left as from an emptied bin, minor clutter. Is it odd that in a mind so reduced to vacuity what is left so often is filth, with a leaning to excrement? It suggests that this is a last resort of a cancelled mind.

A result of what is an establishment/Tate Gallery paternalism dominating fashion in the art market is a slamming of doors to artists made unacceptable by sincerity and competence. What commercial gallery with a living to earn wants the intrusion of such competition? The real artist is a pariah.

What is it then that lays such degeneracy upon what was the world of art? These people, men and women, who are its priests, are they isolated eccentrics? They are symptoms, almost marionettes in a dismal dance to a social sickness. The name of the sickness is urbanism, a condition of the mind.

Our species has lost its sense of what nature made it; most menacingly it has got above itself. Originally, finding itself bewildered and in fear, it created for its comfort a protective God - sex male, appearance, reassuringly in its own image. Well enough that served; but such simple adulations have loosened, disintegrated before the march of human ingenuity. The foundations have crumbled. For the gap so left, a successor has not been slow. Our species in its brilliance has found technology. We have begun to wonder, so pleasingly, that perhaps after all it is we, so admirably clever, who are the true updated God. We can do it all; we are in control. Up to a point almost it could appear so. Undoubtedly very persuasively, there have been astonishing penetrative advances; almost day by day we must wonder what new, hardly credible brilliance will be upon us. But at this point of congratulation it is cautionary, even vital, that we remind ourselves that still we are entirely ignorant as to what is life, what is consciousness. We do not seem in the least likely to know. What life is made of, that is known. The knowledge takes us no further. The wall remains.

Never, more than now, has there been a time when it is salutary to recall essential facts of having life on earth, thus to be more rational in our use of it.

First then, we are animals. As worms, birds and badgers are animals, so are we. We are of earth, as are all the animals, all the plants. Of earth we are born; by earth we are sustained. We have no independence of earth, and that is a gift, if allowed to be, immeasurably lovely. And this we must never cease to acknowledge, every day, for every moment of life, to earth we are bound by an umbilical cord; nor can any ingenuity of the human brain, so much larger than that of other animals, change that. However clever we may be we are a part of a delicacy, vastness, interdependence that is life on earth. Being so gifted with a larger brain, we should, we must, by the consciousness so given, be humble before what we see. The earth as given us, provided a means for fulfilment of all rational desires, and indeed of sublimities. Earth's functioning, of such vast but intimate complexity, woven of incalculable diversities of species, of infinite subtleties of relationships, in all has an efficiency hardly within our comprehension. For pleasure, multiple delights, fulfilment, are brought about that life on earth shall continue. That there are other factors, fiercely harsh, does but by contrast emphasise the rest. The tragedy of mortality, individually of such sorrow, is of that immortality which is the passing on the materials of life, ensuring the endless succession of life.

Sometimes as I read, a creature, minuscule, insignificant, will cross the page very privately engaged. I puff it on its way, anxious that needless death shall not cease its essential part in the functioning of its minute niche of being. What it is, this thing just visible, I do not know further than that it is an insect; it is vibrant with life, it scurries on legs too fine for my seeing. But it, this busy speck, is perfect. Perfectly, wholly, it is structured for that niche which is its world - and which is as inseparable from the web of life as am I or an elephant or the blue whale. And, I think watching this busy mite, had I microscopic power of sight, almost certainly it would reveal that the creature, brought to largeness, has a sculptural beauty of shape, as so often insects have.

Whatever are the infinitesimal creatures of that niche - is there beauty for them in the obscurities of their perception? What tantalising scope there is for wonder. It has been said often enough that beauty has no intrinsic being, but is relative. It must be said, fervently, that that is not true. It is the *capacity* of the individual to perceive beauty which is relative. How then we must wonder; go as far as we may beyond our normal limits of vision, in places even of no light, beauty is to be found - but with no eye to see it? Then why? Within our *capability* of seeing, always there is beauty, often consummate. Nature's use of it as a persuasive means is not difficult to see. In the wondering consideration of such evasive mysteries, the danger is constant of slipping into anthropomorphism. And some will certainly say, some too confident in their objectivity, it is all accident anyway. But is not that anthropomorphism?

Riddles of nature, so elusive, are by most happy fortune, not to be resolved. Knowledge too far may be destructive to creative imagining. It is such enthralments of ignorance that have so much to do with stimulation to art. And what more than this mystery so intoxicates those of a kind to go fishing? They, the anglers, are of many kinds (in our time there have come those not of right philosophy). But in anglers of the truest kind there are constants. Walton had the word; angling, he said, is for contemplative men. Contemplating the drugging mystery of life in water, wholly entrapping of the imagination, there is, very tantalisingly, a little lifting of the curtain, a hinting glimpse of nature's miracles. Many anglers, probably by no means thinking themselves of the poetic kind, are experiencing a poetic response to the ineffable beauty of nature's workings - so sensitively to be seen in water.

Very late in earth's history nature put man into the first perfection; the Bible's allegory of Adam and Eve is very apt; very well it expresses that *Homo sapiens* was to be an unconforming species intrinsically, inevitably, destructive. At first, by degrees isolated, not apparently connected, where man came, he came with an effect of withering. Other species began to slip into extinction in his proximity, but so little to be observed as not to seem significant. Then wandering hunter-gatherer man began settlement, he began to farm, thus starting first distortion of nature's perfect economy; by that thrusting urging more species into extinction.

CHAPTER XXVI

Hereafter

A MORE than usually long life, unless very severely hedged by monotony, may seem in retrospect as a circuitous corridor from which open many rooms. The Wessex room in which now I live, was opened by Chris Yates.

We have lived in Wiltshire for many years, in its eastern part, with little consciousness of neighbouring Dorset and Somerset. Then in Stockbridge there was a launch party for a book by Mick Lunn. There we met Chris Yates; from that has stemmed much else. No great time later Chris was bookshop browsing in Blandford in Dorset. There among the books, was another man. Said he to Chris, "Excuse me, do you know if Bernard Venables's new book is here?"

"Yes," said Chris, "down there on the bottom shelf."

Then, as anglers will, fell they at once into easy talk, ripening quickly into friendship. The other man was Tony Hayter, Dr Tony Hayter. Early upshot of their meeting was that they and I should meet on the bridge that spans the Wylye at Great Wishford, a seed from which has sprung a plant of great burgeoning. On that day I remember we caught some grayling.

As with Chris and Tony it had been, so it was with Tony and me. From first moment, standing on the bridge over the Wylye's crystal current we fell immediately into easy concord.

At about this same time, with that most warmly trusted of old friends, David Sanders, I fell into a benignly tranquil annual practice. Each time, often about September, we stray away. We go with no compulsive purpose, with no urgency. We take fishing tackle and sometimes we fish; we wander, finding ourselves in places, often with delight that chance should lead us with such unerring instinct to places of such hidden pleasure. We find little pubs of so much bucolic seclusion that we wonder that they should have public enough for their support.

So, purposelessly, we have wandered up and down through the celtic secrecies of the Teifi river country, threading its plunging verdant valleys, through its ravels of brook and lane. In Cornwall we have paused for the fishing of the Camel, and in another year wandered loosely in a hinterland of obscurely tangled lanes, as it seems, unpopulated and, surely, beyond the power of map for interpretation. In Scotland we have idled through the Isle of Mull, fished and dawdled about the valley of the Aberdeenshire Don where trout are wild and large and raking.

In so much peregrination it could not be that we should not go to the country of the Wye which, once known, must forever demand return. I, in my earliest time of fishing the Wye, once had been taken upstream to Builth Wells. It had been but straight there, a glimpse, then back to Hay. But by that glimpse, its touch to the thrilled imagination never ceased to beckon. Never, I thought then, had I seen country of such idyllic loveliness, seeming to me, then young, something of imagination. That was more than sixty years ago, an interim which had shown me many places of surpassing loveliness. And now, I returned to that country about Builth, a magic of cwm and moor and mountain. I knew now that nowhere had I seen country to surpass it. It started in me an evasive sense of recognition of something just beyond grasp. What that was came to me when, thinking of the place, I found running in my head Rutland Boughton's music and the words for 'The Immortal Hour'.

It was for me a major discovery which probably would never have been made, had we not received an invitation. Just on the edge of Builth, just across the bridge over the River Irfon which flows into the Wye, there is a drive which goes splendidly under its tall trees all the way to Caer Beris Manor. A manor house once it was, but now is an hotel. It is an hotel of the country house kind, in its grounds originally planted as an arboretum and now most nobly mature in its trees, secure against all unseemly bothers of the common world. Peter Smith who owns and has made it, is an angler. It is our great happiness that from time to time we are his guests.

For us Caer Beris has been, and remains, a place of manifold attachment - not properly just to be called pleasures. That has no sense of the passionate indefinables aroused and fed by that celtic Eden. Its fusion of wilderness and the sense of the thousands of human years that have had their continuity there is saturating. I am able only to speak for myself, and I am an angler and an artist and a writer, but for all these selves this place stirs and regenerates them in their inseparableness. For the experience of this country, for its infiltrating haunting of the soul, I think I am the better writer, the better painter.

Since no place can be entirely free of risk by contact in so small a patch as Britain is, even here may come discordant moments. We, David and I, came upon a reservoir. It was man-made, but time and weather had been upon it; it lay in a serene lap of landscape. At a point of parking space there was a car; below, by the water, two men were fishing, the doors of the car were open to allow freest passage for the fullest sound volume of pop-music so that the fishers should not suffer deprivation. They conducted their bawling bawdy conversation competitively. Their accent showed them not to be local. We left, shrunken with shame that we could not deny that we were of the same species.

By this is raised a dilemma of our time, one of insistent nagging.

So harried as constantly we are by the growing and often throttling grip upon our soul of technology, we are often led to its absolute denial, futile as that is. Liking it or not, immovably it is with us. But our sensitivities rebel often painfully; then we remind ourselves that it is this same technology which has given us the lovely boon of recorded music so faithfully done that, with good equipment, we are hearing the music no less well, possibly better, than in the concert hall. For the country liver this is immeasurably a gift. But it is by that same blessed facility that the hooligan noise by the water was made available, enabling its listeners to evade the risk of thought. A dilemma indeed.

The placid routines of Wessex one morning, were stirred by the coming of a buff envelope addressed to me but boldly marked, 'THE PRIME MINISTER'. I handled it a little nervously; what could the Prime Minister want with me? I opened it. The Prime Minister informed me that he had recommended to Her Majesty that I should be made a Member of the Most Excellent Order of the British Empire. If I wished to accept this would I please make a tick in the place provided. A little stunned I made my tick. In May of the following year I was summoned to Buckingham Palace there to attend an Investiture. As a recipient, I learned it to be normal to wear morning dress, but kindly, mercifully, there would be no crossness if I wore merely a lounge suit. I was grateful; the mental picture of myself in morning dress rather alarmed me.

At the Palace I was separated from wife and daughter Hannah. In a state faintly of panic and unprotectedness I was bidden by a sign marked 'Recipients' to the ascent of an imperiously grand flight of stairs.

All indeed was so predictably grand that, notwithstanding the little edge of panic, I found myself taking it for granted. The staircase was most grandly wide, colonnaded, red-carpeted; but it would be, wouldn't it?

That ascended, I found myself absorbed into the gently immaculate flowing of a routine, flawless, hitchless. All who, so to speak, fed us through, were softly reassuring. We were in the Queen's Picture Gallery, corralled within a fat crimson rope beneath the

Bernard Venables OBE, with Eileen and Hannah.

Old Masters. There, of mixed kind, we waited. I found myself next to one of Indian blood, West Indian origin, many years a resident of Britain, a kindly spoken small man. Close by, of enormous height, was a black man; he was entirely superb. His head was neat and small, a perfect finial to the column of height and lofty spread of shoulders. He carried himself easily. I thought it probable that he was an athlete. There was a lady who impressed me a little alarmingly, being both very large and, I thought, intimidating.

Now we were so briefed. We, no doubt an awkward squad, were moulded with deft and gentle hands to a state fit for passing through the web of protocol. Somewhat complex though it was, we were cajoled, calmed, persuaded with a suave mastery polished by a thousand occasions. All was done, as we were told, with the wish that our passage of the Palace process should be one of happiness.

He who was our mentor was superb in his easy professionalism;

perfectly he wore the façade of being invested with royal representation, mingling that with a kindly suggestion of being on our side.

"You will be presented to His Royal Highness the Prince of Wales. You may if you wish address him as His Royal Highness, but once is enough. After that call him Sir - don't be nervous. He will be understanding."

He instructed us closely as to each part of our passing from hand to hand on the way to presentation to the Prince. As if to condition us to the ceremony's climactic end, he was tall, handsome, precisely enclosed in a uniform quietly splendid. He was as though discreetly declining any suggestion of being portentous.

As I waited till I too should be processed into the ballroom and the royal presence, I reflected that this event, cardinal to me as one recipient, had been going on since January at constant intervals, plodding down through the alphabet, an inexorable sequence of us, all to have the required gracious Royal words, the handshake.

Then there at last was I at the entrance to the ballroom; there again a pause. Then advance to a stand just short while my predecessor was done. Then forward to face the Prince; bow, advance three paces, receive the Order on the left chest. The Prince engages me in brief conversation, shakes hands and I note that he has a large hand. I retire three paces backwards; bow, and it is over. I leave the ballroom by the opposite door, there to have my decoration removed from me, put into its formal box. I am now fully processed. But still they come, the rest of the Vs and after them the Ws, perhaps even the XYZs. I thought the prince looked very strained. Then all of us, down the grand staircase under the towering Life Guards, each on his plinth with drawn sword, so totally immobile as not quite to be believed. How trying for them - have they no itches? Under those breastplates too. It has worried me a little since then.

Descending those majestic stairs, I thought of how it had come that I should be descending them. Honours are not easily given. I was aware that largely it had come from the loyal pressures of a great many anglers who worked hard that I should have this honour. I was grateful; I was humbled.

Fishing the Itchen.

Choosing the right fly.

At Izaak Walton's cotttage.

Fishing the Hampshire Avon.

But back to Wessex, back to the domed chalk heights, the calm far drifts of sky. How distant now all the mightiness, the crimson and the gold. Still here the breeze ripples on the grass of the water meadows, carries the river smell. Back to fishing, to painting, to all the long quiet days, friends and fishing.

In fishing now I am grateful for the friends I have, so dependent I am on their help. A fisherman, particularly a fly fisherman, no longer with sight enough for the tying of knots, for the seeing of trout in the transparent water of chalkstreams, is like a horse with three legs but with consciousness enough to have acute awareness of what he is missing. My friends lend me their eyes, kindly they cajole at least as far as may be with secondary sight to make possible the continuance of fishing. In Wessex, western Wessex, there is a Wessex cell of fishermen, close-knit. Of them is Tony Hayter, and to such accord have we come that combined operation fishing of the nymph is partially successful.

Tony spots - "There," he says, "two feet and a bit out from that tussock overhanging from the bank - ah he's moved up a few inches - on the gravel just behind the weed bed, can you see that?" I strain, looking, think that pale glimmer is it.

I cast. "A little more line," says Tony, "about a foot more." I cast again. "Better, you're on his line. He's seen it - wagged his tail - ah, not taking it - showed interest though. Try him again. Think he might take if you induce him."

Another cast. "He's seen it, wagging tail - now." I induce him, hand-draw the fly slightly. "Yes, now!" cries Tony; I strike. The trout is on - so it is if this is one of our proud days. Sometimes for a moment I feel the fish and it is gone.

Towards the end of the coarse fishing season we go pike fishing, Tony, Chris Yates, Ronnie Butler and, helped along, I. Then the joyful fever of trout again and soon the mayfly itself, a greater fever. When summer comes and the days are long and soft and gracious there is the halcyon dream of tench fishing, the rite of summer. But summer passes, the flowers fade, the leaves turn and fall, and the long grey shapes deep against the gravel are the big grayling, haunting the sinking autumn days.

But not only upon fishing does failing sight throw its dreadful threat. A painter must paint, in that is a sublimity, an irradiating compulsion. But, were its capability cut off it could be a torture. So steeply has my sight declined since I came into my nineties its black threat has hung low. Twice it has come to crisis; twice, as by a miracle of a dawn beyond normal allotting, it has passed. I find myself as it seems with a stronger vision - as if having pushed through a darkly hanging curtain I find on its other side a lovely light.

Fate, so often on its occasions cat-like in its play of me, so often with smiling malice, has no less bestowed many delights, many favours. Who could have had better friends than those who are mine? Of them is Ronnie Butler.

Him I first met in a way most appropriate, by the introduction of that other primary friend, Tony Hayter. That it is appropriate is because these two, at a glance so different, essentially have a kinship. Tony is a scholar, effervescent in erudition; Ronnie, a Scot, a businessman, fizzes no less. In both runs that childhood remnant which separates perfectionist from common clay. They are of course devoted anglers.

Now Ronnie, who further is affected by a largeness of the heart, has like many other anglers, been greatly disturbed that I who was the creator of *Mr Crabtree Goes Fishing*, have for that received not a penny. It seemed to him proper that he should turn upon this the full force of his entrepreneurial skills, his acute business acumen. He negotiated with Mirror Group Newspapers, achieved a lease of the copyright of the book, thus to be able to publish a facsimile of the original edition. To me he offered terms spectacularly generous. *Crabtree* so happily reborn is selling well.

How kindly indeed did fate deal with me in my friends; oldest of them all, Eric Thomas, was first instigator of my travels. But for Eric should I have fished in the mountains of Morocco, should I for forty years have had so steadfast a friend. And, need it be said there is Mike Blackall, whom first I met in the old airport at Lusaka. As this book has told, Mike has been initiator of so many of my more stirring experiences.

The return of *Mr Crabtree* would anyway have made epic that year; but the year was 2000, the Millennium, a year fraught with suggestion of destiny. Surely it seemed, a year of great event. In its way it was.

But hardly at all, apart from *Crabtree* was it such a year. Quite early, in April, it had an event that seemed of such promise. My book *A Rise to the Fly*, was with some flourish published; it seemed, still so seems, launched upon a good life. But before that, in February, was an event of quite contrary suggestion. I am a member of the Savile Club; for fifty-one years so have been. On the 2nd of February I attended a lunch there for senior members. Characteristically the occasion had that benign sense which is of such Savile occasions; at its end we descended the gracious curve of the ballroom stairs. The curve was deceptive; I stepped into space, went headlong to the bottom. I was then ninety-three. Untypically I survived but was shaken.

Two days after the glowing launch of *A Rise to the Fly* Eileen broke her ankle and a few weeks later I had a nocturnal fall, so bringing my full weight and the bath's sharp corner into impact on my shoulder blade.

I survived that; we survived the year 2000 though that at times had seemed dubious.

Now the year is gone, over; the great millennium so laden with assumed significances, so burdened with mishap, is little more than irrelevance. And I, willy nilly, was suspended in that sequence, which linked two epochs which to the historical eye is a momentary flash. Not quite a century ago I was born. That briefest of all centuries separated modes of life as separate from the present as the Iron Age. I, as I hear of great age, as I feel, am at a pause; by the acceptances I now should be settled in the declining drift out of life, no more a part of it. How can it be? Can I for whom life has been so intense of Living consent to this migration out of being?

Still I know the ecstasies of summer mornings; still the butterflies, ephemerally lovely, demonstrate the unending rhythms of beauty that are the fibres of nature's structure. How can I leave all that and, if still I know anything, will know so still it is, but I not there to love it? All those thrills of being, all loves of kin, of friends, all stopped.

But so much of that, dear familiar things of life, are being pushed aside by onrushing stridencies. But so late as it is, we must not abandon hope. So much of conjectured future, guessed on present evidence, must induce cringing dread. But, again, we who are a plague species trailing our destructive smear, are also from whom came Shakespeare, the Italian Renaissance, Mozart and Beethoven, Wren and Rembrandt, all demonstrations of the human spirit. They mostly are not men of society's mastery; their sensitivity is too commanding of them for them to be commanding of their peers. But, just perhaps, in social extremity, the quiet glory of their voices might give lift to the gathering unreason that shadows us more as we advance into the 21st century.

I shall not see, must faintly hope. For years that still are mine as long as my eyes can co-operate I must paint. Our technological era, whatever its faults, does give means of continuance for writing. So much still there is to do.

Postscript

HANNAH VENABLES

I was recently in Salisbury college and met again a lecturer who I hadn't seen for nearly twenty years. He was soon recounting the point at which he had realised who my father was. During an early lecture he had mentioned a passion for angling and so I said I loved fishing. As he was aware of my surname, he then said, "I s'pose you're going to tell me that your father is Bernard Venables." "Well, yes, actually," I said. This had prompted the usual response of surprise and pleasure and then the recounting of the huge impact of the books on a young fisherman. His description of the books and the illustrations in particular was so warm and vivid that I could see that he could picture them as though he were holding them in his hands there and then.

This is an example of the 'Bernard effect'. I am going to try and describe the Bernard effect on a family with three young children growing up.

I suspect that my brothers and I had a fairly abnormal upbringing. We lived in a large, but falling down farmhouse that was a mile away from the nearest road. There wasn't much money; not many outings, nor clothes, nor any luxuries. But, we had a great deal of a great many other things.

We were surrounded by books, by words and pictures. Outside, we were surrounded by the fields, trees, lanes and ponds. We seemed to spend days wandering through woods, along tracks, exploring and discovering the natural world. We were taught to appreciate it. We could recognise and name the flowers, the trees, butterflies and birds. We learnt to be still, to really see the natural world. Dad was forever pointing out colours in the landscape or gazing at an impressive sky. Unfortunately this could lead to trouble when being driven by Dad. On occasions as I stared out of the car window, I realised that the verge was getting farther away. This was because Dad was so intently studying a cloud formation that he had ceased to be aware of the road. Mum would shriek "Bernard!" and we would be OK again.

Whilst we were growing up, Mum and Dad were attempting to be organically self-sufficient. We reared chickens, geese and goats and grew vegetables. Our waste was recycled as much as possible and Dad developed an impressive system of compost heaps. This lifestyle slotted into our deeply rural surroundings.We were not shielded from the cycles of the country. We knew the fate of the cute lambs that were born in front of us. The geese that we had to dodge all year were the geese that Dad killed and we plucked for Christmas.

We waged a constant battle against rats. Not only were they a threat outside but they were intent on living inside with us. They were capable of gnawing through walls and once in, would run up and down between the floors with their hob-nail boots on. Hours before Dad left on a long trip to Africa, he hurriedly went round laying poison bait. Unfortunately they all died in the walls and floors, and the stench in the house was unbearable for weeks.

This self-sufficiency was not only a means of producing healthy and cheaper food. It was also a reflection of his discontent with mass-food production, globalisation and the chemical abuse of the environment. These concepts were regular meal-time topics of conversation. As children, we were familiar with Schumacher and 'small is beautiful' and the principles of the soil association. Above all was the knowledge that the natural world was beautiful, fascinating and precious, but finite.

Some of Dad's varied jobs did have advantages as far as we were concerned. We are the proud owners of a Tom Baker as Dr Who autograph for instance. Dad and I went to a river with a photographer. Dad cut a hazel from the hedge and made a rudimentary rod. We then struggled to catch a fish on it, which eventually we did. Whilst we were at school, Dad was making schools' nature programmes and I can remember sitting in the classroom listening to his voice on the radio. For one programme we were enlisted to construct a den for the pamphlet. We prided ourselves on our den building so there was much at stake. We built the finest den ever and its picture duly graced the pages of the booklet. Dad also did a programme about the rats in the London sewers and I can remember being mortified at being prevented from going down with him.

In the absence of proper family holidays, instead we would have days out. These consisted of locating ancient earthworks in remote fields. Then we would go off for a pub lunch. I expect many of you know how my Dad felt about beer. He was vitriolic in his loathing of 'keg'; he would say the word as though spitting out poison. In those days there were not many pubs that not only sold real beer but also kept it in the correct manner. It felt like hours that we drove through village after village searching for the right pub.

We are all an amalgam of our genes and upbringing. I am grateful for the bundle that I received. I can't pick up a book without smelling the paper . . . I can't pick up a book without wanting it. Paper, paint . . . colour gives me intense pleasure. I want my children to have these simple pleasures. They are learning all the plant names and are learning to appreciate their natural surroundings. They love to wander through woods looking for fungi or the signs of badgers. What better legacy.

My sweetest memory of those childhood days is of being in the garden on a summer's day, with the sound of the tapping of a typewriter wafting from the studio window.